Counselling for
Eating
Disorders

SECOND EDITION

Sara Gilbert

Los Angeles | London | New Delhi
Singapore | Washington DC

First edition first published 2000
Reprinted 2002
This second edition first published 2005
Reprinted 2007, 2008, 2010

SAGE Publications Ltd
1 Oliver's Yard
55 City Road
London EC1Y 1SP

SAGE Publications Inc.
2455 Teller Road
Thousand Oaks, California 91320

SAGE Publications India Pvt Ltd
B 1/I 1 Mohan Cooperative Industrial Area
Mathura Road, New Delhi 110 044
India

SAGE Publications Asia-Pacific Pvt Ltd
33 Pekin Street #02-01
Far East Square
Singapore 048763

British Library Cataloguing in Publication data

A catalogue record for this book is available
from the British Library

ISBN 978-1-4129-0278-6
ISBN 978-1-4129-0279-3 (pbk)

Library of Congress Control Number available

FSC
Mixed Sources
Product group from well-managed
forests and other controlled sources

Cert no. SGS-COC-2482
www.fsc.org
© 1996 Forest Stewardship Council

Text pages are FSC certified

Typeset by C&M Digitals (P) Ltd., Chennai, India
Printed on paper from sustainable resources
Printed in Great Britain by TJI Digital, Padstow, Cornwall

Contents

Preface

I first became interested in working with this client group when working in an obesity clinic in the late 1970s. At that time, the only eating disorder truly recognised was anorexia nervosa. People who were overweight or of normal weight and who could not control their eating fell sadly between two stools. Either they were forced to fit into medically oriented dietetic or nutrition clinics, where their apparent lack of motivation to do as they were advised was viewed askance by the people who tried to treat them; or they were assumed to be depressed or even personality-disordered and offered temporary shelter under a psychiatric umbrella – just as inappropriate. It became increasingly clear that what these people needed was something different, something which addressed the specific problems of these disorders and which did not force them to pursue an answer which relied on their problems having an entirely physical origin or to be labelled as suffering from some form of insanity.

While the origin of eating disorders remained poorly understood, it made increasing sense to treat them with a cognitive behavioural approach, encompassing as it does a collaborative therapeutic style, the teaching of self-control to clients and a way of exploring the meaning of the disorders together with clients. Since the publication of the first edition of this book, cognitive behaviour therapy has become more firmly established as a treatment of choice for the eating disorders, and I have updated the literature and references cited in the book to take account of new developments in theory and practice.

In this book, I have attempted to describe how to counsel people with eating disorders from a cognitive behavioural point of view. In doing so I must acknowledge that the origin of many of my descriptions is influenced by a combination of many sources, including my reading of the works of Aaron Beck and his colleagues, and Christine Padesky in relation to cognitive therapy for depression and other disorders, and of Hilde Bruch, Christopher Fairburn, David Garner and Paul Garfinkel, and Kelly Bemis Vitousek, among others, in relation to eating disorders.

I have not attempted to write a comprehensive 'how to do it' book with instructions of a flow-chart nature. I have assumed a basic knowledge of cognitive behavioural and counselling techniques and have not detailed exactly what to do word for word as this is, by the very nature of eating disorders, different in every single case. (For more details of how to use cognitive behavioural techniques to elicit and answer, for example, negative automatic thoughts and to arrive at underlying assumptions, I would refer readers to Judith Beck's [1995] excellent manual.) Instead, I have taken an integrative stance and drawn on ideas from the cognitive and behavioural fields, many of them researched in practice, which can be tailored in varying combinations to the treatment of individual clients. For example, I have drawn on ideas about enhancing motivation for treatment, schemas about the self and interpersonal relationships, and eating disorder as a means of coping with negative affect. I have avoided giving exact prescriptions of exactly when and where to introduce specific techniques as it will be up to individual counsellors to decide together with their clients at what point in therapy each approach might be most useful.

In the following chapters, I have on many occasions used the pronoun 'she' to refer to clients, rather than the more clumsy 'she/he', and have made this choice merely because most sufferers are female. However, the ideas may apply equally to male sufferers, who have much in common with female sufferers.

The case histories I have described are not those of real people. Rather, they are composites derived from clients I have met, and with the details of their stories and their names changed so as to preserve the confidentiality of the real people on whom they are loosely based.

Finally, this book could not have been published without the work and encouragement of several people. Windy Dryden, series editor, suggested that I write the book several years ago. His constructive criticism of drafts of the first chapters helped me to set the style for the book as a whole. Despite the many obstacles to my meeting deadlines, Windy was unfailing in his patience and in his belief that I would complete it as promised. I should also like to acknowledge the hard work of the editorial staff of Sage: Melissa Dunlop, Justin Dyer for his relentless and painstaking editing of the text, Kate Scott, Louise Wise, Rachel Burrows, and in particular Susan Worsey for her support and encouragement over long periods when personal circumstances made it impossible for me to write.

Sara Gilbert, November 2004

Acknowledgements

The author and publisher wish to thank the following publishers for kind permission to reprint material: the American Psychiatric Association for quotations from *Diagnostic and Statistical Manual of Mental Disorders* (4th edn) (1994) (© 1994 American Psychiatric Association) (diagnostic criteria for anorexia nervosa and bulimia nervosa; research criteria for binge eating disorder); the Guilford Press for a table from W.R. Miller and S. Rollnick, *Motivational Interviewing: Preparing People to Change Addictive Behavior* (1991) (Table 4.1); Plenum Publishing Corporation and the authors for permission to adapt a table from D.M. Garner and K. Bemis, 'A cognitive-behavioral approach to anorexia nervosa', *Cognitive Therapy and Research*, 6 (1982) (Table 7.1); the Nutrition and Dietetic Department of Northwick Park and St Mark's NHS Trust for the leaflet 'Eat for Health' (HEO2/9705) (Appendix 3); Quartet Books for permission to adapt material from Anne Dickson, *A Woman in Your Own Right: Assertiveness and You* (1982), pp. 29–36 (Appendix 7).

1 What is an Eating Disorder?

Interest in eating disorders has mushroomed in the past twenty years. Until the early 1980s, most people knew about the existence of anorexia nervosa, but few mental health professionals or dietitians would have considered it necessary to have more than the ability merely to recognise the disorder so that they could pass a case on to a specialist worker or unit.

Obesity, although comparatively common, was poorly understood, and obese people had to rely for help largely on medical interventions of uncertain efficacy and often questionable ethics. Few overweight people would have admitted to an eating problem if they had one, and for help with motivation to diet they had only a range of slimming organisations of variable quality on which to rely. As an alternative, some who complained of problems with control were referred for psychiatric help, only to be re-referred to their own doctors as not having qualified for treatment for clinical depression.

Until recently, people of apparently normal weight who had problems around food and worries about their weight were likely to be dismissed at the primary care level as not having a problem at all because they did not fit into any previously known category of psychiatric or physical disorder.

Dietitians have often been the sole point of referral for these three groups of people, but with a background mainly in nutrition and little knowledge of psychological factors, they too were baffled by the complex motivations of people apparently unable to prevent themselves from abusing their bodies and could often do little more than hand out a diet sheet.

In the last twenty years or so, help has become increasingly available for people with specific diagnoses of bulimia nervosa and anorexia nervosa. In recent years also, mental health professionals have begun to address the problem of binge eating disorder in overweight people. Awareness of the need for specialist units and therapy has meant that someone with an eating disorder is more likely than previously to be referred for psychiatric or counselling help or can at least receive advice from a self-help group. At the same time, there has been a growing acceptance of the need for every professional in the therapy and counselling fields to have some understanding of people with eating problems, and dietitians and general practitioners too have begun to espouse the use of a psychological approach towards working with people with an eating disorder. They have become more keenly aware of the need not just to provide therapy for people with clear eating disorder diagnoses, but to address themselves to the problems of a wide range of people with disorders of eating and weight, including obese people.

This book is an attempt to provide a practical basis for working in the area of eating disorders both for those counsellors with a psychological, psychiatric or general background, and for dietitians and nutritionists. Its aim is not only to include ways of working with people with a specifiable eating disorder, but also to offer ways to improve the methods by which nutritional advice and counselling are offered to obese people and to those who by virtue of their problems are unable to eat in a health-promoting way.

This chapter will describe the behaviour, eating habits and physical symptoms to look for in people with disorders of eating. It will define and describe the conditions known as 'anorexia nervosa' and 'bulimia nervosa', and discuss some of the other eating problems which counsellors may meet in people with atypical, less easily definable eating disorders, such as binge eating, binge eating in people who are over-weight, or inability to eat for reasons other than fear of becoming fat. It will also dis-cuss the question of the relationship between eating disorder and weight; in other words, it will raise and discuss the question of how far people at a very low weight or a very high weight in relation to height may or may not have an eating disorder.

A note about psychiatric diagnosis

Psychological disturbances are generally classified under two parallel psychiatric classification systems. These are the American Psychiatric Association's *Diagnostic and Statistical Manual of Mental Disorders* (DSM) (American Psychiatric Association 1994) or the World Health Organisation's *International Classification of Diseases* (WHO 1992). In this book, I have used the *DSM-IV* classification system as a basis for describing the disorders under discussion and the results of research about the efficacy of their treatment.

If we are to work with people and their problems, we need some way of defin-ing the problems so that we all know that we are discussing the same phenome-non. In this regard, psychiatric diagnosis is a useful system. It also helps us to draw conclusions from research into treatment. However, the distinctions between the so-called 'disorders' are by no means firm and immutable. There is much overlap of symptoms and characteristics between disorders. It is also important to remember that the conditions we are referring to are not necessarily illnesses or conditions which a person can 'have' in the same way as they can 'have' multiple sclerosis or epilepsy, or which they can 'catch' in the same way they can 'catch' pneumonia or HIV. As yet there are no clear links with physiology or brain chem-istry. As John Marzillier, an experienced psychotherapist and research psycholo-gist, has pointed out:

> the experiences that lead people to be diagnosed as 'mentally ill' are experiences that all of us can have in some form at some stage. This is why, despite over a century or more of research, psychiatrists are no further forward in defining and understanding – let alone successfully treating – any major psychiatric 'illness'. (Marzillier 2004: 392)

The people we meet in therapy for eating disorders may have common symptoms but the way they respond to therapy will be a function of the complex interaction between their symptoms and many other factors, including physiology, personal-ity, past experience and current circumstances. Counsellors may experience some discomfort in trying to attach labels to the real people they meet in their consulting rooms. However, 'diagnosis' is merely a starting point from which to explore the indi-vidual needs of clients and apply the general principles and individual techniques of cognitive behavioural therapy.

Recognition of eating disorder

The American Psychiatric Association's *Diagnostic and Statistical Manual of Mental Disorders (DSM-IV)* (1994) defines an eating disorder as characterised by 'severe disturbances in eating behaviour'. Strictly, the definition 'eating disorder' applies only to the specific diagnoses of anorexia nervosa and bulimia nervosa, both of which require a disturbance of body shape and weight as an essential feature. A broader definition of eating disorder is offered by Fairburn and Walsh, both psychiatrists who have been at the cutting edge of eating disorders research for the past twenty years. They propose: 'a persistent disturbance of eating behaviour or behaviour intended to control weight, which significantly impairs health or psychosocial functioning. This disturbance should not be secondary to any recognised general medical disorder ... or any other psychiatric disorder' (Fairburn and Walsh 2002: 171). This definition has the advantage that it encompasses a range of disorders and eating difficulties beyond the specific diagnoses of anorexia nervosa and bulimia nervosa.

Recognition of the widespread nature of problems around food and eating stemmed from three areas. The first and perhaps most public of these was the feminist movement. Susie Orbach's book *Fat is a Feminist Issue* (1978) drew a great deal of attention to the movement through its novel discussion of so-called 'compulsive overeating' which talked not so much about 'fat' itself but about the fear of fat and the place held by that fear in the culture of women in the context of their relationship with men. This led to a rash of books around the area of dieting and body image, most of which carried the implication, either directly or indirectly, that dieting and obsession with body image has something to do with the place of women in a sexist society.

Another source of recognition was in mainstream psychiatry. Gerald Russell (1979), known for his work with people with anorexia nervosa, commented on the existence of an anorexic-like syndrome in women of normal weight. These women had previously been anorexic and, although of normal weight on follow-up, were still obsessed with weight and shape. They binged frequently but went to great lengths to control their weight by means of vomiting, taking laxatives or starving themselves in between binges. He called this syndrome 'bulimia nervosa' as opposed to anorexia nervosa.

A third source of recognition was from epidemiological research. 'Bulimia', as it was called in the United States, or 'bulimia nervosa', as it was called in Britain, was recognised to exist on a wide scale among women who had never approached their doctors for help.

However, there is no doubt that the existence of the popular word 'binge', and the phenomenon itself, has its basis in the obsession with dieting that prevails in the western world. Very many men and women of all ages diet habitually. In this setting, it is sometimes difficult to assess how far someone is actually suffering from an eating disorder. On the one hand, dieting and a negative attitude to fat are condoned and often highly valued by people as an indicator of self-control both in themselves and in other people. Hence it is possible for someone who is suffering intensely with an eating disorder to hide the fact not only from themselves but from the very people who might be able to help. On the other hand, inability to diet and a tendency to binge eat, or reluctance to eat during times of stress, are often mistakenly interpreted as signs of a primary eating disorder rather than as the symptoms of some other serious distress that they often are.

The relationship between weight and eating disorder

Eating disorders are largely defined by characteristic behaviours around food and weight control and attitudes to weight and shape. An eating disorder can never be diagnosed from weight or shape alone but, a person's weight is an important feature of an eating disorder. A person's degree of overweight or underweight is commonly described by a measure known as the body mass index (BMI). This is derived from the formula W/H^2 (weight in kilograms divided by the square of height in metres). Weight can be plotted in relation to height and the resulting graph has been reproduced in widely available table form depicting the upper and lower limits of the weight range. The normal range for the body mass index is between 20 and 25. Below 20 are increasing degrees of underweight. From 26 and above are increasing degrees of overweight: grade 1 (overweight): 26–30; grade 2 (clinical obesity): 30–40 and grade 3 (severe obesity): 40 and above.

Anorexia nervosa

Anorexia nervosa is a state in which the sufferer, usually female, refuses to eat enough to maintain normal body weight for her height. Usually she claims to want to lose weight to be slimmer; sometimes she says that she does not feel hungry or that it is uncomfortable to eat.

One currently accepted definition of anorexia nervosa is given in the fourth edition of the American Psychiatric Association's *Diagnostic and Statistical Manual (DSM-IV)* and has four criteria:

1   Refusal to maintain body weight over a minimal normal weight for age and height.
2   An intense fear of gaining weight or becoming fat, even though underweight.
3   A disturbance in the way one's body weight or shape is experienced, undue influence of body weight or shape on self-evaluation; or denial of the seriousness of the current low body weight.
4   In females, absence of at least three consecutive menstrual cycles when otherwise expected to occur. (American Psychiatric Association 1994: 544–545)

The weight criterion by which to define anorexia nervosa is given in the tenth edition of the *International Classification of Diseases (ICD10)* (WHO 1992) which specifies that weight is maintained at least 15 per cent below that expected or, in adults, body mass index (BMI) is below 17.5kg/m². In younger people, instead of actual weight loss, there may be failure to gain weight as expected during puberty or childhood.

All anorexics refuse food and count calories, and many eat as little as 200–300 calories per day. They may also take strenuous exercise, and often appear 'faddy' with their food. Some take an immense interest in cookery and in cooking for other people, although they will avoid eating the food they cook themselves.

Anorexics are also thought to have a distorted body image, in that they often appear to grossly overestimate their own size or weight. A great deal of research in the 1970s was devoted to the question of how far anorexics overestimate their body size. This is in common, however, with many other people with abnormal eating habits and the emphasis more recently has been on sufferers' attitudes to weight and shape. Peter Cooper and Christopher Fairburn (1993) have pointed out the distinction between 'dissatisfaction with body shape', which may or may not be experienced by women with eating disorders, and 'overvalued ideas about body shape and weight', which they hold are a necessary diagnostic feature for both bulimia nervosa and anorexia nervosa.

In addition, anorexics are specified as 'restricting types' or 'binge eating/purging types'. Several studies have pointed to the fact that anorexics are divided between those who keep their weight down solely by restricting their food intake and are not currently purging or binge eating, and those who also binge eat and purge themselves by vomiting or by taking laxatives, diuretics or enemas. The relative numbers of bingers *vis-à-vis* restrictors are on average about 50 per cent across studies, which have pointed to some consistent differences between the two groups. For example, while more of the bulimics have had heterosexual experience and are married, their social adjustment is no better than that of the restrictors, as they also describe themselves as more anxious and depressed, more guilty about their eating habits, and more aware of difficulties in interpersonal relationships. The bulimics are also significantly older when they present for treatment and have been ill for longer. More of the bulimics appear to seek help for themselves, while the restrictors often deny that they have a problem at all. However, the bulimics also appear to carry a worse prognosis, and in addition are more likely to exhibit impulsive behaviours such as stealing, drug abuse, suicide attempts and self-mutilation. (See also Da Costa and Halmi 1992; Gilbert 1986.) Garner and his colleagues (Garner, Garner and Rosen 1993) have suggested an entirely different division of anorexics, between those who purge and those who do not. They have suggested that this avoids the problems of defining a binge. It also makes sense in that many anorexics purge without bingeing, and that there is a strong association between purging behaviour and level of psychopathology, chronicity and length of illness (Favoro and Santonastaso 1996; Tobin, Johnson and Dennis 1992).

Attempts to characterise types of anorexic have their limitations, as individual sufferers vary widely in their presentation. In addition, many are diagnosed as suffering from clinical depression – up to 63 per cent in some studies, according to Herzog, Keller et al. (1992), and up to 35 per cent have been described as having an obsessive compulsive disorder (OCD) (Rastam 1992). There is even some question about whether or not all anorexics have a drive for thinness. Several authors have pointed out the fact that up to 20 per cent of anorexics, in particular in the Far East, do not appear to be afraid to get fat: these patients are more likely to attribute fear of eating to some other phenomenon, such as stomach bloating or pain, loss of appetite, lack of hunger (see Ramacciotti et al. 2002 for a discussion).

Anorexia nervosa currently has a very high profile. However it is important to bear in mind that a search throughout the world literature has shown that it affects on average less than 0.5 per cent of young women (see Hoek and Van Hoeken 2003).

Table 1.1   Incidence and prevalence of eating disorders

Anorexia nervosa	
Incidence:	8 cases per 100,000 population per year
	(1 in 19 male)
Prevalence:	0.3% for young females
Bulimia nervosa	
Incidence:	12 cases per 100,000 per year
Prevalence:	1% in young women
	0.1% young men
	90% are female, 10% male

Source: Hoek and Van Hoeken

Between one in 16 and one in 19 anorexics is male. Sufferers are usually in their adolescence but the disorder can appear at any time between 12 and 44 years, and there are recent reports of its appearance in young pre-pubescent girls (see Lask and Bryant-Waugh 1986 for a review). Together with bulimia nervosa, it has tradition-ally been described in both clinical and research studies as being overrepre-sented in the upper social classes. A recent examination of the social class status of patients referred to a specialist treatment centre in London over the past 33 years has led the authors to conclude that social class distribution of anorexia nervosa is still consistently weighted towards social classes one and two (McLelland and Crisp 2001). Anorexia nervosa was also thought to be confined to white people, both in the United States and in Great Britain. However, the disorder is reported increasingly in women of all classes, and in Asian and Afro-Caribbean women. It is reported also to exist at a rate higher than expected in the young homeless (Freeman and Gard 1994). These findings suggest that eating disorder may be linked to the cultural and family difficulties engendered by immigration and change rather than to social class or culture *per se*. In fact, Gard and Freeman have cast doubt on the widely accepted belief that eating disorders are linked to higher social class (Gard and Freeman 1996). In a review of several studies dating back to 1973, they noted that the belief that anorexia nervosa in particular is more preva-lent in high socioeconomic groups is based on flawed evidence from small biased samples; they point out that the number of more recent studies reporting either no relationship or one which points in the opposite direction far outweigh those which do report a relationship with high social class. Nevertheless, the relation-ship between eating disorder and class is still under debate. In a recent national survey of health registers in Sweden, where access to health services is fairly equi-table, the factors most strongly associated with inpatient treatment of anorexia nervosa were having parents from northern, central or eastern Europe (as opposed to southern Europe, the Middle East or Africa) and coming from a white-collar household (Lindberg and Hjern 2003).

The disorder takes a physical toll on sufferers. Long-term starvation causes muscle weakness and loss of muscle strength, which also affects the heart. Sufferers may develop cardiac abnormalities and arrhythmias. They may have dry skin and excessive growth of dry brittle hair over the nape of the neck, cheeks, forearms and thighs, called 'lanugo' hair. They often have cold hands and feet, and peripheral oedema (swelling). They can suffer from constipation. Long-term amenorrhoea (lack of menstrual periods) may lead to premature bone loss and place sufferers at risk of osteoporosis. Indeed, there is evidence that young women with anorexia nervosa have an increased risk of fractures in later life (Lucas et al. 1999).

What happens to people who have anorexia nervosa?

Most anorexics have just one episode of the disorder and eventually return to a normal weight. Of those who are treated in clinics and survive, between 40 and 80 per cent have been reported to achieve normal weight by between two and ten years after they are first seen. However, many continue to have abnormal attitudes to food and weight for a very long time and about half of previous sufferers do not return to eating normally. Between 13 and 50 per cent do not get their periods back. About 60 per cent of those who continue to maintain a low weight and have problems with eating manage to live apparently normal lives, and hold down jobs. According to Steinhausen (1999), 5 per cent of anorexics die of anorexia nervosa, and the all-cause standardised mortality ratio for anorexia nervosa has been estimated at 9.6 per cent (Nielsen 2001), putting anorexics at about three times the risk of dying as people with other psychiatric illnesses (NICE 2004). Poor outcome has been associated with a later age of onset of the disorder, a longer duration of the disorder, psychiatric comorbidity, poor family relationships and low body weight at discharge from treatment (see Fichter and Quadflieg 1999; Ratnasuriya et al. 1991). A fatal outcome has been associated with longer duration of illness, bingeing and purging, comorbid substance abuse, and comorbid affective disorders (Herzog, Greenwood et al. 2000).

Bulimia nervosa

Bulimia nervosa is perhaps in some ways a more dangerous condition, if only because it is not easily recognised by other people. Bulimics are usually of normal weight. They are usually young women who have powerful urges to overeat which they alternate with periods of starving themselves, or worse still of vomiting or purging in order to control their weight. It is possible to suffer from bulimia nervosa for many years without even close family members guessing that the person has a problem. Bulimia nervosa was first described by Gerald Russell (1979) in a group of ex-anorexics, and he defined sufferers as experiencing a morbid fear of becoming fat, powerful and intractable urges to overeat, and as avoiding the fattening effects of food by self-induced vomiting or purging, or both.

DSM-IV criteria for bulimia nervosa are as follows:

1 Recurrent episodes of binge eating, characterised by:

   (i)   eating, in a discrete period of time an amount of food that is larger than most people would eat during a similar time period or under similar circumstances.

   (ii) a sense of lack of control over eating during the episode.

2   Recurrent inappropriate compensatory behaviour in order to prevent weight gain, such as self-induced vomiting, misuse of laxatives, diuretics, enemas or other medications, fasting or excessive exercise.

3   The binge eating and inappropriate compensatory behaviours both occur, on average, at least twice a week for three months.

4   Self-evaluation is unduly influenced by body shape and weight. (American Psychiatric Association 1994: 549–550)

The bulimia nervosa may be of the purging type or of the non-purging type. Purgers are currently engaged in self-induced vomiting or the misuse of laxatives, diuretics or enemas. Non-purgers have used other inappropriate compensatory behaviours, such as fasting or excessive exercise, but have not regularly engaged in purging behaviours.

Many bulimics start the day by eating nothing or very little, then possibly are 'good' at lunchtime with a yoghurt or an apple. Typically, bulimics eat low calorie meals, with an emphasis on fruits and vegetables when they are not bingeing. As the day wears on, they may be overtaken by the urge to eat more and will find themselves unable to stop. After eating perhaps a meal, or even only one snack item, they may go on to eat several meals or several items of food, typically high in calories, carbohydrates and, in particular, fats – packets of biscuits, confectionery, cereals, etc. They may stop eating only when uncomfortably full, or if interrupted. After an eating binge they experience extreme guilt and anxiety. Days of binge eating bouts may alternate with several days of strict dieting or starving. Bulimics usually binge in private, hiding the problem from other people, with whom they will appear to eat normally. Often, they do not eat normal meals at all, for fear of overeating, or of eating foods too high in fats or carbohydrates. Some have reached a stage where they have difficulty in experiencing hunger or knowing when they have reached 'fullness' at the end of a meal. Ironically, despite repeated attempts to eat less or to diet, many bulimics eat more calories altogether than do normal eaters as their meals may be larger and consist primarily of dessert and snack foods, and contain a large percentage of additional fat (Weltzin et al. 1991). Some researchers have suggested that some bulimics can consume up to 5,000 kcal in one binge, and others have suggested that bulimics can consume between three and 27 times the recommended daily caloric intake. (For a discussion of binge content see Fitzgibbon and Blackman 2004.)

For many bulimics, eating may be followed immediately by vomiting, perhaps once, or several times, until the sufferer feels her digestive system has been 'flushed out'. Some vomiters will use this means of purging themselves perhaps on two or three occasions per week. Others find themselves vomiting up to five or six times a day, directly after eating any but the most 'slimming' foods. Some bulimics can vomit only after consuming a very large amount of food. They can therefore become trapped in a vicious cycle. Once having discovered the possibility of vomiting, they will use it whenever they have broken their self-imposed dietary restrictions. Hence if they overeat on only one occasion or eat one item of 'forbidden' food, they may decide to vomit and therefore eat to fullness in order to do so.

About 27 per cent of bulimics have used laxatives, most commonly of the stimulant type (Colton, Woodside and Kaplan 1999). A small proportion of people with more severe forms of eating disorder also use chewing and spitting out food without swallowing as a means of ridding themselves of excess calories (Kovacs, Mahon and Palmer 2002).

Sufferers are usually women between the ages of 18 and 34, with an average age of 24 years. The disorder has its onset on average between ages 16 to 18, and in the majority of sufferers follows a period of extreme dieting and loss of weight. People present themselves for treatment between one and five years after the disorder has started.

Because of the hidden nature of eating disorders, in normal-weight bulimia in particular, there is growing awareness that they may be more prevalent than we currently realise.

Since Russell's first description of the disorder, it has become clear that it affects a wide range of people, including anorexics and ex-anorexics.

Christopher Fairburn, in Oxford, conducted a series of carefully run surveys to estimate the prevalence of binge eating and bulimia nervosa in the general population, from which he concluded that the point prevalence of bulimia nervosa among adolescent and young adult women is between 0.5 per cent and 1.0 per cent, with a lifetime prevalence closer to 2 per cent, reflecting the fact that the disorder has a limited life-span (see Fairburn and Beglin 1990; Fairburn, Hay and Welch 1993). Meanwhile, researchers in the United States have conducted surveys which suggest that the problem is widespread there too.

Estimates of the prevalence of the disorder have varied as widely as between 1 and 20 per cent – largely because of the wide variations in definition. However, when studies using comparable strict criteria are examined, prevalence appears to be about 1 per cent of young adolescent and adult women (Fairburn and Beglin 1990).

Little has been said about males with bulimia nervosa, but Carlat and Camargo (1991) have reviewed the literature between 1966 and 1990 and have concluded that it affects approximately 0.2 per cent of adolescent boys and young adult men, and that 10 to 15 per cent of all bulimics identified in community-based studies are male.

Since the early descriptions of bulimia nervosa, there has been a vast amount of interest in the disorder and its treatment. There has also been considerable discussion about the criteria necessary for defining it. One reason for this appears to lie with the increasing awareness that there is a great deal of overlap between the behaviour of anorexics, bulimics and indeed some obese people. For example, about one quarter of sufferers may have been anorexic in the past, and between 30 and 40 per cent of sufferers have previously been overweight. Also, there is a large question-mark over the necessity for sufferers to use purging behaviours in order to qualify for a diagnosis of bulimia nervosa. According to the *DSM-IV* criteria, vomiting or some other form of purging is not necessary but is seen as equivalent to dieting, fasting or vigorous exercise. This possibly reflects the fact that binge eating in the presence of extreme concern about weight and shape is experienced to a pathological degree by very large numbers of people, women in particular, many of whom have never attempted to rid themselves of excess calories by any means other than strict dieting.

Nevertheless, most research and treatment studies have focused mainly on bulimics who purge. In a review paper addressing the subtyping of bulimics, Mitchell (1992) notes that several authors have suggested that the purgers have more body-image disturbance and more anxiety about eating than do the non-purgers, greater problems with concentration, feelings of guilt, worthlessness and more suicidal ideation. Non-purging bulimics, however, tend to be overweight as well as older, and they binge eat less often than do purgers. In fact, most people who come for treatment are likely to use purging of some form or other.

Tobin, Johnson and Dennis (1992) found that in a sample of 245 bulimics nearly 80 per cent used two or more forms of purging behaviour, and only 16 per cent of those who did purge relied on vomiting alone. Frequency of purging is often seen as a marker of severity, but Tobin and his colleagues point out that previous authors have failed to show any correlation between the frequency of any one purging strategy and psychopathological symptoms such as depression, or response to treatment. The results of their own studies appeared to suggest a relationship between number of purging behaviours and psychiatric disturbance.

With regard to psychiatric disturbance, many authors have noted that bulimics have an increased prevalence of other disturbed behaviour such as abuse of alcohol and illicit drugs, shoplifting and suicide attempts. Hubert Lacey (Lacey and Evans 1986) has gone so far as to suggest that these people have more specific problems with impulse control, and has proposed a subtype of bulimia nervosa called 'multi-impulsive' bulimia. Others, however, see this phenomenon as largely part of a continuum linked with severity of clinical disturbance (Newton, Freeman and Munro 1993). This notion fits in with clinical experience which suggests that the more disturbed and upset the person, the more likely she is to resort to other means of improving her mood such as drugs and alcohol, the more likely she is to discover the utility of stealing to obtain large supplies of food, and the more likely to be driven to attempts at suicide.

An additional area for concern has been the nature and extent of the binge eating itself. A binge is, by its very nature, private, inaccessible to the public eye, and diagnosis is therefore largely reliant on self-report of varying clarity and reliability. In order to ensure at least some uniformity across cases, the *DSM-IV* criteria specify a minimum average of two binge eating episodes per week for at least three months. It is, of course, possible to experience binge eating without actually fulfilling the *DSM-IV* criteria for an eating disorder. Estimates of admitted binge eating in females have ranged from 20 per cent in a community survey of women of reproductive age to 90 per cent in a sample of college students.

Definition of a binge

In common parlance, the term 'binge' is used differently by different people. For example, while one person might consider that they have binged after eating two meals plus a packet of biscuits and a box of cereal, others may consider themselves to have binged after only a couple of bars of chocolate and two apples. While some researchers in the field have relied on their own varying definitions of a binge, others have followed those prescribed in successive revisions of the *Diagnostic and Statistical Manual of Mental Disorders* of the American Psychiatric Association. These have evolved from: 'rapid consumption of a large amount of food in a discrete period of time, usually less than two hours' (*DSM-III*: American Psychiatric Association 1980); to 'rapid consumption of large amounts of food in a discrete period of time' (*DSM-III-R*: American Psychiatric Association 1987: 68); to the most recent definition, which specifies that a binge is characterised by both 'eating, in a discrete period of time, an amount of food that is larger than most people would eat during a similar time period or under similar circumstances' and 'a sense of lack of control over eating during the episode' (*DSM-IV*: American Psychiatric Association 1994: 549).

Like anorexia nervosa, bulimia nervosa can take its toll physically on the health of sufferers. Some bulimics experience amenorrhoea, some experience oedema and possible kidney disfunctions. The vomiting itself causes potassium, chloride and hydrogen ions to be lost in the vomitus, resulting in symptoms of muscle weakness, constipation and headache. Sufferers also experience palpitations, abdominal pain, easy fatiguability, sore throat and swollen salivary glands. The disorder leads to a predisposition to cardiac arrhythmias. Many bulimics have dental problems, and indeed their condition may first be picked up by their dentists, as the continual presence of vomitus in the mouth can cause tooth enamel to dissolve.

What happens to people who have bulimia nervosa?

While a great deal is known about recent improvements in treatment for bulimia nervosa, less is known about outcome than about anorexia nervosa. The course of an eating disorder varies greatly between individuals. However, a meta-analysis in 1999 found that just under half of bulimic patients recovered, about a quarter showed improvement and a quarter remained chronic cases. The relationship between duration of illness and outcome is not clear, with different studies citing different opinions except on three findings: that borderline symptoms, suicide attempts and alcohol abuse are related to poor outcome. Also, several authors have concluded that recovery is more likely the earlier the person receives treatment (see Reas et al. 2000).

Atypical eating disorders (Eating Disorders Not Otherwise Specified – EDNOS)

Until recently, the term 'eating disorder' applied largely to either anorexia nervosa or bulimia nervosa. As with many classification systems this produced the difficulty that if a person had an eating problem which did not fit neatly into one of these two descriptions, health professionals would try very hard to make it 'fit' one or other description, possibly ignoring the features which singled the person out as being different; or they would assume that the person did not really have an eating disorder at all. It is now recognised, however, that many people fit some but not all of the criteria for either anorexia nervosa or bulimia nervosa even though they suffer from an eating disorder. For example, they may have all the features of anorexia nervosa but without a disturbance in their experience of body weight or shape; or all the features of bulimia nervosa but without any apparent attempt to counter the 'fattening' effects of food.

There is much discussion in the research literature about how to characterise people with so called 'atypical' eating disorders and about whether these people merit assignment to a specific psychiatric diagnosis. This is largely because the nature of the difficulties varies so greatly and because as yet they have no easily definable common 'course' or outcome. Currently, they are relegated in the *DSM-IV* to a group titled 'Eating Disorder Not Otherwise Specified' (EDNOS) and the criteria for this group are known as 'research criteria'.

Binge eating disorder

The largest group of people with EDNOS are those people described as having binge eating disorder (BED). This is a group of people, most but not all of them obese, who experience marked distress about binge eating but who cannot be diagnosed as having bulimia nervosa. As the criteria are as yet preliminary, the diagnosis of binge eating disorder remains in the *DSM-IV* under the temporary status of 'research criteria'. Robert Spitzer, with several other researchers in the obesity field in the United States, conducted a large survey of several weight control programmes together with a large community survey. This group was the first to suggest that the disorder, which includes the key aspects of loss of control and distress about the binge eating, affects about 30 per cent of people attending hospital-based weight control programmes but only 2 per cent of normal-weight people and 4 per cent of obese people in the community (Spitzer et al. 1992). They concluded that, in general, binge eating disorder was associated with a lifetime history of severe obesity and frequent significant weight fluctuations, and in the general population may have a prevalence slightly higher than that of purging bulimia nervosa. In support of their contention that the disorder be added as a diagnostic category distinguishable from EDNOS, they carried out a second multi-site study, as a result of which they pointed out that this group of people also experience several additional problems which could qualify for psychiatric disorder, including impaired work and social functioning, overconcern with body shape and weight, general psychopathology, and a strong history of depression, alcohol or drug abuse and of treatment for emotional problems (Spitzer et al. 1993). They found that, unlike bulimia nervosa, binge eating disorder was only slightly more common in females than in males in the weight control samples and was equally common in males and females in the community non-patient and college samples.

Another important difference between people with binge eating disorder and those with bulimia nervosa is a difference in the temporal relationship between weight worries and dieting behaviour, and the start of binge eating. Whereas, for most bulimics, dieting preceded binge eating, for many people with binge eating disorder, bingeing long preceded dieting as a major problem. In one research study, 45 per cent of BED sufferers reported dieting before starting to binge eat, whereas 55 per cent reported binge eating before their first diet (see Spurrell et al. 1997). The 'binge-first' group had started binge eating at a younger age than did the 'diet-first' group, and also had a history of more psychiatric problems.

The questions which revolve around whether or not binge eating disorder is a distinct clinical entity focus in three areas: how far it can be distinguished from bulimia nervosa or anorexia nervosa; how far it is simply a variant of bulimia nervosa; and how far it is a subtype of obesity, for as body mass increases, so do rates of binge eating. (For a fuller discussion see Devlin, Goldfein and Dobrow 2003.)

Whether or not the phenomenon of binge eating disorder is definable as a recognisable psychiatric disorder, there is a large group of people for whom the symptoms pose a great social and emotional, if not also physical, health problem – BED is linked with obesity and sufferers are more likely to have poorer social functioning, higher levels of disability and more health problems than do people without eating disorders (see Wilfley, Wilson and Agras 2003).

Any counsellor who is asked to treat people with eating disorder is likely to be faced with the need to provide an effective treatment for the condition, however labelled. This consideration becomes increasingly important with the rapid rise in the population of obesity. In the United States, over 30 per cent of adults are obese. The rest of the western world is fast catching up with this epidemic. In Britain in 1980, only 7 per cent of the adult population was obese. This figure had more than doubled by 1993 to 15 per cent, and about half the population has a body weight higher in relation to their height than the desirable range (Wiseman 1996).

Binge eating in obesity

Possibly 50 per cent of obese people suffer with binge eating problems. The only difference is that they do not often compensate for overeating in the same way as bulimics and so are prone to putting on weight faster. The question often arises as to how far obesity is itself an expression of eating disorder, and therefore it is relevant to discuss it briefly here.

Obesity results from an excess of energy intake over expenditure. However, as, on average, obese people have been found to expend more energy than normal weight people, they must, on average, take in more food in order to remain obese (see Garrow 1988). This idea has for a long time formed the basis of the assumption that obese people must indeed eat more than lean people in order to be fat. However, the vast amount of research time and effort that has been expended on the question of whether obese people eat more than do people of normal weight has yielded inconclusive results. Even if it were proven that obesity is caused by overeating, the question would arise as to how far the cause of this increased intake has to do with the extremes of lack of control over eating behaviour typical of people with eating disorders. Obese people, knowing themselves to be prey to comments such as 'he/she shouldn't be eating that', seldom admit to overeating, even if they perceive themselves as doing so; and until recently, the idea of the 'jolly' fat person has often been accepted. When bulimia nervosa was first described, the emphasis was on binge eating in people of normal weight and descriptions of fat people distressed by overeating were fairly rare.

One of the first descriptions of binge eating in fat people was given by Stunkard, who noted that a small proportion of his patients (less than 5 per cent) binge ate, some of them at night (Stunkard 1959). Hilde Bruch (1974) pointed to a higher proportion of her patients with similar problems, but her numbers would naturally have been greater as she was a psychiatrist who was known to have an interest in people with problems in controlling their food intake. More recently, there has been some evidence, both from clinical observation and from research, in particular with weight control programmes, that up to 50 per cent of obese people binge eat (Gormally et al. 1982; Keefe et al. 1984; Loro and Orleans 1981; Marcus, Wing and Lamparski 1985; Telch, Agras and Rossiter 1988). At least a small proportion could be said to meet the *DSM-IV* criteria for bulimia nervosa, given that the criteria do not make it necessary for purging or vomiting to exist, only that sufferers make some attempt in between binge episodes to counter the effects of bingeing, such as dieting or starving for a few days. Nevertheless, there are some obese people who binge eat to varying degrees but who do not make clear attempts in between binges to counter the effects of bingeing. In fact, obese people are very much less likely in general than are normal-weight bulimics to engage regularly in purging or other compensatory behaviours (Marcus et al. 1992). There is a question therefore as to whether these people can be said to have an eating disorder, and if so, is this the same as bulimia nervosa? In comparing obese binge eaters with normal-weight bulimics, it has been suggested that while some binges are objectively similar to those of bulimics as described in the *DSM-IV*, others are rather more subjective episodes and either may consist of only a small number of calories or may present not as a discrete proscribed episode but as an episode lasting for several hours.

   DSM-IV research criteria for binge eating disorder are as follows:

A. Recurrent episodes of binge-eating characterised by:

   1   eating, in a discrete period of time, an amount of food that is definitely larger than most people would eat in a similar period of time under similar circumstances
   2   a sense of lack of control over eating during the episode

B. The binge-eating episodes are associated with at least three of the following:

   1   eating much more rapidly than normal
   2   eating until feeling uncomfortably full
   3   eating large amounts of food when not feeling physically hungry
   4   eating alone because of embarrassment about amount eaten
   5   feeling disgusted with oneself, depressed, or very guilty after over eating

C. Marked distress is experienced regarding binge-eating
D. The binge-eating occurs, on average, at least two days a week for six months
E. The binge-eating is not associated with the regular use of inappropriate compen-satory behaviours (e.g. purging, fasting, excessive exercise) (American Psychiatric Association 1994: 731)

Other causes of weight loss or gain or unusual eating behaviours

One possible danger of broadening the characterisation of eating disorders is that people with atypical symptoms may slip through the medical net and be referred for counselling when in fact the symptoms they have are signs of other psychiatric illness or of underlying medical conditions rather than of a primary eating disor-der. Even more problematic is the case where a true eating disorder is exacerbated by medical illness which is therefore not diagnosed because of the concordance of its symptoms with that of the original disorder.

   Both some schizophrenic and some depressed patients may lose weight and show signs of food avoidance, the former perhaps in response to delusions about specific foods and possible poisoning, and the latter as a result of true general loss of appetite or anorexia, and both may experience amenorrhea in response to starvation. Neither, however, will demonstrate the intense drive for thinness nor disturbance in body image seen in anorexics, and the depressed person is unlikely to appear to be starving him- or herself on purpose.

Some medical causes of weight loss or reduced calorie intake include gastro-intestinal disorders such as Crohn's disease and coeliac disease, and a variety of central nervous system disorders, including lesions of the hypothalamus (the centre in the brain controlling hunger), many infections such as tuberculosis, and most commonly malignancies involving in particular the gastrointestinal tract, pan-creas and liver. Most of these sufferers will experience genuine anorexia or lack of hunger, unlike the person with anorexia nervosa, who may claim to have lost all desire for food but who with careful interviewing is likely to admit to a voracious hunger accompanied by intense fear of satisfying that hunger and of losing con-trol around food and gaining weight, together with disturbed attitudes and beliefs about weight and shape and their importance in that person's life. Because of the strong tendency of some anorexics to deny hunger, and to deny problems around weight and shape, it is possible for people with some other illnesses to be referred after even a thorough medical or psychiatric assessment. Their very denial will be interpreted as evidence of eating disorder, and they arrive in the consulting room of the counsellor with a diagnosis of eating disorder and a request for psycholog-ical treatment. Therefore it is essential that counsellors who express an interest in treating people with eating disorder are on the lookout for such possibilities, which do occur, if rarely.

Medical causes of overeating may include central nervous system lesions, such as tumours involving the hypothalamus or frontal lobes, traumatic brain injuries and some degenerative disorders, including the later stages of Alzheimer's dis-ease, central nervous system infections and seizure disorders, in particular those involving the temporal lobes. (For a full review of medical illnesses associated with weight loss and binge eating, see Kaplan and Katz 1993.)

Essentially, the person with an eating disorder will always exhibit psychopatholog-ical features such as a drive for thinness, a fear of fatness, an abnormal preoccupation with body weight and shape and an unusual investment in these considerations as a basis for their self-esteem and self-confidence. It is towards these features that counselling must be directed. A major consideration to take into account, then, is that of what features in a client's life or personality may have rendered them vul-nerable to acquiring these disorders, and what factors might have helped to fix and sustain the behaviour and attitudes which characterise them.

The following chapter will focus on causes of eating disorders and will pay some attention also to the psychological aspects of obesity and the difficulties faced by people attempting to lose weight.

2 Causes of Eating Disorders

Many causes have been attributed to eating disorders, and each one has lent itself to the development and practice of a variety of treatments. However, given the complex nature of these disorders, and the very different way in which they present in individual people, it is likely that different causal factors will influence their development in each person. Thus, most workers in the field now accept the notion that eating disorders are multidetermined in nature. Where treatment is concerned, some consensus has been built up between specialists, with many centres offering similar sounding therapy programmes. However, the number of ideas that exist about which treatments are the best ones to use bear little relation to the body of research evidence. In Britain in 2004, the National Institute for Clinical Excellence (NICE) published a guideline paper about the treatment of eating disorders. The group of professionals responsible for preparing the paper researched all of the available evidence. It was notable that the size of the body of opinion about the efficacy of treatments bore an inverse relationship to the number of good (randomly controlled) trials actually reported (NICE 2004).

This chapter will describe the range of causes put forward to explain eating disorders. Where relevant, it will describe the treatment methods that have been developed in response to these ideas, and their effects.

Early medical sources looked for a physical cause for eating disorders, anorexia nervosa in particular. The idea of a hypothalamic disturbance was posited, given that the hypothalamus is the part of the brain thought to control appetite. Indeed, hypothalamic changes can be seen in anorexics, but these changes revert to normal as sufferers are cured of their disorder, and it is likely that the physical changes are a consequence rather than a cause of the disorder in the first place. Moreover, even the presence of amenorrhoea has been disputed as a necessary diagnostic factor in the disorder, as there are many people who exhibit all the other characteristics without amenorrhoea (Garfinkel et al. 1996). There are certainly medical conditions which cause either extreme weight loss or bulimia, but, as noted in Chapter 1, the factors notably missing in all these conditions are the psychopathologic features found in anorexia nervosa and bulimia nervosa, namely the drive for thinness, the fear of fatness and the extreme concern with body shape and weight. Some current medical research, therefore, is beginning to focus on isolating the biochemical mechanisms which may combine with extreme stress in some people to produce a drive towards self-starvation.

Psychosomatic theories

The earliest psychological explanations for anorexia nervosa and overeating were couched in psychodynamic terms. Psychoanalytic psychology emphasises past and early experience as an important causal factor influencing psychopathology and uses as its method of discovery a series of sessions with individual 'patients', by which term clients would be referred to, in which they recall and explore issues to do with their early upbringing and relationships with parents and other important people in their lives. (For a full overview of psychodynamic models of eating disorders, see Dare and Crowther 1995.) Psychoanalytic thinking dominated the therapy field until the second half of the last century. However, it was traditionally a lengthy treatment, and available only to a limited number of 'suitable' patients, even in its shorter forms. While some patients have been helped by this form of treatment, the majority remained unaffected and the proponents of the treatment have made little or no attempt to produce evidence for its efficacy.

Early theories postulated that the refusal to eat in anorexia nervosa was a symbolic repudiation of sexuality, especially fantasies and wishes surrounding oral impregnation and implicating strongly the presence of oedipal conflict. But, as Goodsitt has pointed out in his chapter in a key text, *Handbook of Psychotherapy for Anorexia Nervosa and Bulimia*, such theories do not explain other anorexic symptoms such as denial of thinness, body image distortions and disturbances in thinking (Goodsitt 1986). Neither do they explain the belief widely held among people with eating disorders that fat is to be despised and weight gain to be avoided at all costs. Later, the influence of Hilde Bruch (1974), a psychiatrist who worked largely with women with eating disorders, moved some way from this kind of interpretation towards an understanding that anorexia nervosa and other eating disorders were disorders arising at an earlier stage of childhood. She based this idea on her perception that patients displayed major deficits in self-identity and autonomy. She concluded that eating disorders were secondary to an underlying disturbance of personality which arose from the child having a faulty relationship with a mother who consistently misinterpreted her child's signals of hunger, distress or other needs at an early age. Hence the child does not learn to know when she is upset what she really wants or needs by way of comfort, and comes to use food as a cure for all ills. Such a child typically would be seen as a 'good' child, anxious to please, and would rarely make her needs or wants heard, but as a result would experience a paralysing sense of ineffectiveness. Hilde Bruch suggested that such a child may be triggered into dieting when faced by new and stressful experiences such as going to a new school or away from home to summer camp. The child may be vulnerable to criticism and may diet as a way to gain acceptance by her peers.

Based on these ideas, Bruch favoured what she called a 'fact finding, non-interpretive approach' to treatment (1974: 336). She abandoned the traditional use of interpretation as a result of her experience of using this method and concluded that for a patient with an eating disorder, such an approach 'may mean the devastating re-experience of being told what he feels and thinks, confirming his sense of inadequacy and thus interfering with his developing true self-awareness and trust in his own psychological faculties' (1974: 336). She described her work as 'collaborative' and held that this approach 'leads to a repair of their cognitive distortions … thus they can become more realistic in their self-appraisal' (1974: 337). Bruch called her approach 'the constructive use of ignorance' (1974: 338), by which she meant that the therapist attempts to adopt an objective approach to working together with patients to understand their difficulties. In a sense, Bruch's work was very much a precursor to the cognitive therapy approach as described later by Aaron Beck in relation to the treatment of depression (Beck et al. 1976) and subsequently in relation to a range of other disorders. Although Bruch's work did not include a behavioural element, a cognitive behavioural approach to the treatment of the eating disorders can be seen as a natural corollary of her work rather than as an entirely novel approach.

Arthur Crisp's work (1980) is also couched in psychodynamic terms, but has a different theoretical basis from that of Hilde Bruch. He has conceptualised anorexia nervosa more specifically as a disorder of adolescence, triggered by the onset of puberty. The sufferer is frightened by the physical and emotional changes she is going through, the challenges involved in growing up, and by the growing realisation of her sexuality. She literally stops the process by starving herself down to a prepubertal weight, so that fear of losing control of that weight takes over from the more real fears of adulthood and the changes involved in achieving it. Treatment involves a combination of refeeding using varying degrees of coercion, couched in loosely behavioural terms, family therapy and individual broadly psychodynamically oriented therapy. The aim of the behavioural element of the treatment is to expose the sufferer to the feared stimulus, in this case food and eating, with the aim of desensitising her to the fear, at the same time as achieving the target of weight gain.

Stress-induced eating

All psychosomatic theories have in common the idea that overeating, especially in the obese, is a response to emotional distress, particularly anxiety and depression. However, empirical support for this idea is equivocal. While several studies have drawn links between self-reports of overeating and obesity or eating disorder, few studies have been able to demonstrate a link between overeating and anxiety where attempts have been made to standardise anxiety stimuli.

Nevertheless, the notion that some people eat more than others when under psychological 'stress' is one that has received more attention in the popular literature than in scientific circles. We all think that we know what we mean by the word 'stress', but it is in fact problematic to work with largely because of the difficulties of definition and measurement. This is true in relation to both 'stressors' derived in laboratory experiments and those experienced in real life, all of which pose varying levels of threat to different individuals, and even in the same person at different times. One area of study has extrapolated from evidence in the animal literature about the effects of stress on animals. For example, Antelman and his colleagues (Antelman, Roland and Fisher 1976) found that rats would gnaw, eat or lick at food when their tails were pinched. Other studies have also shown increased eating in response to other physical stressors such as electric shock. Extrapolation to humans, however, is difficult, and the exploration of stress-induced eating in humans has focused on hypothesised individual differences between people. One line of thought is based on the psychosomatic account which suggests that obese people cannot distinguish between hunger and anxiety because they learned to associate them at an early age or because, as Bruch suggested, they never learned to distinguish between them. Based on these ideas, Stanley Schachter and his colleagues predicted that while normal people could label gastric contractions as hunger, overweight people could not, and would therefore continue eating regardless when under stress (Schachter, Goldman and

Gordon 1968). This idea was the basis for the 'internal–external' hypothesis, which came to underlie much of the research into obesity in the 1960s and 1970s. This was the notion that normal-weight people, because they are aware of gastric, inner cues, are internally oriented where food is concerned and will therefore not eat when under stress because they are aware of reduced gastric activity. Obese people, on the other hand, are 'externally' motivated, in that they are less responsive to internal cues to eat and will therefore eat more in response to stress (because they are unaware of reductions in gastric motility) and will eat more in response to external cues such as the time of day and the sight of food. In fact, this idea has received little support as the results of studies investigating it both in the laboratory and in the natural environment have been equivocal. (For a review of stress-induced eating, see Greeno and Wing 1994.)

Interpersonal stress and life events have been cited as triggers for the onset of eating disorders in the majority of women with eating disorders. However, there do not appear to be major differences between women who report onset of their disorder in response to a provoking event and women who do not (Schmidt, Troop and Treasure 1999). Hence it is unclear how far a trigger event can be said to be causative.

Comfort eating

Another idea which fits in with psychosomatic theory, and which makes more sense in relation to the subjective experience of some obese and eating-disordered individuals, is the idea, widespread in common parlance, that people who overeat do so as a means of deriving comfort and well-being from food. Overeaters have described eating as a way of giving to themselves, as a way of filling a large 'hole' or of avoiding feelings of 'emptiness'. It has been suggested therefore that bulimics are unable to nurture themselves in other, non-food-related ways. In a rare attempt to investigate this idea, Lehman and Rodin (1989) gave a series of questionnaires covering questions about self-criticism, reactivity to positive and negative events, self-efficacy and 'self-nurturance' to groups of bulimics, and dieting and non-dieting controls. They found that the bulimics were less likely to react positively to positive events, more likely to react negatively to bad events, and had decreased levels of self-efficacy and higher levels of self-criticism than did the comparison groups. Interestingly, they found that each of the three groups were as likely to use food to comfort and support themselves, but that bulimics were less likely than the other groups to nurture themselves in ways unrelated to food. Hence it is possible that while 'comfort eating' may be a universal phenomenon, the focus on food as a sole means of looking after oneself, rather than as one feature in a repertoire of self-nurturing behaviours, may be more pronounced for people who develop an eating disorder.

Such is the power of 'comfort eating', that it has often been described by people who overeat as a 'compulsion' or 'addiction'. The term 'compulsive overeating' is widely used, and there is a theory that people who overeat are addicted to food, or at least to foods of a certain type such as those containing sugar and starches. This is indeed the basis of several widely used treatment programmes such as Overeaters Anonymous, particularly in the United States. Superficially, there are strong similarities between drug or alcohol abuse and binge eating, such as cravings, use of the behaviour to relieve negative feelings, difficulty with stopping the behaviour, and subjective feelings of loss of control over the 'addictive' behaviour. However, whether or not these similarities can be attributed to the same underlying process is questionable. There are several studies, both clinical and research, which suggest that carbohydrate consumption, in particular consumption of simple carbohydrates, results in a temporary reduction in negative mood states in individuals experiencing a variety of different types of emotional and physical disorder. These disorders include premenstrual syndrome, seasonal affective disorder, withdrawal from tobacco and alcohol, bulimia and obesity (see Christenson 1993 for a review of the mood-regulation effects of food). This phenomenon has led to speculation that carbohydrates must produce their mood-altering effects through their effects on neurotransmission of serotonin in the brain. However, there is no conclusive evidence to date that this is the case, and in general no credibility is given to the idea that food, like drugs such as tobacco and alcohol, is addictive in the biological sense. Moreover, the abstinence or disease model of eating disorder has implications for treatment which are unhelpful. The model prescribes increased dietary restraint, with avoidance of specific binge foods and increased control of eating patterns. However, most bulimics have already attempted, on the basis of intuitive common-sense ideas, to tackle their symptoms in these ways, but have merely replicated past failures to get their eating under control. (See Wilson 1993a for a fuller discussion.)

The family as a source of eating disorder

Clinical observations of families with an anorexic or bulimic member have led to many attempts to identify the common characteristics of such families. One line of work carries with it the implication that the families of people with eating disorders carry a kind of psychiatric/psychological morbidity which happens to express itself as eating disorder, perhaps as an attempt by the sufferer to claim some kind of individuation for herself. Some workers have suggested that such families are characterised by disturbed relationships, for example where a marriage is good on the surface but where the couple is masking a high degree of dissatisfaction. Minuchin and his colleagues (Minuchin, Rosman and Baker 1978) have identified a number of characteristics which they believe are typical of anorexic families – over-protectiveness, rigidity, lack of conflict resolution, and an atmosphere which allows for little privacy so that the anorexic child is involved in unresolved marital or family conflicts. In one study post-treatment where subjects were asked to describe the factors that had been most helpful in relation to improvement, not one subject cited family members as contributing to their cure. On the contrary, most said that family members had been unhelpful (Rorty, Yager and Rossotto 1993). In another study, family factors prior to treatment were stronger predictors of outcome of a short-term therapy than were any other measures. The bulimic patients who did not improve reported their families as being highly controlling, organised, moralistic, achievement-oriented and unexpressive (Blouin et al. 1994). In a study of 69 patients with a diagnosis of anorexia nervosa, family dysfunction was the factor most frequently mentioned by the patients as a cause of their disorder (Tozzi et al. 2003).

Another line of thought suggests that certain families carry a specific tendency to pathology in the area of eating and weight *per se*. For example, a family history of anorexia nervosa or obesity may be taken to imply that eating disorder could be carried through families. In support of this idea, about one quarter of the anorexics in one study had at least one relative who had at one time suffered an eating disorder. Other examples would be: a family with an unusual interest in weight, food or shape; or one or other parent working in the food or fashion industry. Many researchers in the area of eating disorder have noted that parents with eating disorders do not eat in front of their children or do not behave in a positive way towards their children during mealtimes (Waugh and Bulik 1999). None of this, of course, necessarily implies a genetic link, and could equally well be explained by the influence of environment and learning. Indeed, in one American study the mothers of a group of young women with high scores on a measure of eating disturbance were compared with the mothers of a group who scored low on the same measure. The mothers of the daughters in the identified group had more disturbed eating themselves than did the comparison mothers; they thought that their daughters should lose more weight, and were more critical of their daughters' appearance (Pike and Rodin 1991).

The results of two studies by Chris Fairburn and his colleagues in Oxford provide some possible evidence about how such links might be developed and maintained. One study looked at mothers with eating disorders and their 12- to 14-months-old infants and compared them with a group of mothers without eating disorders (Stein et al. 1994). They found that, compared to the controls, the index mothers expressed more negative emotion towards their infants during mealtimes but not during play. The infants' weight was found to be inversely related both to the amount of conflict during mealtimes and the extent of the mother's concern about her own body shape. In another study, the authors compared the eating habits and attitudes to food of mothers of children with non-organic failure to thrive with those of the mothers of normal children (McCann et al. 1994). The mothers of the failure to thrive children were more careful about their own diets and 50 per cent of them were restricting their child's intake of 'sweet' foods while 30 per cent were restricting foods they considered 'fattening' or unhealthy. Hence, it is apparent that erroneous beliefs about food and eating and maladaptive uses of eating behaviour itself can be fostered at a very early age. What is more, a young woman's experience of a mother's inappropriate use of food to improve mood and a high level of teasing about weight may influence the formation of bulimic symptoms in later life (MacBrayer et al. 2000).

Another way of looking at the link between eating disorder and family is to suggest that some factors may put children more at risk of eating disorders than others. For example, Fairburn and his colleagues compared 67 women with a history of anorexia nervosa with 204 healthy control subjects, 102 people with other psychiatric disorders and 102 people with bulimia nervosa. They found that perfectionism and negative self-evaluation were both more common in the people with eating disorders than in either of the other groups and that bulimics were more likely than any of the other groups to have obese parents, a parent with psychiatric disorder, or themselves to have had an early menarche (Fairburn et al. 1999). There may, conversely, be some family factors which protect children from eating disorder. In one study in Connecticut, girls with symptoms of eating disorder reported significantly lower levels of family 'connectedness' (feeling cared for, sharing activities), family communication (discussing problems and misdemeanours) and connectedness with friends or other adults than did girls without symptoms (Fonesca, Ireland and Resnick 2002).

Eating disorder and child sexual abuse

The idea of inadequate support in early life and the possible links between early unresolved trauma and eating disorder has been explored in a slightly different way in relation to the idea of a link between child sexual abuse and eating disorders. Many researchers have pointed to the possibility that women with eating disorders have experienced a high rate of sexual abuse in childhood compared with expected figures for normal women (for example, see Palmer et al. 1990; Sloan and Leichner 1986). It has been suggested that bulimic women are likely to binge more frequently if they have been abused and that the frequency of bingeing is particularly high if the woman reports being abused by a relative, in a way that involves force, or before the age of 14 years. They are also more likely to vomit more frequently if the abuse was intrafamilial (Waller 1992). There is, however, no clear consensus about the nature of the links between sexual abuse and specific symptoms or severity of eating disorder. Nevertheless, the clinical experience of many writers has led to a view that binge eating, starvation or chronic purging behaviours may develop as an attempt, albeit maladaptive, to cope with or escape from the negative thoughts and feelings engendered by prior sexual abuse and as a focus for an attempt to bring control into an otherwise chaotic life.

An alternative view regarding the link between child sexual abuse and eating disorder comes from more recent research which suggests that an eating disorder may be just one manifestation of disorder in people who have been abused, and that sexual abuse is not necessarily more prevalent than in depression or substance abuse disorders. For example, workers in Michigan (Folsom et al. 1993) noted that a majority of subjects with either eating disorders or general psychiatric disorders studied by them (about 70 per cent) reported a history of sexual abuse, and about 50 per cent of both groups reported histories of both sexual and physical abuse. Rates of sexual abuse did not differ between subjects with bulimia nervosa, anorexia and bulimia nervosa, affective disorder or borderline personality disorders. Nor did eating-disordered subjects experience more severe forms of sexual abuse than psychiatric subjects.

In a review of several studies of child sexual abuse, Connors and Morse (1993) conclude that about 30 per cent of eating-disordered patients have been sexually abused, but that this figure may be comparable to that found in the female population in general, and lower than numbers found in some other psychiatric groups.

Notwithstanding the arguments for and against a specific link between child sexual abuse and eating disorder, the existence of a history of child sexual abuse may be important from the point of view of its effects on self-esteem, and in particular negative beliefs about the self. Although the majority of instances of child sexual abuse are said to be extrafamilial, abuse could in some cases have a mediating role where there are other strong predisposing factors, including negative family factors such as difficulties with management of conflict, lack of support, or physical or emotional neglect. In one study of American university students, the existence of a history of child sexual abuse combined in an additive manner with a history of a dysfunctional family environment to increase the risk of bulimia (Hastings and Kern 1994). In another study of young girls in therapy for psychiatric problems, girls who displayed impulsive and drug using behaviour following sexual abuse were also more likely to show disordered eating (Wonderlich et al. 2001). Thus, a history of abuse, whether it be physical, emotional or sexual, can be a central feature in the development and maintenance of an eating disorder where the route is via self-destructive and impulsive behaviour rather then dieting based on low self-esteem.

Family therapy as a treatment for eating disorder

Given the widely held view that the family may in part be responsible for the origin and maintenance of eating disorder in its members, family therapy has been offered widely as a treatment of choice, at least to young women still living at home. Treatment approaches have been influenced largely by the work with anorexic patients of Selvini Palazzoli (known as the Milan method), and of Salvador Minuchin, based on the systems theory approach (Selvini Palazzoli 1974; Minuchin, Rosman and Baker 1978).

Selvini Palazzoli adopted the view that the family is a self-regulating system based on a number of rules. She concluded that the members seem to be sure enough of their own communications but that they deny the content of what other people have to say. No one in the family is prepared to be responsible for leadership, and any decisions made are said to be for the good of someone else. The central and most serious problem is the system of alliances between members, which is based on a large number of secret rules. In addition, the parents of eating-disordered clients are concealing a deep disillusionment with each other which they are unable to resolve, with the result that the client has become the go-between. Based on these assumptions, Selvini Palazzoli devised a short-term form of therapy, involving the whole family and consisting of a maximum number of 20 sessions. The content of the sessions was based not on head-on confrontations, but on positive connotation. So, for example, an overclose relationship between a daughter and the family would be redefined in terms of love and concern. Following on this, the 'symptom' or problem of which the family was complaining, or which had been observed in sessions, would be 'prescribed'. The theory behind this paradoxical treatment was that the therapist was now in a position of power because the family was unable to contradict her; but by prescribing the symptom, the therapist of course implicitly rejects it.

There has been no research looking specifically at this therapy, but the effectiveness of the use of paradoxical intention with individuals suggests that aspects at least of the therapy might have some utility in clinical practice. The therapy would also use the technique of circular questioning – whereby each member of the family is asked to describe a problem from his or her own point of view, with the aim that the family arrive at a new perspective on problems. Interestingly, this technique has parallels in cognitive behaviour therapy in its emphasis on investigating and reattributing the symptoms of the family.

Minuchin's therapy method is based on 'systems theory'. He believed in the need to create a change in the system by challenging four basic family character-istics: enmeshment – overinvolvement and blurring of boundaries; overprotec-tiveness; rigidity – which maintains the status quo; and inability to resolve conflict. The therapy traditionally begins with a family lunch in which the thera-pist may either underfocus or overfocus on the eating issue depending on the particular family circumstances, but will soon move on to other issues to do with parental control in younger patients or autonomy in older patients. The aim of the therapy is to create stress in the system, and rejuggle the alliances between family members. Again, research has been limited, but Minuchin and his col-leagues themselves followed up 53 patients for between one and seven years. They claimed 86 per cent recovery both of the anorexia and of problems with eating behaviour.

More recently, workers at the Institute of Psychiatry in the United Kingdom have conducted a series of controlled studies of family therapy with adolescent and adult outpatients, some of whom had previously been hospitalised in their unit. In their work, they have found little evidence to suggest that there is a spe-cific type of family constellation or style of family functioning that is invariably associated with an eating disorder. In an early study, 57 patients with anorexia nervosa who had been hospitalised were randomly allocated on discharge to family therapy or individual supportive therapy. The family therapy was 'eclec-tic', with contributions by the methods of Haley (1976), Minuchin, Rosman and Baker (1978) and Selvini Palazzoli (1978). Family therapy was found to be more effective than individual therapy in patients whose illness was not chronic (that is, less than three years) and had begun before 19 years. At one year, nine out of ten of the family therapy patients were rated as having a good or intermediate outcome. However, only two out of 11 patients in the group who were treated individually made a good or intermediate recovery. In contrast, individual therapy was more effective for older patients. A follow-up study showed that outcomes for family treatment continued to be superior to individual treatment five years after treatment was completed (see Eisler et al. 1997; Russell et al. 1987). The Maudsley group have also looked at differences between kinds of family therapy. Conjoint therapy (where the whole family is seen together) was compared with family counselling (where the parents are seen separately from the children). The family counselling approach fared marginally better than the conjoint approach, and appears to be more successful where there are high levels of family criticism. This suggests that therapeutic involvement of all family members *per se* may have more utility than attempts to re-align family members (Eisler et al. 2000; Le Grange et al. 1992).

The Maudsley group's results have to some extent been supported recently by the research of Robin and others (1994) in the United States. They compared 'behavioural family systems therapy' with individual therapy which also included separate meetings with a therapist for the parents. The treatments were on aver-age 16 months long (12 to 18 months). Both groups gained significant amounts of weight, the family therapy group gained more weight (increases in body mass indices of 5.1 versus 2.7 for the individual group). Both treatments produced com-parable changes in eating attitudes, body shape dissatisfaction, depression and eating-related family conflict.

Eating disorder and other psychiatric diagnoses

Depression

Some workers have suggested that anorexia nervosa and bulimia nervosa are really forms of affective disorder, akin to major depression; in other words, sufferers and their families have a predisposition to general neurotic morbidity which may be genetic. In support of this idea, they note that many anorexics and bulimics describe themselves as depressed. Also, several studies have suggested a high prevalence of affective disorder, anxiety disorders and alcoholism both in patients with eating disorder and in their first-degree relatives (Halmi et al. 1991). However, if indeed eating disorder in these people is an expression of affective disorder, it is not clear why the individuals concerned should develop an eating disorder in particular. Also, it is possible that the depression is, on the contrary, secondary to, and perhaps results from, eating disorder, as the depressive symptoms often appear after the eating disorder and usually improve with improvement in the eating disorder.

In line with the idea that eating disorders may be a form of affective disorder, some centres, in the United States in particular, have advocated the use of antidepressant drugs as a treatment of choice.

There have been few controlled trials of the use of antidepressants in anorexia nervosa, with no significant response. No pharmacological treatment has been demonstrated to show clinical improvement in anorexia nervosa, and in fact the use of any medication is dictated not by the diagnosis of anorexia nervosa but by the judgement of the professionals involved in relation to what other symptoms the person expresses (see Walsh 2002).

However, several trials have shown a clear advantage of antidepressant medication over placebo in the treatment of bulimia, whether or not the patients are depressed (Mitchell, Raymond and Specker 1993; Walsh 1991). While the use of monoamine oxidase inhibitors (MAOIs) is inappropriate in the case of people with no control over their eating behaviour because of their potentially dangerous side-effects, several trials have demonstrated the efficacy of tricyclic antidepressants such as imipramine and desipramine, and fluoxetine. Bulimic patients who were not depressed before treatment show as much improvement on antidepressants as do patients who were depressed, which suggests that the mechanism by which the drugs work is different from that in depression, and hence the disorders themselves may not be comparable. On average, patients receiving active medication achieve a decline in binge frequency of about 69 per cent. However, only about 20 per cent of the patients stop binge eating altogether and in many trials patients have been able to maintain their improvement only through continued use of the antidepressant drugs. Also, while antidepressant therapy may bring about symptomatic improvement, there is no evidence that drug treatment has any effect on the patients' attitudes to weight and shape. This points strongly to the notion that any treatment must address the specific thoughts and feelings of people with eating disorder in order to have any lasting effect.

Obsessive Compulsive Disorder

In addition to depressive disorders, obsessive compulsive disorder (OCD) has been reported to have a high lifetime prevalence in people with eating disorders.

Prevalence figures vary between researchers but it seems likely that as many as 30 per cent of both anorexics and bulimics suffer with OCD in addition to their eating disorder (see Milos et al. 2002). The symptoms of the eating disorders themselves often appear similar to those of an obsessive compulsive disorder: excessive dieting, checking of weight and food, worries about weight and eating, and rituals around mealtimes can have an obsessional character. Some writers have suggested considering anorexia nervosa as a form of OCD. The symptoms of bulimia nervosa have been compared to those of obsessive compulsive disorder because of the way in which sufferers use purging as a means of 'undoing' the negative effects of overeating, so that purging is negatively reinforced by reducing the bulimic's fear of weight gain (Bulik et al. 1992). Another similarity between people with obsessive compulsive disorders and eating disorders is a tendency to being perfectionistic and self-critical. Given the similarities between these disorders, it might follow that the psychological treatment of choice for obsessive compulsive disorder, exposure with response prevention, would also be effective in relation to people with eating disorders. Several studies have compared the use of exposure and response prevention, first described by Rosen and Leitenberg (1982) with cognitive behavioural programmes. They have shown that the cognitive behavioural approach is more effective than the more behavioural exposure and response prevention approach, albeit that the former may include aspects of the latter within the treatment programme (Agras 1993). This too is evidence that people with eating disorders need help to address their specific concerns about food, eating and weight, as opposed to either a purely symptomatic or a purely medical approach.

Body Dysmorphic Disorder

Many anorexics begin dieting in order to cope with a specific defect they have noticed in their body, which may have nothing to do with weight and size. Some of these people may have body dysmorphic disorder (BDD), a diagnosis given to patients who are preoccupied with an imagined or slight defect in the appearance of some part or parts of their body (American Psychiatric Association 1994). This preoccupation and the associated distress are extremely difficult to treat and may have an almost delusional character. Up to 40 per cent of anorexics in one study were found to be suffering from BDD in addition to their eating disorder. The BDD had preceded the anorexia nervosa and was more prevalent in the group of patients with the earliest onset of their illness and the greatest severity of disturbance (Grant, Won Kim and Eckert 2002).

Personality disorder

Eating disorders are often chronic, and many sufferers appear to have longstanding personality and emotional difficulties in addition to or pre-dating their eating disorder. These difficulties may include patterns of unstable and intense personal relationships, an unstable self-image, chronic feelings of emptiness assuaged only by bingeing on large amounts of food, and impulsive and potentially self-harming behaviours. Several researchers have suggested that up to 70 per cent of inpatients with eating disorders also suffer with a personality disorder as defined by *DSM-IV*. Counsellors might expect clients with personality disorder (PD) to be more difficult to treat. However, there is no clear evidence about the effect of PD on the course and outcome of an eating disorder (Grilo et al. 2003).

Anorexia and bulimia nervosa as sociocultural phenomena

The disadvantage of characterising the eating disorders as psychiatric disorders or of linking them with other known disorders is that this may not lead to greater understanding where specific diagnoses do not link in with effective treatments.

An alternative to the 'psychiatric disorder' explanation is that anorexia nervosa and bulimia nervosa are both diseases of our modern society, which idolises slimness and health and denigrates fatness. For example, Garner and his colleagues (1980) studied the pictures of *Playboy* magazine centrefold girls and of winners of the Miss America pageant from 1959 to 1978. During this time period, the weights of both women and men were on the increase. However, the ideal shape of women was increasingly thinner over the years as judged by the measurements of both the centrefold girls and the Miss America winners. At the same time, the authors of the study noted a significant increase in the proportion of space given to material about diet and slimming in six major women's magazines between 1969 and 1979. In more recent years, a great deal of publicity has been given to this kind of pressure on women, and many people are under the impression that it no longer exists to the same degree. However, Wiseman and his colleagues (1992) continued the study on through the years 1979 to 1988, only to find that the overvaluation of thinness continues. While the numbers of articles in women's magazines on diet alone have decreased slightly since the 1970s, the numbers on exercise, and in particular on exercise combined with diet, have increased. Hence thinness, couched in terms of health, is now sought through both dieting and exercise. What is more, we continue to be exposed to media images of thin women. Not only have the models photographed in the most popular magazines become thinner since the 1980s, but the extent to which the figures of the models are revealed in full body shots has increased (Sypeck, Gray and Ahrens 2004).

In this context, very many adolescent and pre-adolescent girls are self-conscious and very sensitive to fatness and changes in body shape, and it is an easy thing for dieting to be triggered by a chance remark or by contact with other dieters.

Several surveys have been carried out to explore the prevalence of dieting and attitudes to weight among both men and women of all ages. Estimates have varied widely, but even the most conservative suggest that dieting and negative attitudes to current weight in people of normal weight are fairly common. At least 50 per cent of women and young girls would like to be slimmer (for example, see Wardle and Marsland 1990), and as many as 50 to 75 per cent have tried dieting at least once in their life (see, for example, Jeffery, Adlis and Foster 1991).

Where young adolescent women are concerned, dieting is particularly common. A series of surveys carried out in Leeds, England, by Andrew Hill and his colleagues suggests that up to 70 per cent of adolescent girls have tried dieting (Hill, Oliver and Rogers 1992). The results of one large American survey found that 44 per cent of female students and 15 per cent of male students were dieting at the time of the survey (Serdula et al. 1993). What is more, in studies carried out in girls' schools, researchers have found that concerns about weight and dieting are developing increasingly earlier in life, with girls as young as age 9 believing themselves to be overweight. Sadly, these ideas are likely to be acquired from other children, as being at a school where there are more older girls was associated with identifying with a thinner ideal shape, being more likely to have dieted, and having lower self-esteem (Wardle and Watters 2004).

Behind this behaviour there lies a general attitude to weight and body shape which is given credibility by the notion that fat is synonymous with ill-health and thinness is synonymous with health. A history of obesity has been associated with several chronic conditions, such as arthritis, diabetes mellitus and gall bladder disease, and life-threatening diseases, such as coronary artery disease, and certain cancers, in particular cancers of the gastrointestinal system and breast cancer. Epidemiological studies, particularly those conducted in the United States, have concluded that overweight people in general die earlier than people of average weight (Simopoulos 1985). Hence, the rational need for people to be within a normal weight limit set down in relation to insurance company figures confers respectability on the idea that fat is 'bad' and slimness is 'good', and indeed on the whole of the diet industry. This is the case despite the fact that the evidence from longitudinal studies that weight loss in obese people increases longevity is in fact equivocal (for reviews of the evidence about the effects on health and mortality of weight loss, see Andres, Muller and Sorkin 1993; Williamson and Pamuk 1993).

An independent factor influencing attitudes to fat people is that of a prejudice against fat and against fat people which is all-pervasive. Fat children are seen as 'dirty', 'stupid', 'sloppy', and as less likeable even than children with physical deformities by other children (Richardson et al. 1961; Staffieri 1967) and by adults, even those who are themselves overweight (Maddox, Back and Liederman 1968). There is some evidence that fat people are less likely to be offered high-powered jobs than are thin people, and a person's appearance as either fat or thin may have a powerful influence on the attitude to his or her health and capacity to do the job of a prospective employer (Klesges et al. 1990). This prejudice is endorsed by the medical profession (Maiman et al. 1979), and even trained dietitians have been found to have negative attitudes to obese people (Oberrieder et al. 1995). Negative attitudes are encouraged even at an early age, in all kinds of subtle ways. Susan Wooley, an American researcher, tells the story of how her colleagues went out to look for fat children whom they could photograph. When asked in the park if they would allow their children to be photographed, all the mothers of normal-weight children said 'Yes' and all the mothers of the fat children said 'No'. But it is not only parents who subtly convey the idea of shame to their fat children. Even in their earliest reading material, characters, often with negative or comic characteristics, are described as 'fat', but no author would think of describing a character as 'thin' nor dare to describe someone as being 'black', 'coloured', 'disabled' or 'blind' except in a very positive setting.

Hence, dieting, seen as the way to achieve slimness and avoid being fat, is condoned, even applauded, by society, by the media, and by the medical profession.

Prevalence rates for the eating disorders are far higher among women than among men, which raises the major question not only about why this gender-related difference should exist, but about how it comes about and how it is maintained. It has been argued that women are at far greater risk than men because of the way in which women are socialised in society and encouraged to develop their gender identity while at the same time being expected to fulfil a variety of additional roles – such as career woman, mother (Striegel-Moore 1993).

The question that arises is how far eating disorder is triggered by the stress of dieting alone, and how far it arises as a result of a combination of factors. It is not surprising that young women who diet seriously are indeed more likely than other women to be preoccupied with their weight and to have serious problems with binge eating (Huon 1994). In groups where there is a high pressure to be slim in order to succeed in a chosen career, there is some evidence that the prevalence of eating disorders may be higher even than in the general population. In both athletes, for whom leanness or the maintenance of a specific weight are important, and ballet dancers, for example, significant symptoms of eating disorder, in particular binge eating, are extremely common, and the prevalence rates for anorexia nervosa have been reported to be as high as 4 to 16 per cent.

However, dieting, while clearly a risk factor for eating disorder, is not the sole prerequisite. In many cases, dieting is not a precursor to eating disorder at all. Two studies of women with binge eating disorder have reported that binge eating preceded a first diet in 55 and 37 per cent of cases respectively (Brewerton et al. 2000; Spurrell et al. 1997). The group who reported having binged first had started bingeing at an average of 12 to 15 years of age, as compared to an average of 26 years for those who started by dieting. One of the research studies noted that the people who started with bingeing were also more likely to have a personality disorder and to have psychiatric problems. These findings imply that there may be different pathways into an eating disorder, with different triggers, which may have implications both for what causes an eating disorder and for the nature and course of the treatment offered. Dieting, engendered by a range of factors, including media influence, may be the trigger for an eating disorder in about half of sufferers. However, for a large number of other people, binge eating, perhaps started in an attempt to cope with difficult emotions, may itself trigger a spiral into eating disorder.

Where dieting does appear to be the chief trigger, it is certainly not the only cause. Ballet dancers and athletes, who need to maintain a low maximum body weight, are known to be at higher risk than are other people of becoming anorexic or bulimic, but some are more amenable to cure with simple advice and counselling than are other people with eating disorders. In one study of female athletes, the 16 per cent who had an eating disorder had significantly lower self-esteem and mental health than the other women (Hulley and Hill 2001). There is a difference between a normal dieter who simply wishes to be more physically attractive and more socially acceptable, or who needs to maintain a low weight for her career, and the young woman who is at risk of an eating disorder. For the at-risk person, problems with low self-esteem, and wider issues to do with control over her life, may act as predisposing factors for eating disorder in the context of an interest in dieting.

An additional consideration to take into account when exploring vulnerability factors in eating disorder is that of cultural differences. Most theories of causation assume that weight concerns are central and that the emergence of eating disorders in non-western cultures can be attributed to a process of westernisation, whereby great value is placed on thinness. However, high levels of eating disturbance have been noted in groups of Asian, Caribbean and Muslim women espousing traditional cultural orientations (Rieger et al. 2001). It may be that thinness is valued in some cultures for different reasons than in western culture, and the search by a young woman for autonomy in the face of authority figures may be just as salient in other cultures as it is in our own, if for different reasons.

Eating disorder as learned behaviour

The idea that in some cases eating disorder is preceded by dieting has led to the notion put forward originally by Peter Slade (1982), among others, that eating disorder might become rewarding to some young women, not in the sense of being pleasant, but as a way, albeit destructive, out of an impossible emotional turmoil. He suggested that the behaviour of non-eating may start as a means of avoiding obesity, but may take over in the presence of various 'setting conditions'. In his view, adolescent conflicts arising from problems in the family of an anorexic girl could combine with interpersonal problems to contribute to a general sense of dissatisfaction with life and with the self. Another predisposing factor of perfectionistic tendencies operates together with this condition to create a need for control. Under these conditions, dieting, which may be triggered by critical comments or a chance remark or simply because her friends are doing it, may be positively reinforced by feelings of success. The fear of weight gain is negatively reinforcing and serves to strengthen the dieting behaviour. Bingeing too, if it occurs, has a negative reinforcement value in that it makes the person feel bloated, uncomfortable, out of control, and the consequent dieting, starving or purging behaviour becomes extremely rewarding as a consequence. Hence the sufferer is in a vicious circle from which she cannot escape.

Eating disorder as a corollary to dieting and food deprivation

This latter idea is given added strength by the notion that dieting itself, or at least starvation, may render some people more vulnerable to bingeing behaviour. Dieting is also one of the most well-established risk factors for the development of anorexia nervosa. Several studies of dieters have suggested an association between dieting and disordered eating. For example, in a study of 440 high-school women in Australia, those girls who dieted most frequently and for whom the discrepancy between their actual and ideal weights was the largest, had the highest scores on a scale of binge-eating frequency (Huon 1994). This kind of study does not of course explain direction of causality, in that it could be that the heavier women have a greater need to diet simply because they binge eat. However, while most women diet or are exposed to the diet culture, only a small proportion develop an eating disorder. Moreover, only a proportion of obese women binge eat. In one study, obese binge eaters scored more highly on measures of psychiatric morbidity than did obese non-binge eaters and the authors suggest that rather than bingeing in response to dieting, the women were using binge eating as a way to regulate mood and cope with depression and anxiety (Bulik, Sullivan and Kendler 2002).

Some plausible evidence for a causal link between dieting and eating-disordered behaviour comes from studies of people who are food-deprived in circumstances other than dieting to lose weight.

An example of this is a much-cited study of Second World War conscientious objectors (Keys et al. 1950). In an attempt to study the effects of starvation as a means of understanding the experiences of many people in wartime Europe, the researchers dieted a group of young men over a three-month period to approximately 74 per cent of their initial weight. During the starvation period, the men displayed symptoms akin to those of anorexics. For example, they became irritable and worrying, depressed, unable to concentrate, they talked constantly about food, even hoarded it. The men were subsequently refed to their initial weights, but despite having the freedom again to eat whatever and whenever they liked, some of the men reacted to the refeeding by continuing to eat when full, and some began alternately to diet and binge eat in an uncontrolled way.

In an attempt to produce further evidence for a possible link between deprivation and binge eating, Polivy and colleagues (1994) retrospectively studied a group of Second World War prisoners of war (POW) and compared their eating habits with those of a control group of combat veterans who had not been captured. Subjects were asked whether they had experienced episodes of uncontrollable binge eating since being liberated. In comparison to the combat veterans, the POWs had suffered serious food restriction during the war and lost an average of 15 per cent of their body weight. They reported significantly more binge eating since their wartime experiences than did the control group. Hence, there does appear to be a link between deprivation and subsequent binge eating, which cannot be explained by, for example, stress alone. However, it is not clear how far this effect may have a physical rather than a psychological basis.

There has also been some research in support of the idea that dieting has negative physiological consequences. It has been suggested that people who diet may find it increasingly difficult subsequently to lose the same amount of weight on successive occasions. Research with animals has suggested that there may be an underlying metabolic basis for this in that rats fed on exactly the same reducing diet on two subsequent occasions took longer to reach their target weight on the second occasion than on the first (Brownell, Nelson Steen and Wilmore 1987). Athletes needing to maintain competition weight find this increasingly difficult to achieve from year to year. Brownell and his research team (Steen et al. 1988) compared a group of young wrestlers who 'cut' their weight several times in a season with wrestlers who did not. The group who dieted were called the 'cycling' group because their weight went up and down in cycles, whereas the group whose weight remained the same were called the 'non-cycling' group. The average height, weight and percentage body fat of the men was the same in both groups. But the resting metabolic rate of the cycling group was significantly lower than that of the non-cycling group. This could be explained either as the effect of dieting on metabolic rate, or as the result of people with initially lower energy requirements having to work harder to achieve a low weight. However, a similar effect has been claimed in obese dieters on closely supervised reducing diets. In one study, for example, weight loss during a second cycle of dieting was significantly lower than during the first (Blackburn et al. 1989). It is known that dieting reduces metabolic rate, but whether or not this change is permanent is debatable. Nevertheless, people who need to diet frequently may become increasingly frustrated and hence diet in increasingly unhealthy ways. Either way, dieters who frequently fail to achieve their targets, overeat, gain weight and then diet again ('weight cyclers') may unwittingly compromise their ability to diet successfully and render themselves vulnerable to cyclical bingeing and dieting behaviour.

The Restraint Hypothesis

It is possible that the mere thought of having to control their eating can act as a stress on some individuals, as evidenced by the suggestion that the prevalence of eating disorder in diabetics, who need to control their intake of certain foods, is greater than in the normal population (Rodin et al. 1986).

This concept is based on the idea of Nisbett (1972) that some people are underweight with regard to a biological set-point. This means that some people, both normal and overweight, are chronically hungry and therefore very vulnerable to external, social stimuli which have to do with food and eating. Based on this idea, Herman and Mack in 1975 proposed the concept of restrained eating, and devised a questionnaire to measure it.

'Restrained' eaters are constantly dieting, constantly worrying about their weight, and spend a great deal of time thinking about food. 'Unrestrained' eaters, on the other hand, are not bothered about their weight, eat what they like, and rarely diet. In several experiments, researchers gave their experimental subjects small amounts of food, called 'preloads', prior to testing their responses to various experimental conditions involving offers of more food of varying types. They found that people who described themselves as restrained eaters according to the questionnaire failed to compensate for preloads by eating more instead of less afterwards, while the unrestrained eaters ate less afterwards. (They called this 'counterregulation'.)

What is more, restrained subjects ate more if they thought they had a high-calorie preload than if they thought they had a low-calorie one. They ate more if they were anxious, and they ate more if they thought the preload had contained alcohol.

Herman and Polivy (1980) interpret these findings as suggesting that for some people their attempts to control their eating become disinhibited in the face of anxiety or when they think they have already eaten something fattening or something that will take away their control: in other words, that anxiety and cognitive manipulations can have a disinhibiting effect on normally restrained people. In some more recent work attempting to clarify the determinants of overeating, Polivy and Herman (1999) have suggested that the disinhibition of eating noted in their studies may have a psychological function for individual dieters. In a further taste-perception experiment, they manipulated dieters' and non-dieters' experiences of success and failure in tests of cognitive ability. Eating did not appear to reduce anxiety or provide comfort. However, the restrained subjects (dieters) were more likely than were unrestrained subjects (non-dieters) to attribute their negative feelings in the experiment to overeating than to their poor performance on the 'tests'. The authors suggest that the dieters may have eaten more in order to distract themselves from negative feelings, and also that distress about the (over)eating may have served to mask the real cause of the negative feelings.

This can, of course, only be a very superficial explanation of the theory. Since it was first described there have also been many arguments over the content of the Restraint Scale itself – some people have suggested that it measures two things, concern with diet and weight fluctuation, and that therefore a fat person who is unrestrained but whose weight fluctuates could score very high. Nevertheless, it underlines the notion that the reasons why people eat more or less at different times are complex, and that differences between obese people and thin people may be less important than those between dieters and non-dieters.

A natural corollary to the idea that some people develop binge-eating problems as a result of dieting is that therefore these people need to be helped to give up dieting itself. This has been a core idea behind the treatment offered by members of the feminist movement, such as Susie Orbach (1978). Polivy and Herman (1992) have themselves evaluated a short-term programme aimed at raising conscious-ness in chronically dieting women about dieting and teaching ways of eating normally. Most of the women in their pilot group were overweight. At the end of the programme, most of the women scored lower than before therapy on the Eating Disorders Inventory (see Chapter 4), had significantly higher scores on measures of self-esteem, were less likely to be bulimic, were less likely to be clinically depressed, and maintained their gains over a six-month period. However, the women remained the same weight, suggesting that while this kind of programme may be extremely useful in helping people to give up an obsession with dieting and weight, it cannot be used as an alternative means of achieving weight loss.

Conclusions

In summary, many different causes have been put forward for eating disorders, and there is clearly no one factor that can be said to be responsible for them. What is more likely is that there are several paths to eating disorder and that different factors play varying roles to different degrees from one individual to another (see Figure 2.1). In order to be effective, any treatment needs to have both the capacity to take into account what these factors are, and the flexibility to address itself to those which are most relevant in each case. The results of a study set up to assess the perceptions of women about the cause of their disorder support this idea. In addition to the notion of family dysfunction, the women also cited, in descending order: weight loss or dieting, perceived pressure or stress, inappropriate comments, control, family weight and food issues, and sexual abuse (Tozzi et al. 2003).

To date, the search for a purely medical cause for eating disorders, or the sug-gestion that they may be carried genetically through families, has not borne fruit. On the contrary, approaches which have been helpful in terms of alleviating suf-fering have focused on changes which clients can make themselves, based on the development of a changed understanding of their symptoms and the role of weight and eating in their lives. A cognitive behavioural approach begins to make sense of many current ideas with regard to causation in relation both to individual clients' attitudes to themselves and to society's attitudes and expectations about eating, weight and shape. It allows client and therapist the flexibility to work at the level of either symptom or underlying beliefs, at the pace chosen by the client. It allows for the creation of new solutions based on a shared understanding of the individual nature of the client's disorder.

Figure 2.1   The many paths to eating disorders

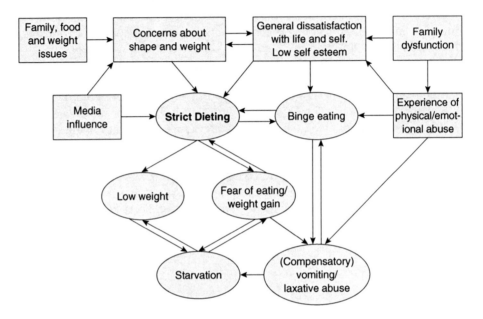

3 A Cognitive Behavioural Approach to Eating Disorders

What is cognitive behaviour therapy?

Cognitive behaviour therapy (CBT) is a time-limited psychological therapy approach developed originally in the United States by Aaron Beck for the treatment of depression (Beck 1967; Beck et al. 1976). Beck had been trained as a psychoanalyst but was disappointed in the limited improvements depressed patients were able to achieve with the psychoanalytic method. He came to believe that the negative thinking characteristic of depressed people is not just a symptom but also a diagnostic feature of the disorder, and that it needs to be treated directly. Beck believed that negative thinking could be triggered by life events such as the loss of a loved one, but arose from the activation of dysfunctional assumptions which were developed in childhood – for example, 'In order to be loved, I have to be perfect.'

Cognitive therapy has evolved both in scope and in complexity. Initially extended by Beck and his colleagues for the treatment of anxiety, it has since been used in the treatment of other disorders, including substance abuse and personality disorders and has been further developed theoretically and clinically by several clinicians and researchers. The term 'dysfunctional assumption' has sometimes been used interchangeably with the term 'schema', to describe the way in which a person organises his or her experience and perception of the world and which dictates the way he or she deals with new experiences. Dysfunctional assumptions are not necessarily the sole cause of a problem – we may all have beliefs about ourselves and about the world that are to some extent mistaken. It is when events occur that drive us, because of our beliefs, to behave in consistently dysfunctional ways, that they become a problem. The therapy focuses on helping people to modify initially the negative automatic aspects of their thinking and then to protect them from future relapse by modifying the underlying dysfunctional assumptions on which the thinking is based.

Clinicians and researchers vary in the degree to which they attribute priority to different levels of thought and belief in clients. Some place more emphasis on the deepest level of thinking – core beliefs or negative schemas (see Figure 3.1). Core beliefs are seen as lying beneath assumptions. They are absolute, and can include beliefs about the self, the world and other people: 'I am a failure', for example, may underpin the assumption 'In order to succeed I have to be thin'. Once the nature of clients' negative schema has been assessed and discussed with clients, the therapy moves directly to using a range of cognitive and behavioural techniques in order to modify the schema directly.

Figure 3.1   Levels of thinking in CBT

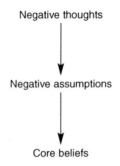

Negative thoughts

Negative assumptions

Core beliefs

An outline of the characteristics of cognitive behaviour therapy

Cognitive behaviour therapy is a 'structured, short-term, present-oriented psycho-therapy' (for a clear step-by-step introduction, see J.S. Beck 1995: 1). It is based on the idea that behaviour, thoughts and feelings are learned, and can therefore be unlearned or modified. The therapist helps the client to formulate problems in cognitive terms, and is constantly inviting feedback from the client to ensure that he/she feels understood and can learn to contribute jointly with the therapist to the treatment.

The therapy requires a sound therapeutic alliance and a collaborative relationship between client and therapist. It is very much a problem-solving approach. Goals are set in behavioural terms and potential solutions are tested out in practice: clients are encouraged to explore options for change and evaluate outcomes by comparing progress with previous experience and hence are encouraged to take an objective, scientific, view of their problems. Clients are often taught to set up behavioural experiments to test out the validity of thoughts or to try out new ways of thinking and behaving (see also *The Oxford Guide to Behavioural Experiments in Cognitive Therapy* by Bennett-Levy et al. 2004). In this way, clients are taught, in theory, to become their own therapists and are thus prepared to deal with relapse and problems if and when they arise in the future.

Cognitive therapy has a strong educational element. The basis of therapy is to teach clients to conceptualise their disorder in cognitive terms. This means that clients learn about the 'ABC' of behaviour and thoughts: they learn to make links between antecedents, or triggers, behaviours or thoughts, and their consequences, which may be related either to mood or to self-damaging behaviours. Clients are also taught about the nature of their disorder in general, so that they have the tools to protect themselves from more serious problems and are motivated to aim for change. In the case of an eating disorder, this means, in addition, teaching about the physical consequences of the disorder and of abnormal eating behaviours and of any attempt to make changes. It also means teaching the principles of normal eating behaviour and nutrition.

The method uses 'Socratic questioning'. This involves the therapist in asking questions of clients which help them to explore problems and possible solutions.

The questions themselves often raise further questions. In answering these questions, clients are helped to examine and test out alternative ways of looking at problems and consider novel ways to view their situations.

Another important aspect of the therapy is the setting of homework tasks. Clients are frequently asked to monitor and record behaviours relating to key problems, or any attempts they may make to modify habitual behaviours. In the case of eating disorders, this may involve, in the first instance, keeping a record of eating and drinking, together with any incidents of purging and the situations in which they took place. Homework is also used by the therapist to give clients practice in following through new ways of looking at a situation, and in modifying old habits.

Sessions in cognitive therapy usually follow an agenda, often set the week previously. This ensures that therapist and client keep strictly to task. The client can change the agenda at the beginning of a session to accommodate urgent considerations.

In the first part of therapy, there is usually a strong focus on teaching clients to recognise and record their negative automatic thoughts. Cognitive theory holds that negative thinking results in negative affect or moods, so that replacing negative thoughts with alternative, more rational thoughts will lead to the development of more positive feelings. Negative automatic thoughts reflect the private, and in some cases unhelpful, commentaries people give themselves on events occurring in their lives, both external and internal. For example, a depressed person might record thoughts such as 'I'll never get any better', often reflecting a theme or recurring frequently. Sometimes the therapist is able to help clients to become more aware of specific themes occurring in their thinking, such as fear of social or more personal threat. Clients are trained to modify their negative automatic thoughts in the direction of creating commentaries which are more helpful and optimistic, and which still truthfully reflect their situations rather than merely rehearsing positive self-statements proffered by the therapist as a sensible alternative to negative thoughts. The idea underlying this technique is that if people can practise saying more positive things to themselves, as long as the statements reflect the truth and are credible, then through practice they will be able to develop and learn to believe in a more positive view of their situations. This will, in turn, lead to improvements in their symptoms of depression or anxiety.

As the therapy proceeds, it moves on from the symptomatic level to working at a deeper level, on modifying underlying assumptions, or 'if ... then' statements and, finally, core beliefs. The rationale behind this is that if core beliefs can be modified, the client will become less vulnerable to relapse or further distress in response to future trigger situations or life stresses. Core beliefs are ascertained by a process of questioning, similar to that used to elicit negative automatic thoughts. They are then challenged and modified using a range of techniques including those used for modifying negative thoughts.

The nature of cognitive behaviour therapy as applied to eating disorders

Cognitive behaviour therapy has been applied to a wide range of emotional disorders of varying degrees of severity, including anxiety, sexual problems, obsessional problems, drug and alcohol abuse and personality disorders. It has been applied to eating disorders by several different research groups. Their methods have differed somewhat from Beck's original descriptions of therapy in taking account of their idiosyncratic conceptualisations of the cognitive basis for the disorders. Two modifications of cognitive therapy were first applied to the treatment of eating disorders in the early 1980s. One of these was first described by Christopher Fairburn (1981) for the treatment of bulimia nervosa, and the other by Garner and Bemis (1982) for the treatment of anorexia nervosa. It has since then been subject to detailed research, in particular in relation to the short-term treatment of bulimia nervosa, both in Britain and in the United States. The theoretical basis of the treatment has come largely from a cognitive view of the maintenance of eating disorders. This view is based on restraint theory (see also page 32) and the link between dieting and chronic hunger and overeating or counterregulation on the one hand, and the notion that the automatic thoughts and underlying assumptions of dieters reflect overvalued ideas about dieting and weight loss on the other. The theory also requires the presence of low self-esteem, which is maintained by binge eating and vomiting.

The methods used usually combine behavioural with psychoeducational and cognitive approaches in helping clients both to monitor and change behaviour and to explore and evaluate their ways of thinking about their eating disorder and the world and experiment with alternatives. The treatment involves treating the symptoms directly, in a behavioural way. Behaviour therapy methods are focused on modifying eating disorder symptoms and on building up skills to cope with relapse. At the same time, cognitive therapy methods are focused on treating the associated disturbance in attitudes to eating, weight and shape. Clients are helped in the first instance to recognise negative thought patterns and related dysfunctional behaviour and to learn to substitute alternative, more 'rational' thoughts. In a second stage of therapy, aimed at maintaining therapy gains and preventing future relapse, clients are helped to recognise underlying dysfunctional assumptions and to modify these in favour of more helpful ones.

In the case of an eating disorder, the practical, behavioural and educational approaches and the work on beliefs and underlying assumptions are applied to two main subject areas. These are, on the one hand, the subjects of eating and weight and, on the other hand, the more general psychological functioning of the sufferer, including themes such as self-esteem and confidence, interpersonal and family issues. Garner (1986) has called these 'first-' and 'second-track' issues. The earlier part of therapy places greater emphasis on the first track, switching to second-track issues later on. In practice, there may be much switching from one track to another and back during the course of therapy, although this tendency to switch will vary from one treatment centre to another.

The Oxford research group, responsible for a large number of the controlled studies completed to date, described itself initially as being rigorous in its adherence to a treatment manual which is published in a book entitled *Binge Eating: Nature, Assessment and Treatment* and co-edited by Christopher Fairburn and Terence Wilson (see Fairburn, Marcus and Wilson 1993). Their treatment followed three distinct stages. In the first stage, a cognitive view is presented of how bulimia nervosa is maintained, and behavioural techniques are used 'to replace binge eating with a stable pattern of regular eating'. In the second stage, there is more emphasis on giving up dieting as well as eating healthily. The main focus of this stage is on 'cognitive procedures' aimed at modifying beliefs and attitudes to the problem. This comprises a problem-solving approach to dealing with stressors that provoke overeating, and a 'cognitive restructuring' approach to recognising and modifying negative automatic thoughts and underlying attitudes relating to body shape and weight. A third stage comprises three sessions aimed at maintaining progress, practising the techniques learned in earlier sessions and preparing for relapse. Most of the research detailing the efficacy of CBT for the eating disorders has broadly followed this scheme.

A broad interpretation of cognitive therapy for the eating disorders

The specific protocol-based view of the maintenance of eating disorders described above does not necessarily take into account the different developmental paths by which people come to their idiosyncratic expressions of disorder (see Chapter 2). A cognitive therapy approach needs also to take into account additional factors such as the use of excessive food consumption or deprivation as a tool for positive coping, and negative core beliefs about the self (see also Cooper, Todd and Wells 2000: 238–244). Some therapists and researchers have moved beyond the application of traditional, and specifically protocol-based, cognitive behaviour therapy techniques in a quest to resolve the more complex and enduring aspects of eating disorders. They have borrowed from two therapies devised originally for the treatment of personality disorders, which by definition are harder to treat, and more resistant to short-term psychotherapies.

Schema-focused therapy
Schema-focused therapy is a form of cognitive behaviour therapy first described by Jeffrey Young (1999). The aim of the therapy is to 'enable patients and therapists to communicate about deeper level phenomena that have not yet been incorporated into most short-term cognitive behaviour therapies' (1999: 7). In his book *Cognitive Therapy for Personality Disorders*, Young describes a form of cognitive behaviour therapy that bypasses the initial work at the level of negative thoughts which is characteristic of conventional CBT. The primary emphasis of the therapy is on the deepest level of cognition, which he calls the 'early maladaptive schema'. According to Young, these schemas are unconditional beliefs and feelings about oneself and the environment. They are developed early in life and are very resistant to change, as they are cumulatively reinforced by the person's experience. For example, a woman with an 'unlovability' schema will interpret being abandoned as just one more piece of evidence that she is unlovable. These schemas are tied to a high degree of emotional arousal and can lead directly or indirectly to a range of psychological disorders, including the addictions and eating disorders. On the basis of his work with patients, Young has hypothesised a series of 18 early maladaptive schemas, which he groups into five schema domains. These are: 'disconnection and rejection' (for example, mistrust); 'impaired autonomy and performance' (for example, defectiveness); 'impaired limits' (for example, insufficient self-control);

'other directedness' (for example approval-seeking); and 'over vigilance and inhibition'.

These schemas are seen as operating through three main processes. The first is 'schema maintenance': the person highlights information that confirms the schema and ignores or denies information that contradicts it (for example, operating in the same way as prejudice). The second is 'schema avoidance': whenever the schema is triggered, the individual develops a habit of avoiding negative feelings in a variety of ways such as behavioural avoidance (for example, not going out); cognitive avoidance (denial); affective avoidance (including not experiencing emotions such as anger or sadness or positive attempts to block them out such as distraction through eating, compulsive behaviour or even self-harm). The third process is 'schema compensation' where the person overcompensates for an early maladaptive schema. For example someone with a dependency schema battles through life never asking for help.

Schema-focused therapy begins with an evaluation session in which symptoms and problems are identified with the help of a life history questionnaire and a question-naire designed to detect signs of the 18 early maladaptive schemas (see Chapter 4). Next, clients are educated about the nature of schemas. Clients are then helped to identify their own maladaptive schemas. They learn to recognise them 'live' in current events and through triggering past memories with the help of imagery. The therapy proceeds through the conventional cognitive behaviour therapy strategies for change with an emphasis on constant practice in challenging schemas. An additional emphasis in schema-focused therapy is an emphasis on experiential techniques drawn form Gestalt therapy in order to trigger schemas in the sessions, promote catharsis and practise change strategies. There is also increased emphasis on the relationship with the therapist in terms of disclosure and the provision of a 'limited re-parenting role', for example in terms of providing reassurance of competence, or discipline, within the bounds of a professional therapeutic relationship.

The work of modifying schemas is not necessarily restricted to the purely verbal techniques usually characteristic of cognitive therapy. CBT therapists are beginning to borrow from other disciplines such as Gestalt psychology in order to effect change through multisensory paths. For example, Vartouhi Ohanian (2002) has described the use of 'imagery rescripting' to modify core beliefs. Imagery rescripting has been used in the treatment of borderline personality disorder and is similar to the image change work often done with victims of sexual abuse and post traumatic stress disorder. The aim of this work is to modify core beliefs not by means of verbal logic but through imagery, based on the notion that many early schemas are laid down, sometimes predating the acquisition of language, in a form that is not amenable to adult logical description. In therapy, the client is asked to image and describe a critical traumatic event as if in the present, from the child's point of view, with the child's attributions. They are then asked to bring an adult perspective to the image – perhaps by imagining the same situation with the addition of a 'rescuing' adult who can view the situation with a different set of beliefs about attributions of responsibility. In a single case study, Ohanian describes a dramatic reduction in bulimic behaviours after one such session of treatment in a woman who had previously benefited from standard CBT.

Dialectical behaviour therapy

Dialectical behaviour therapy (DBT) is an 'integrative' psychotherapy first developed in the 1990s by Marsha Linehan (1993a; see also Heard and Linehan 1994). It is integrative in the sense that it recognises differences rather than ignoring them or avoiding them and includes novel methods in the therapy process as a means to deal with these differences. It was developed originally as a treatment for suicidal and parasuicidal individuals who are not readily amenable to responding to change therapies, and subsequently for borderline personality disorder and substance abuse (see also Linehan 1993a, 1993b). It has also been adapted as a cognitive therapy for preventing relapse in depression (see Segal, Williams and Teasdale 2002).

There are many features in the therapy which lend themselves to the treatment of certain individuals suffering from an eating disorder. In the standard model of DBT, clients commit themselves to one year of outpatient treatment. The philosophical basis or 'dialectic' of DBT is the necessity to accept patients as they are within the context of trying to help them change. There is an ongoing tension between a focus on learning to accept distress but not necessarily to act on the feelings generated, and a focus on creating positive change. The model is based on the idea that a combination of emotional vulnerability and an invalidating environment have worked together to prevent certain people from learning to regulate emotions and tolerate distress. These problems in turn make it difficult for the person to use behavioural coping skills or learn to give up dysfunctional behaviour.

A key feature of the therapy is the use of Zen psychology which focuses on validation and acceptance without judgement. Treatment strategies related to unconditional acceptance of the client's behaviours are integrated with behavioural and cognitive behavioural strategies which promote change. While the behavioural aspect of the the the therapy actively teaches change strategies, the Zen aspect teaches the client to allow and observe urges without acting upon them. In this way, the experience of the client who feels that he or she cannot change is validated, the idea being that 'if one observes the urges without reinforcing them through action, the urges will naturally decrease over time' (Heard and Linehan 1994: 65).

The targets of treatment include: therapy interfering behaviour; the skills of mindfulness, distress tolerance, emotion regulation and interpersonal effectiveness. Therapy interfering behaviour can include any behaviour which makes it difficult for the client to benefit from therapy, such as not completing food diaries, refusing to be weighed, or an absence from treatment because of the need for inpatient medical intervention. Mindfulness practice includes attention to the skills of observing, describing, focusing on one thing at a time, and the development of a 'wise mind' which is the synthesis of 'emotion mind' (feelings, wishes) and 'rational mind' (thought, logic and facts). Distress tolerance skills concentrate on acceptance of distress, distraction and self-soothing rather than trying to avoid the distress through strategies such as drinking or overeating. The emotion regulation module is based on traditional behaviour therapy. It includes teaching clients about the function of emotions, ways to decrease emotional vulnerability and ways to increase positive emotions. The goal of interpersonal effectiveness is to reduce interpersonal chaos and increase balance in one's relationships.

Dialectical behaviour therapy has been adapted by several centres for the group treatment of binge eating disorder in a model where emotional dysregulation is seen as the core problem of BED, as opposed to the view that the primary cause or maintaining factor is dieting. Treatments have adapted Marsha Linehan's original treatment manual specifically to target eating problems. Patients are taught mindfulness skills, emotion regulation skills and distress tolerance skills (see also Robins and Chapman 2004; for a more detailed discussion about how DBT might be applied to eating disorders, see Wisniewski 2003).

A 'transdiagnostic' approach

Recently, the Oxford group has also extended their definition of cognitive behavioural therapy to embrace a 'transdiagnostic' approach which may be applied to any one of the diagnostic categories of eating disorder in whichever combination is most appropriate for the person in question. This approach includes additional treatment modules which are also aimed at dealing with those aspects of eating disorders which are harder to treat and which the group sees as maintaining mechanisms in cases which are less amenable to their standard treatment. These mechanisms are mood intolerance, clinical perfectionism, core low self-esteem and interpersonal functioning. Where seen as appropriate, cognitive therapy methods are applied to the treatment of the first three of these aspects, and an 'interpersonal therapy' protocol is applied to the treatment of interpersonal problems. The offer of interpersonal therapy is based on the evidence from research that interpersonal therapy was shown to be almost as effective in the treatment of bulimia nervosa as was CBT in some of the initial research studies, although the time taken to improve was longer.

The theoretical basis of cognitive behaviour therapy in relation to eating disorders

Cognitive behaviour therapy lends itself theoretically to the treatment of eating disorders for several reasons. One of these has to do with the connection between eating behaviour and belief, the relationship between attitudes to weight and shape, and dieting as a consequence.

Cognitive therapies and attitude change

Most theories of causation take on board the notion that eating disorders are connected with an overvaluation of the importance of weight and shape and a consequent fear of fatness. It is possible that these factors underlie, at least in part, both the non-eating behaviour of anorexics and the binge-eating behaviour of normal-weight bulimics, as well as of some people with binge eating disorder. These attitudes result in severely restrained eating in an attempt to achieve an improved, or even perfect, figure. This restraint is perfected by restricting anorexics, but is, of course, broken by bulimics, who are trapped in a cycle of overeating and purging fired by the belief that to stop would be to result in the disastrous consequences of overweight.

With regard to bulimia nervosa in particular, cognitive behavioural treatments borrow from restraint theory, which suggested that some people attempt to keep their weight below a set point through dieting, and are therefore chronically hungry and prone to overeat. As a consequence they attempt to purge themselves or starve and are thus caught in a vicious circle of binge eating and purging and spiralling low self-esteem. In fact, the evidence for restraint theory is as yet inconclusive, and there is evidence that for some women with a high drive for thinness, purging to control weight precedes binge eating, which sometimes begins in response to purging.

In order for sufferers to give up their eating disorder, it is necessary for them first to see links between their eating behaviour and their thoughts and feelings, and then to break those links by finding alternative responses to stress or negative feelings. Second, they need to become aware of sometimes-unarticulated beliefs underlying their eating behaviour. This is true both for those people who find their own behaviour unacceptable, and also for people for whom their behaviour is entirely acceptable. The first category includes people who purge and those whose bingeing behaviour is out of control. The second category includes those who see no need to change; there are restricting anorexics, on the one hand, and some purging bulimics, on the other, who see their symptoms as a necessary evil and a lesser problem than their expected weight gain should they dare to give up their symptoms.

An overvaluation of the importance of weight and shape, together with distorted ideas about eating, has been regarded in cognitive behavioural models of eating disorder to be the main psychopathological disturbance. Sufferers appear to believe that the achievement of a thin body is essential as a source of happiness and that failure to achieve this state is synonymous with failure as a person. For example, Amanda believed that if she were curvaceous people would think she was 'tarty' and would not take her seriously. She assumed that through dieting she could reduce her bust and hip measurements and believed that the only way to do this was to stick to her diet continuously. Underlying these beliefs were the core beliefs that she was unattractive and that no one respected her. In order to modify her eating behaviour and her dysfunctional beliefs she needed to find new ways of developing self-esteem as an alternative to basing her feelings of self-worth on her ability to achieve and maintain a perfect 'ideal' shape.

The use of a cognitive therapy approach makes it feasible to directly explore and question common assumptions about the importance of weight and shape. Having aired these assumptions, clients can decide whether they wish to continue to espouse them, modify them, or replace them with alternative ones.

At a deeper level too, the approach makes it feasible to address more personal issues regarding self-worth. So, while the therapy takes on board the task of tackling individual assumptions about the importance of weight and shape, it also challenges underlying core beliefs about the personal identity of sufferers, thus fitting in with, for example, the theory of Hilde Bruch in relation to the personalities of young women with eating disorders.

There are additional factors at work in relation to people with binge eating disorder who are overweight. Here, the overvaluation of the importance of weight and shape is relevant but may be less so than other factors. For example, clients who are obese often have highly unrealistic goals for weight loss and speed of weight loss. This means that any degree of weight loss is often unacceptably small and is not maintained for long. Some clients are depressed and need to focus on alternatives to overeating as a means of dealing with their depression.

Empirical evidence for differences in underlying schemata between people with and without eating disorders

Much of the evidence for the idea that people with eating disorders have idiosyncratic assumptions about the importance of shape and weight which underlie their problems is, of course, based on clinical descriptions rather than empirical research.

There is, however, a small body of literature which suggests that there are measurable differences in attitude to weight and shape between people with eating disorders and normal eaters. For example, some studies have used questionnaire measures of outcome which have shown up differences in degree of self-esteem, and in ideas about the importance of shape and weight. In one follow-up study by Fairburn and his colleagues (Fairburn, Peveler et al. 1993), those patients who at the end of treatment had the highest residual levels of attitudinal disturbance were the most likely to relapse subsequently. In another attempt to address the thought processes of eating-disordered people in contrast to normal subjects, Myra Cooper asked groups of patients with eating disorders to think out loud whatever thoughts they had while engaged in three tasks: looking at themselves in a full-length mirror, weighing themselves, or eating an 'After Eight' mint chocolate. In comparison with normal non-dieting controls, patients with bulimia nervosa were particularly concerned with weight and appearance, and anorexics were more concerned with eating, as shown by the relative numbers of negative self-statements each group produced about eating and weight (Cooper and Fairburn 1992). In further research, using the 'Eating Disorder Belief Questionnaire', the authors found that in comparison with other types of psychiatric patient, patients with eating disorders scored more highly on assumptions relating to eating and weight (Cooper and Hunt 1998).

Differences with regard to assumptions and beliefs have been noted in other domains as well as those of shape and weight, indicating that the psychopathology in eating disorders goes deeper than merely an idiosyncratic disturbed attitude to shape and weight. Glen Waller and his colleagues have examined the role of more general core beliefs in the cognitive content of bulimic disorders. In one study, they compared the responses of a group of 50 women with a diagnosis of bulimia nervosa with 50 women with no eating disorder on Young's Schema Questionnaire. They found that the bulimic women scored more highly than the controls on three beliefs: perceived Defectiveness/Shame, Insufficient self-control, and Failure to achieve. Moreover, the bulimics' Emotional Inhibition beliefs predicted the severity of their bingeing, while their Defectiveness/Shame beliefs predicted the severity of their vomiting (Waller et al. 2000). In a further study, Waller compared a group of women with no eating disorder with a group suffering from bulimia nervosa and a group suffering from binge eating disorder. The two clinical groups scored more highly than the non-clinical women on pathological core beliefs. Among the binge eating disorder group, binge eating was positively associated with several core beliefs including social isolation, abandonment, incompetence, and dependence (Waller 2003).

Not only do people with eating disorders have core beliefs that differ from those of other people; but there is also some evidence of a link between negative thoughts and beliefs and behaviour. Cooper and her colleagues found that bingeing 'seemed to provide an initial distraction in some cases from negative automatic thoughts and images, negative self-beliefs and negative emotional states' and that patients with eating disorders believed that dieting was a way to counteract the negative implications of their beliefs about themselves (Cooper, Todd and Wells 2002, see also Cooper, Wells and Todd 2004).

An attempt to provide a more direct measurement of the specific cognitive disturbance which is believed to characterise people with eating disorders has been made in a group of studies using the Stroop colour-naming test (for example, see Long, Hinton and Gillespie 1994). In this test, subjects are presented with a series of words printed in one of four primary colours. The experimental card consists of words which are considered emotionally significant to sufferers, such as 'food', 'cream', 'heavy', 'stomach'; and a control card consists of neutral words matched to the experimental words for length and frequency of use in everyday language. Instead of reading the words, subjects are asked to name the colours in which the words are printed. In general, people with anorexia nervosa and bulimia nervosa have been slower to colour name words related to food and shape than groups of normal-weight women of the same age. In addition, Waller and his colleagues have reported on the results of some experiments that show slower colour naming for food and shape-related words, after presenting subjects with abandonment cues (words such as 'alone', 'deserted', 'ignored') (Meyer and Waller 2000).

The results of these experiments are by no means entirely consistent and therefore the test cannot have the status of a categorical test of pathology. However, they do support the existence of a general concern with shape and weight under-lying the behaviour of people with eating disorders and raise the question of the need to work with clients at the deeper levels of assumptions and schemas about the self, other people and the world in general, in addition to the more accessible beliefs about weight and shape.

Cognitive therapy and the sociocultural model of eating pathology

Taking a wider focus, a cognitive therapy approach makes sense also from the point of view of what is seen as the contribution of our modern culture to the establishment and maintenance of eating disorders. There is even some research evidence for the notion that viewing slender images leads to greater levels of body dissatisfaction in young females than viewing neutral images (see Groesz, Levine and Murnen 2002). Beliefs about the importance of a thin shape and low weight may be fairly wide-spread, especially among some groups of young people. This is often used as a reason by individual clients for holding on to unhelpful beliefs about the importance of looking a certain way. However, in order to give up an eating disorder, clients are often forced to question these views and consider the possibility of giving up the quest for a perfect body. They are forced to explore the consequences of having a less than perfect figure and face the need to build up the confidence to confront their peers without the mask of invisibility conferred on fashion look-alikes.

Cognitive therapy and individual expression of eating disorders

A cognitive therapy approach can, of course, also take into account the individual motivations of sufferers. The most widely chronicled and researched versions typically espouse certain assumptions built into the treatment such as the notion that eating disorder stems from dieting in response to society's condemnation of the fuller figure. The value of cognitive therapy, given its wider interpretation, however, is that in assessing and treating psychological problems it provides therapists with the tools to make assessments of and treat a range of psychological and emotional difficulties. This is because by its very nature it has the capacity to allow therapists to understand the idiosyncratic paths by which each sufferer reaches his or her own version of distress. It matters not whether, for example, bingeing is preceded by dieting, or vice versa. The aim of the therapy is to help individual clients to arrive at an understanding of what maintains their difficulties and to promote change through enabling them to modify the schemas underlying the thoughts and feelings involved in triggering and maintaining those difficulties. Hence, in a situation where bingeing predated dieting, for example, the focus of therapy might be to enable the sufferer to recognise the links between bingeing and other behaviours and feelings and to create alternative ways of dealing with distress. In this instance, therapy might in practice look very similar to cognitive therapy for depression, or anxiety: there would be less emphasis on alternative eating habits than in a 'traditional' eating disorder treatment programme and more emphasis on recognising negative mood states, monitoring and answering negative thoughts and identifying and addressing underlying assumptions and schemas.

The structure of cognitive therapy for eating disorders

The structure of the therapy also lends itself well to the treatment of people with eating disorders. One key aspect of the cognitive therapy approach is the important place given to educational methods. The counsellor's aim is to teach clients what they know about their problems so as to enable them more easily to make changes. Both overeating and under-eating to excess have grave physical concomitants, the effects of which the client needs to recognise and understand in order both to make the decision to give up her disorder and to work out how best to go about doing so. Unlike other therapy approaches, cognitive therapy not only allows, but encourages, the therapist to impart salient information to the client. The therapist is there in the role both of teacher and of listener, and the two roles are not incompatible, as they might be in other therapies.

This feature of the therapy process comes from the notion of collaboration. The therapist and client work together to solve the client's problem. The therapist is neither authoritarian dictator nor blank screen, but is a teacher in the sense of guiding and sharing information, on an equal footing, with the client. Incidentally, this collaborative role was very much endorsed by Hilde Bruch, who is famous for her work with people with eating disorders. Originally a psychoanalyst, she held that traditional psychoanalytic methods were inappropriate in relation to treatment of eating disorders as the work had to be collaborative in order to be effective.

The importance of the therapist taking a collaborative stance was exemplified strongly in the case of Alice, who, at the age of 16, was referred by her GP but came reluctantly with her parents. She had been suffering from anorexia nervosa for about a year and had dropped from her normal weight of nine stone to around six and a half stone. She was sullen and uncommunicative. Her typical response to any question was to shrug slightly, and say 'I don't know'. The only way to win this young girl's confidence was to let her know that she had an ally, that it would be safe to express her ideas and feelings without being forced immediately to eat or to give up her freedom to make choices.

If people are to change the way they think and feel about their eating disorder, they need to understand, at least on an intellectual level, the causes of their physical discomfort. For example, the anorexic needs to understand that a constant feeling of stomach fullness and bloating is a symptom not of being fat but of starvation; and that until she is once again within the normal weight range, she is likely to have a large stomach. Lack of hunger at mealtimes may in part be due to slower gastric emptying in anorexics than in people of normal weight, for reasons not yet fully understood. Similarly, the puffy cheeks of a bulimic are not a sign of fatness but the result of swollen salivary glands acquired through repeated vomiting.

At a more basic level, the educational aspect of the cognitive approach is valuable in relation to the encouragement of changed eating habits. Therapists often claim that people with eating disorder know more than anyone else about correct diet and about the nutritional value of foods. However, this knowledge is usually heavily biased by the person holding a plethora of erroneous beliefs about food and nutrition. For example, binge eaters often believe that it is possible to gain two to five pounds in weight merely through eating a large meal and, conversely, that a period of rigorous purging can result in large real immediate weight losses. Many have beliefs about fats or carbohydrates being uniformly 'bad' for people who need to modify their weight. The cognitive therapy approach, with its use of 'Socratic dialogue', allows for an exploration of the nature of these beliefs and offers the possibility of challenging them within the therapeutic framework, which is necessarily non-critical. Often, a client will admit to knowing 'that it's not true really but I can't help believing it'. Cognitive therapy, with its method of eliciting and answering automatic thoughts, allows the client to experiment with alternative views and practise replacing erroneous, unhelpful beliefs with more realistic, helpful ones. Kate, for example, was on the borderline of anorexia nervosa and was also bulimic. She believed that if she allowed herself to eat her forbidden foods of chocolate and biscuits and used any fats in her diet such as oil in her cooking or butter on her bread, she would immediately gain the equivalent weight in fat. In therapy she was persuaded to experiment for one week with allowing herself a small amount of these items without purging after she ate them. At the end of the week, when she got on the scales and found that she had not gained weight, she was able to begin to accept that her previously held belief might be erroneous and was prepared to learn to modify her view of what constituted a healthy diet.

The acceptability of cognitive therapy for eating disorders

One of the attractions of the cognitive behavioural approach for the person with an eating disorder is its face-value acceptability. This is particularly the case for those sufferers whose symptoms are ego-dystonic, in other words their behaviour and feelings are contrary to the way they would like to behave and feel. For example, binge eaters and purgers alike are often very relieved to be given behavioural 'tips' about ways they might change their behaviour using stimulus control methods. These might be as simple as limiting eating to certain times of day, or controlling the availability of certain foods. Similarly, sufferers are very pleased to be given help to cope with relapse which is geared towards the learning of problem-solving skills, on the one hand, and which recognises the fallibility of people who are 'cured', on the other.

Cognitive behaviour therapy, because of its collaborative stance, also lends itself well to the treatment of people at different stages of readiness to change. There is continuous checking back with the client about understanding, about acceptance of the rationale for therapy, about readiness to try out suggested homework tasks, and even about the agenda set for the session. This makes the therapy very amenable to tackling disorders where motivation is a particular problem. Bulimia nervosa and binge eating disorder are often described as being 'ego-dystonic' in that sufferers see their problem as being foreign to themselves, a part of the self that they would like to eliminate. Restricting anorexia nervosa, however, is more often 'ego-syntonic' in that sufferers are pleased to be dieting strictly and often see this as an achievement to be proud of rather than as a problem to be treated. Where this is the case, simply launching straight into treatment would be highly inappropriate, and the client needs first to achieve some level of discomfort with her disorder in order to reach a stage at which she is ready to change. Cognitive therapy lends itself well to this dilemma, for incorporated in the therapy is the necessity of checking back with clients at every stage. Topics covered always include clients' level of understanding of the therapy tasks, and of where they see themselves in terms of change; level of willingness to do homework assignments, and even an investigation of exact reasons for not carrying these out. Therefore, where motivation is itself a problem, this becomes the focus of therapy. Clients may be asked to weigh up advantages and disadvantages of particular courses of action in an attempt to uncover attitudes underlying an unwillingness to change. This process can itself help to tip the balance towards motivation for change as opposed to passive resistance resulting from the belief that the rewards of change are not strong enough to outweigh the disadvantages of staying in the same place.

Contrary to popular belief, cognitive therapy is not just about changing the way people think. Clients can be helped to access and change feelings as well as behaviours and thoughts, and the newer modifications encompassed by schema-focused therapy and dialectical behaviour therapy afford therapist and client a degree of choice in terms of the focus of therapy: whether it be an increase or a decrease in restraint together with experimental change; or an increase in tolerance for the emotional distress which underlies or triggers an eating disorder.

How effective is cognitive behaviour therapy for eating disorders?

Cognitive behaviour therapy and bulimia nervosa

So strong is the evidence base for cognitive behaviour therapy in the treatment of bulimia that there is a recommendation to use it in preference to any other psychological treatment as the treatment of choice in the United Kingdom NICE guideline for the treatment of eating disorders in the National Health Service (NICE 2004). Cognitive behaviour therapy has been widely researched in several studies in relation to bulimia nervosa and has been found to be more effective than other treatments in reducing bingeing and purging, and improving attitudes to weight and shape.

Cognitive therapy has shown itself to be effective in the short term for many sufferers. The first study to demonstrate the efficacy of cognitive behaviour therapy (CBT) was carried out by Christopher Fairburn in 1981. Out of 11 patients treated individually, nine were binge eating and purging less than once a month at the end of treatment and had improved attitudes to food and eating, weight and body shape. In subsequent studies, Fairburn and his colleagues went on to compare the effects of CBT in a series of randomised controlled trials with behaviour therapy alone, and another form of psychotherapy called interpersonal psychotherapy. Cognitive behavioural treatment was superior to the psychotherapy condition in reducing binge eating and purging, in overall clinical improvement, improvements in attitudes to weight and shape, and in the subjects' rating of outcome.

Other controlled studies have underlined the efficacy of CBT in comparison with alternative treatments. In a 1991 treatment review, Craighead and Agras summarised the results of ten controlled treatment studies of psychological inter-ventions in bulimia nervosa. Combining the results on binge eating and vomiting, they concluded that CBT produces reductions in binge eating and vomiting ranging from 52 to 96 per cent at the end of treatment. The percentage of patients in remission at the end of treatment ranged from 15 to 90 per cent, with an average of 57 per cent. In a more recent summary, three eating disorder experts have combined forces to conclude that the 'most recent and best controlled studies' show a percentage reduction in binge eating ranging from 93 to 73 per cent and in purging from 94 to 77 per cent (Wilson, Fairburn and Agras 1997). They quote mean remission rates for binge eating ranging from 51 to 71 per cent and for purging from 36 to 56 per cent. In other words, given a trial of CBT, about half of sufferers can expect to have stopped bingeing and vomiting completely at the end of treatment.

Several studies have also pointed to other improvements brought about by CBT. For example, dietary restraint is reduced, and sufferers increase the amount of food they eat between meals and have improved attitudes to shape and weight (see Wilson 1996 for a review).

The long-term maintenance effect is one of the most attractive features of CBT. The treatment shows good maintenance with follow-up to one year and even six years after the end of treatment. Wilson (1996) cites several studies showing good mainten-ance of six months to one year. In Fairburn's original 1981 study, of the six patients who were followed up one year after the end of treatment, one had relapsed, four had occasional lapses, and one was no longer binge eating or vomiting.

CBT also appears to have an advantage over medication. Several studies have shown that pharmacological treatment is more effective than either no treatment or placebo medication, and medication is often a first line of treatment offered in psychiatric clinics, presumably because it is considered a more rapid and less costly solution than that of offering psychological therapy. Interestingly, clinical practice often reflects more closely the beliefs and prejudices of practitioners than research-based findings. In fact, CBT has been shown to be more effective than medication, and there is evidence that it also results in better long-term maintenance than medication in most follow-up studies (see Mitchell 1991; Wilson 1996).

Moreover, from the point of view of costs, Freeman (1997) has examined the comparative costs of administering CBT on both an individual and a group basis with those of administering medication. He comments that the cost of CBT, both individual and group, is slightly lower than the cost of the medication treatment, inclusive of the cost of the drugs and of the psychiatric assessment involved initially and at follow-up sessions.

Cost is, of course, an important consideration where any treatment for a potentially long-term and harmful disorder is concerned. This has driven the production by several treatment centres of self-help manuals to be used either alongside regular treatment or as a first line of treatment in advance of allocation to a therapist (see also Palmer et al. 2002). It has also raised the question of how far the educational component of treatment alone might be sufficient to produce treatment gains. There is evidence that brief educationally-oriented treatment alone can lead to significant behavioural change in some clients when administered either on a group basis or individually (see Garner 1997), leading to significant reductions in binge eating and vomiting in some of the least symptomatic bulimics. Indeed, so strong is the evidence for CBT self-help treatment that the NICE guideline recommends that people suffering with bulimia nervosa be encouraged to try an evidence-based self-help programme as a possible first step in treatment.

A central aspect of CBT is the educational, homework component. Research using self-help manuals has pointed to the importance of this aspect of the therapy. In one trial, 50 people who had persisted with a programme of supervised self-help using a manual were followed up one year later. They had maintained their gains well, and on average the frequency of bulimic episodes and self-induced vomiting had decreased by 84 and 87 per cent respectively since the beginning of their treatments (see Cooper, Coker and Fleming 1996). This finding testifies to the importance of the educational, homework component of any CBT programme, even if the client is also undergoing therapy with a counsellor.

If cognitive behaviour therapy works, the question arises as to how far this can be attributable to the behavioural component of therapy alone. In fact, the behaviour therapy component is likely to be just as good as CBT at reducing binge eating, if not better (see Wolf and Crowther 1992), and better at reducing self-induced vomiting. However, it is not as effective at modifying dieting or attitudes to shape and weight (Jones et al. 1993). Nor is it as effective in the long term. In one long-term follow-up of up to six years, only 20 per cent of behaviour therapy subjects were in remission (that is, not currently suffering from an eating disorder) compared with 60 per cent of subjects who had received CBT (Fairburn et al. 1995). In short, CBT may have a less immediate effect on symptoms than treatments which are more focused, but appears to produce a more lasting general improvement in people with bulimia nervosa (see also Thackwray et al. 1993).

Cognitive behaviour therapy and binge eating disorder in obese people

There is now mounting evidence that cognitive therapy has a role to play in the treatment of binge eating disorder (see Smith, Marcus and Eldridge 1994).

However, a major question raised by the cognitive therapy approach to obesity and overeating is that of what should be the most acceptable outcome variable. Where bulimia is concerned, it suffices to be able to predict how many people will stop bingeing after treatment; but where obesity is concerned, everyone, and not least the clients themselves, wants to know how far treatment will help them to lose weight.

One of the chief aims of a cognitive therapy approach to bulimia nervosa in people of normal weight and to anorexics is to persuade clients to give up dieting behaviour. This makes sense in a situation where eating disorder is preceded by dieting. However, people with binge eating disorder often describe themselves as having binged habitually *before* they tried dieting to lose weight, and there are differences of opinion about whether or not the focus should be on not dieting or on dieting more efficiently. Hence, the non-dieting approach has for a long time been the mainstay of the feminist approach to concern about being fat (see Orbach 1978), but with the emphasis of the treatment on psychological well-being, limited evidence has been offered of weight loss occurring as a result of their treatment. In one Australian study, 80 slightly overweight women were enrolled in a ten-session group programme aimed at discouraging dieting and reducing pre-occupation with food, eating and weight. Two years later, they had improved self-esteem, self-image, eating attitudes, body image and assertion, as well as an average weight loss of 3 kilograms. While promising, this degree of weight loss would be unsatisfactory for most obese people. Some cognitive behaviour thera-pists have pursued the alternative approach and encouraged more efficient dieting, and, according to Marcia Marcus, one of the chief proponents of this treatment, binge eating can be reduced by taking part in a weight control programme (Marcus, Wing and Fairburn 1995). Nevertheless, while cognitive therapy may help overweight people to feel better, there is still some way to go before we can confidently assure clients that it will actually help them to lose weight. For example, a three-month psychoeducational package was found to produce improvements in self-esteem, body satisfaction and restrained eating in obese women without, however, affecting weight or blood pressure (Ciliska 1998). Similarly, CBT has been shown to improve body image and self-esteem, and reduce overeating and guilt in obese women, without much effect on weight reduction (Rosen, Orosan and Reiter 1995).

Cognitive behaviour therapy and anorexia nervosa

There are few controlled-outcome studies of the treatment of anorexia nervosa. One reason for this may be the comparative rarity of the disorder. Another is that most programmes treating severely ill anorexics draw on a range of techniques and disciplines, medical, dietary and psychological, in an all-out attempt to offer the best treatment available. In this setting it is difficult to tease out the effects of any one treatment method. Nevertheless, there have been some attempts to investigate the efficacy of cognitive behaviour therapy in relation to anorexia nervosa.

In one study, a group of severely ill anorexic women was randomly allocated to either conventional inpatient treatment including refeeding or a day patient treatment programme using a collaborative, CBT approach (Freeman 1995). At 18 months' follow-up, both groups were doing equally well, but at three years, the women treated as day patients had maintained their improvements better than the inpatients.

Another study designed specifically to compare the effects of outpatient CBT with a standard behavioural treatment used routine hospital outpatient management as a control group. All the groups showed similar improvements and there were no significant differences in any of the measures taken between treatment and control groups. However, patients in the CBT group attended more treatment sessions than did patients in the other groups, which suggests that they may have been more motivated to change than the behavioural or control groups (Channon et al. 1989). This motivational aspect of CBT is highlighted similarly in the first controlled trial of CBT for anorexia nervosa. Thirty-three patients were discharged from hospital and randomly allocated to either one year of cognitive behaviour therapy or one year of nutritional counselling. The patients in the CBT condition did significantly better than those in the nutritional counselling alone condition, not only in terms of achieving a good outcome but also in terms of their significantly lower rate of relapse and dropping out of treatment (Pike et al. 2003).

Thus, CBT appears to hold promise for the treatment of anorexia nervosa, at least in relation to its ability to help patients to maintain treatment gains and avoid relapse.

Dialectical behaviour therapy (DBT) and eating disorders

In both an uncontrolled trial and a randomised controlled trial at Stanford, California, more than 80 per cent of patients with binge eating disorder became abstinent from binge eating at the end of a programme of treatment with DBT (Telch, Agras and Linehan 2001). There have also been improvements in people with bulimia nervosa (Safer, Telch and Agras 2001).

In the United Kingdom, Robert Palmer and his colleagues have devised a DBT programme for a group of hard-to-treat people with eating disorder and comorbid borderline personality disorder, all of whom had engaged in acts of self-harm. All of the patients showed reductions in minor self-harm and eating disorder symptoms and the improvements were maintained for 18 months after the end of the programme (Palmer et al. 2003). There was no comparison group in this study, but the combined findings of clinicians and researchers to date suggest that DBT may hold promise for the treatment of some people who are unable to respond to standard cognitive behaviour therapy methods alone.

Conclusions

Cognitive behaviour therapy lends itself well to the treatment of eating disorders for several reasons: it is effective in the reduction of symptoms; it is educational; it is effective in modifying the underlying disturbance in attitude to eating, weight and shape; it can be used in the treatment of emotional states triggering and maintaining symptoms; and it can be applied both to common symptoms and to idiosyncratic expressions of disorder. Cognitive therapy has lent itself to the development of standardised treatment protocols but has also been used in its more newly developed forms, including schema-focused therapy and dialectical behaviour therapy for the treatment of complex and hard-to-treat cases.

The effectiveness of CBT has been demonstrated most clearly in the treatment of normal-weight bulimia. Theoretically, it makes sense also to offer it as a treatment both to clients suffering from anorexia nervosa and to those suffering from binge eating disorder. However, in these areas in particular, much research remains to be done, and it is still very much up to the individual therapist to create an effective programme for each client based on an integration of cognitive therapy principles and clinical judgement rather than on a prescriptive manual-based programme. The following chapter aims to set out ways of beginning this process for individual clients.

4 Beginning the Counselling Process

Engaging the client with an eating disorder can be very difficult. Some clients may have waited for up to five or ten years before summoning up the courage to ask for help. If telling someone for the first time, the client may be experiencing shame, fear, anxiety and a great deal of ambivalence about whether sharing their experience is a good idea at all. It can also be very easy. Many clients live with their disorder on a daily basis and have thought about it a great deal. They know what it is they worry about, they recognise the triggers for obsessive eating behaviours, and they know exactly how much they eat and when, and are eager to explain their predicament.

The initial stages

There are several ways of establishing the exact nature and severity of an eating disorder and the extent to which it may intrude upon a person's life. The initial method is by interview, which can move from an open, non-directive, Rogerian style of interview, towards a more specific format in which the interviewer aims to establish the answers to direct, focused questions.

In beginning this process, a key attitude for the counsellor to adopt is the need for complete acceptance of whatever clients may say about the behaviours that are troubling them. This includes also the avoidance of making assumptions about what clients' aims may be in therapy, in relation either to weight change or to eating behaviour change, or to possible underlying motives or related behaviours or view of the self.

Certain aspects of eating disorder naturally raise many feelings and negative attitudes and no counsellor can be immune to all of these. For example, the shame felt by many women about bingeing on large amounts of unnecessary food when they are not hungry is a natural reflection of an attitude in our society with regard to greed. To many of us also, repeated vomiting would be considered unacceptable and incomprehensible. Clients may resist telling the whole story of their problems or admitting the extent of purging behaviour for just this reason, and it is necessary to question in a non-judgemental way in order to establish the full extent of, or frequency of, a problem.

On the other side, many of us find the idea of self-starvation leading to emaciation equally upsetting, and often frustrating. There is a strong temptation, from the outside, to seize on the apparent problem, the non-eating behaviour, immediately, and to suggest that the person eat something, at least something small, in order to make a start with progress. This temptation may be driven by a variety of factors. First, the client is so obviously in distress, whether or not she admits to having an eating problem. Second, she may have been referred by another professional, perhaps a general practitioner, for specialist help.

There is little to be gained, however, by attempts to speed up the process of engaging the person in therapy and instigating change. On the contrary, the counsellor needs to spend much time in establishing and building up trust so that the client is able to collaborate and become active in the process of change and ask for help where necessary. When things go wrong in this initial stage, the risk occurs that the counsellor will be drawn into a pattern of conflict with the client, similar perhaps to patterns clients have experienced frequently in the past with friends and relatives or even with former therapists.

Moreover, it is important for the counsellor not to be drawn into discussion only of food. As one client clearly put it:

> We've sat here discussing whether or not I'm going to eat an extra yogurt. It always comes back to food. But it's not just about food. I know what I should eat, and I know I'm not eating enough. But I don't need you to tell me that. What I need to know is 'Why am I doing this to myself?' And how can I get it into my head that I can eat normally, that I don't have to ration myself. I'm so afraid to do it, and I don't know why any more.

Many clients have already been in the position of unwilling subject, both in family situations and in past relationships with therapists. The obese binge eater, for example, will have tried many therapies, joined and rejoined one or more slimming clubs, have had several consultations with doctors and dietitians. Each new consultation or therapy will have resulted in the offer of some prescription – in the form of a low-fat diet, a high-protein diet, food replacement plans, drugs to reduce appetite or stimulate metabolism, techniques to use to avoid overeating, perhaps even advice about giving up diets altogether. At the same time, her family may have tried offering support and encouragement, depending on whatever the current diet programme was. 'You're not supposed to be eating those.' 'We're having fish and chips but I've ordered something from the grill for you.' The assumption that the client wishes to lose weight, wishes to make behavioural changes, and wants others to help in these ways has never been questioned.

In the initial stages, therefore, it is necessary both to establish the exact nature of the problem, in some detail, and to ascertain what point clients have reached in terms of their motivation to change, and their understanding of what is needed to enable them to change. Counsellors should bear in mind that the assessment stage is a process which may take more than one or two sessions to complete. While it may be possible to acquire a reasonable overview in the first session, it may be necessary to take one or two further sessions to build up a full picture of the problems.

Assessment of a person with an eating disorder can be aided by the use of a variety of questionnaires, but none of these will serve the counsellor as well as a detailed interview.

First, it is necessary to find out how the client herself sees the problem. The following were some responses from normal-weight bulimics to the question of how they saw their problem:

> I just need help to keep to my diet. (Angela)

> I can't keep my food down. (Diane)

> I want to be able to eat normally like other people without getting fat. (Wendy)

I just want to get rid of this terrible obsession that rules my life. When I'm not eating I'm thinking about food, and when I am eating I'm feeling bad and wish I didn't have to. (Rachel)

Angela saw her primary problem as being an inability to diet. If only she could keep to her self-prescribed regime of 800 calories per day, without bingeing, her problems would be solved. She wanted help to avoid bingeing, but denied that the vomiting was a problem, as she believed that if she could stop bingeing the vomiting would be unnecessary. She believed that she was overweight – she was in fact within the normal range for her height – and that she needed to continue with dieting until she lost a further 10 pounds.

Diane focused on the vomiting. She was aware only that eating engendered such guilt that she felt obliged to vomit after all meals, wherever taken. The vomiting had become almost a reflex action, and occurred in response to a large variety of foods so that the list of foods which were no longer 'forbidden' was now extremely short. She wanted to be able to reduce the range of 'forbidden' foods but had been unable to do this on her own. She could no longer eat with friends or family unless she was reassured about the close proximity of a toilet.

Wendy felt that bulimia was for her a necessary evil. She had been dieting for many years and was now about 14 pounds overweight. She now believed that the amount of food that she could consume without putting on weight was extremely small. She had gone to her general practitioner complaining that she had a very low metabolic rate and enquiring about thyroid gland deficiency. She had been bingeing and vomiting for two years and was convinced that she was unable to eat a normal meal as this would immediately cause her to put on weight. In fact she was trapped in a cycle of bingeing on desired foods, purging herself, and starving for a few days in order to push her weight down, and subsequently regaining the lost weight and more in further binges when she was unable to sustain the strict 'diet' any longer.

Rachel was always on a diet. As long as she kept to her diet, which involved eating only one small meal per day along with occasional small snacks, she was happy. However, she had bouts of extreme hunger. Any slight addition to her diet or change in her plans could lead to her eating in what she saw as an uncontrolled way, and subsequently vomiting, with all the guilt and misery these behaviours carried with them.

Anorexics' conceptualisation of their problems may be equally varied. Responses to the question 'How do you see your problem?' may vary from a silent shrug or 'I don't know' to an impassioned plea for help with the dilemma of wanting to be a normal weight, on the one hand, and wanting to be able to eat as other people do without fear of guilt or retribution, on the other.

Mandy came to therapy – as do many anorexics – because she had been nagged constantly by family and friends. She felt desperate to stay slim, indeed to become even thinner, and was beginning to realise that her dieting had indeed become obsessive to the extent that she could never relax the strict rules that she had made for herself and had become virtually addicted to starving herself.

Ursula had been starving herself for many years, but was frightened by the fact that she had recently begun to eat and to use vomiting as a means of controlling her weight. She felt unable 'to keep anything down' apart from lettuce, cottage cheese and diet biscuits.

Susannah was a keen dancer, and exercised compulsively as well as eating the bare minimum. At 19, she still lived at home with her family, who veered from doing everything in their power to persuade her to eat to ignoring her eating habits altogether. Holding her weight at a body mass index of 17, she refused to accept the need to gain weight, but admitted to feeling unhappy and ill at ease with herself and her appearance.

Sally, on the other hand, had been anorexic for years, and, having been in and out of several hospitals, very much wanted to give up her illness. However, she was unable to push her weight up beyond the body mass index of 16 (which she had reached several years previously as a result of gaining weight in hospital) and was terrified of allowing herself to eat more lest she go completely out of control.

There follows a list of useful questions to ask and areas to probe in confirming or establishing the diagnosis of an eating disorder and assessing its nature. Prior to asking these questions, however, or concurrently, it is important to ascertain the client's body mass index (BMI) which is derived from the formula W/H^2 (weight in kilograms divided by the square of height in metres). The normal range for the body mass index is between 20 and 25. From 26 and above there are increasing degrees of overweight, while people with BMIs of 19 and under are increasingly underweight. A BMI of 17 or below is consistent with a diagnosis of anorexia nervosa. There are several tables available which allow weight to be plotted on a graph in relation to height and which depict the upper and lower limits of the weight range. These allow the counsellor to ascertain to what extent clients are over- or underweight.

Clients often balk at being weighed, some because they are too ashamed of their size to recognise it, others because they themselves have not wanted to accept that they have a problem. However, it is important for the counsellor to weigh the client or to have access to a reliable source for this information. This is helpful in the first instance in terms of confirming the diagnosis of eating disorder as would be defined in *DSM-IV* (American Psychiatric Association 1994) and, second, as a figure against which to measure any change. It is necessary to continue to monitor the client's weight throughout the counselling process.

Some counsellors may prefer to leave the mechanics of weighing to another party such as a dietitian or GP. However, weight or clients' view of their weight is a central part of the problem, and separating this aspect out can merely help to collude with the views of some clients that it is a subject to be avoided or about which to be ashamed. If the client is weighed or reports her weight at the start of the session, the counsellor can record the weight directly afterwards and then continue with the agenda for the day in the knowledge that client and counsellor are both in possession of a complete set of figures for use when appropriate.

In some cases, it may be appropriate for clients to weigh themselves outside the session. Some obese people, bulimics and people with binge eating disorder avoid the scales and fear weighing themselves for the effect this may have on their eating. Others weigh themselves constantly, several times a day. Clients should be positively encouraged to weigh themselves on a regular basis, but not more than once a week, at the same time and in the same clothes. Helping clients to address underlying dysfunctional attitudes to weight is an important part of the counselling process. Thus, while anorexics need to be able to confront and accept their increasing weight, bulimics and obese binge eaters need to learn to attribute less importance to their weight and its fluctuations. The counsellor is in a position to help clients to appreciate the futility of weighing themselves more frequently than once weekly or to cope with the anxiety of dealing with fluctuations in their weight.

Some questions to ask when assessing the person with an eating disorder

1   *The nature of the problem*

- Are you often on a diet or being careful to eat very little?
- Do you overeat?
- Do you binge eat? (Requiring eating a large amount of food and the experience of loss of control.)
- What do you mean by a binge?
- How much food would you eat in a binge? (It is important to ascertain how far the client is in fact consuming objectively large amounts of food as opposed to perceiving an objectively reasonable intake as excessive. See also Wilson 1993b: 235.)
- How often does this happen – times per week, or if every day, times per day?
- How long does a binge last?
- Do you snack between meals?
- Do you think about food a lot even when you are not eating?
- Do you do anything to try to counteract the effects of eating or of binges? For example:

   - Do you diet strictly?
   - Do you miss out meals?
   - Do you stick to a rigid meal plan?
   - Do you ever stop eating altogether for periods of time, i.e. starve yourself completely?
   - Do you ever take measures to rid yourself of food you have already eaten, such as vomit, take laxatives, take diuretics (pills to make you lose water). If so, how often do you do this? Do you try to resist the binges/the vomiting/taking laxatives?

- Do you eat the same foods every day?
- What would be the effect of eating something outside what you usually plan for yourself?
- Are there foods that you avoid eating or that you regard as 'forbidden' altogether?
- Are there situations you avoid, such as going out for a meal to a restaurant or to a friend's house, for fear that you will be confronted with food not allowed on your self-prescribed plan?
- Do you eat in public? If not, what is it that stops you? (for example, do not like the food in restaurants, do not like people to see you eating, prefer to eat alone so that you can savour the taste of the food.)
- How much exercise do you take? (In an anorexic, how far does this appear to be excessive? In a bulimic or obese binge eater, does the person follow a regular exercise plan, or do they avoid exercise as far as possible? One of the chief predictors of success in a diet programme is the maintenance of an exercise programme after the end of a diet, and therefore it is important to ascertain how far the client includes exercise in her daily life or might be able to do so in the future.)
- How long has the problem(s) been going on?

2 *Situational factors*

- Under what circumstances do you binge? Alone in secret/with other people?
- Under what circumstances do you undereat?
- Do you binge eat/undereat/purge in response to specific moods or thoughts? As a result of eating certain foods or classes of food? In response to eating food regarded as forbidden? At what time(s) of day?
- Is there anything that makes the problem worse/better?
- Has there ever been a time when the problem disappeared completely or was better, or was a great deal worse, if only temporarily?

3 *History of weight and dieting*
This should include a history of the client's weight as far back as they can remember, and any attempts to lose or gain weight. In particular the counsellor should ascertain the extent of fluctuations in the client's weight, and as far as possible any relationship of these fluctuations to important life events, a relationship which may or not be apparent to clients themselves. It may also be relevant to ascertain attitudes of other people to the client's weight as these may have a bearing on clients' attitude to themselves and their eating behaviour. Some therapists ask clients to draw a 'time line'. This involves drawing a graph with weight on the vertical axis and time on the horizontal axis. The client plots her weight from as far back as she can remember until the present day. She marks significant points along the line either along the horizontal axis of the graph alone or by use of a vertical line drawn through the horizontal axis to the weight curve with a brief description of the event at the top of the line (see Figure 4.1). In adults, a point on the vertical axis may simply be labelled 'normal weight' as clients cannot be expected to recall exact weight for height figures all the way back into their childhood.

Figure 4.1   Angela's weight graph over time (not to scale)

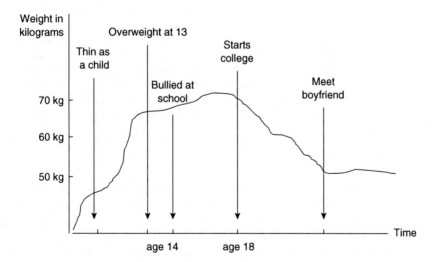

It is also useful to ascertain whether anyone else in the family is overweight, or has been. The likelihood of becoming obese is greater in people who have one obese parent than in those who have none, and greater still if both parents are obese.

- Are you on a diet now?
- Have you dieted in the past?
- How did you go about dieting? (That is, count calories/count fat units/low fat/low carbohydrate/weighing out food according to some published diet plan/just eating less or trying to cut out meals. It is important to establish just what is meant by dieting in order to gauge the person's level of nutritional knowledge.)
- How does dieting affect your eating habits?
- Do you think about food more, or less, when on a diet?
- How successful are you at dieting?
- What led you to diet in the first place?
- What is your eating behaviour when you are not on a diet? (For example, do you tend to eat three meals a day plus snacks, or eat little and often, or eat continuously throughout the day? Many people with eating disorders can barely remember a time when they were not on some self-prescribed diet or what it was like to eat 'normally'.)

4   *History of attitudes to food and eating*

- What was your attitude to food and mealtimes before you ever had a problem?
- How would you describe your eating patterns as a child? As you grew up? In comparison to other people who lived with you at home?
- What were mealtimes like? (For example, to what extent does the client recall taking meals as part of a family, or did mother or carer prepare meals for individual family members and serve them separately at different times, for example when people came in from school or work? Was the client left to her own devices to make her own meals or take snack food from the store cupboard? Was there anything significant about the 'emotional climate' of family mealtimes, for example were meals taken typically in silence, or amid seething rows, solo in front of the television, or with varying members of the family in an atmosphere of ordinariness?)
- What kinds of foods do you like? What did you like before you developed a problem? (What would the client consider to be a normal day's food intake – in the past, as a child, and recently, as an adult? It is useful to ascertain, apart from the client's current attitude to food, whether 'good' or 'bad', what foods they consider to be part of a normal diet. For example, did they historically consume a reasonably balanced diet, taken from a mixture of carbohydrates, vegetables, fruits and proteins, or was their diet largely high-fat, high-carbohydrate? Were meals home-cooked with minimum use of the frying pan, or did they consist largely of high calorie 'take-away' or fast food? Would they consider it normal to include vegetables or fruit in their diet, or are they used to living on a diet of snack foods such as chocolates and crisps or whatever happened to be left in the family refrigerator?)

Elicitation of this kind of information will make it easier to ascertain how far the person might respond to education about diet and changes to be made, so that any referral for nutritional advice can be supported by an understanding by the counsellor of how far the client will need to be helped in making dietary changes, and how far also a preliminary discussion with the dietitian might forestall problems with understanding and compliance. This would seem to be stating the obvious.

However, the reasoning behind this line of questioning is that there are many people seen in therapy who have previously been referred to dietitians and for whom the referral has had no effect. One reason for this is that there is sometimes so large a gulf between clients' knowledge of healthy eating and dietitians' advice that dietitians may be unaware of just how limited is the client's understanding of what they are supposed to do and hence how lacking is their motivation to try it.

5   *Attitude to weight and shape*

- Do you feel that you are too fat? Just right? Too thin? Would you like to be thinner? Fatter?
- Do you want to lose weight? (Or, in the case of someone who is already emaciated – do you want to lose more weight, and if so, how much?)
- What weight are you aiming for? (That is, what is your target weight?) How realistic is the target weight? (In the case of someone who is objectively overweight, and if a weight loss programme taking a year or more is implied, has the client thought about a short-term target(s)? In the case of an anorexic or bulimic client, how far does an unrealistic weight target contribute to maintaining their eating disorder? It is also important to ascertain whether maintaining a slim or thin figure is relevant as an important factor in relation to the person's career, for example in the case of an athlete, a model or a dancer. It may be necessary to disentangle a perceived need to maintain a certain target weight from the person's own idiosyncratic view of the importance of maintaining an 'ideal' weight and shape.)
- What would it mean to you to be fatter/thinner? What would being fatter/thinner say about you as a person? What does being fat/thin say to you about other people you meet?
- What do you think will be the effect on you of losing/gaining weight? (That is, will the client look better, feel better about herself, be meeting expectations of family/significant people in her life? In particular, the counsellor should look for unrealistic expectations of the way in which life will change if the weight is lost, for example, 'Everything will be OK if only I could lose weight' or 'I can only be happy if I know that I can get into a size 10'.)
- How would it affect your life if you knew that you could not achieve this weight?

In assessing attitude to shape and weight, it is also crucial to ascertain how far, on the one hand, the person is merely dissatisfied with her body, and, on the other hand, how far she sees her shape and weight as the most important criterion against which to measure her worth as a person.

- If you would like to be thinner, is there any part of your body that you are satisfied with? Is there any part/s of your body that you are dissatisfied with in particular? (There are some people for whom eating disorder has stemmed from dysmorphophobia – a dissatisfaction with just one body part, for example a belief that her bust is too big, her arms or stomach too fat, or that she has a blemish on her face, which would be less noticeable if she were thinner.)
- Is there anyone else who wants you to lose weight? (For example, a spouse or partner may be putting pressure on the person to lose weight. For example, the woman whose partner promises to marry her if she reaches some arbitrary weight target. In this kind of situation it is as necessary to explore the meaning for the person of her relationship with the potential partner and what that means in relation to her view of herself as it is to explore the history of a problem with eating and weight.)

- Does the way you see the shape of your body negatively affect the way you behave in any way? (For example, does it result in avoidance of certain activities such as swimming, eating in public, or have an effect on personal, physical or sexual relationships?)
- How much time do you spend checking on your appearance?
- How much time do you spend thinking/worrying about your body shape?
- How much time do you spend looking at yourself/a particular aspect of your body in the mirror?

6 *Attitude to dieting for overweight people*

- How much weight do you expect to lose in a week?
- What will losing weight involve for you?
- Does the client expect to have to starve? Eat certain foods to the exclusion of others? Does she know which items in her diet will need to be reduced? Is she aware of the difference between sticking to a time-limited diet versus a long-term healthy eating programme? What life-style changes will the person need to make in order to sustain any physical changes they might achieve?
- What difficulties will be involved in making these life-style changes? How will any attempt to change be affected by work and time pressures, or by financial pressures? How will it be affected by family pressures, such as demands made by family members or by the day-to-day problems involved in catering for a family ('My family won't eat vegetables/brown bread,' etc.).

7 *Symptoms*
It can be useful to explore both physical and emotional symptoms:

- Do you feel unhappy?
- Do you ever feel anxious or shaky?
- Do you ever have giddy spells?
- Do you have any difficulties with concentration?
- Do you feel nervous/have panic attacks?
- Do you have regular monthly periods?

It is not unusual for counsellors to receive referrals of clients who do not have classic symptoms of eating disorder and may be suffering from some other disorder entirely. For example, a client may be referred who has stopped eating, who declares that she is not hungry, who says that she cannot eat. Further questioning may be needed to ascertain whether she is feeling too sad or depressed to eat; whether she feels mainly physically unable to eat; and what her attitude would be to regaining her lost weight. If there is no sign whatsoever that the client fears the idea of being either overweight or normal weight, then other diagnoses may need to be considered and this could merit referral back to a general practitioner for referral elsewhere or for physical investigation.

For example, one woman who was referred to the author ostensibly with an eating disorder reported that she had lost weight recently because she could not 'keep anything down'. It transpired that she was feeling acutely anxious and had been vomiting at mealtimes after one particular anxiety-provoking situation at a dinner party where she had felt extremely nervous and embarrassed. Her anxiety at mealtimes had generalised to a variety of both social and food situations to the extent that she could not eat in public at all and was now convinced of her ability to digest only a limited number of types of food. She was no more than normally concerned about her weight and appearance and had no particular desire to lose more weight. However, because food refusal and vomiting were the chief features of her problem, she had been wrongly diagnosed as having an eating disorder and hence believed herself to have one.

8 *Effect on the client's life*

- How do the problems you have described affect your life in general?
- How do they affect your relationships with family, with friends, with colleagues?
- How do they affect your ability to do your work/study?

9 *History of previous attempts to get help or involvement with counselling*

- If the client has tried dieting, did she get their ideas or advice about what to do from friends, a group, a club, magazines, doctors? Has there been any previous attempt at therapy of a psychological nature? If so, what was the nature of the therapy approach taken? How did the client respond to the therapy? What if anything did she learn from the therapy – about the eating disorder, and about herself? What did she like best about the therapy? What did she like least about the therapy? From these questions it should be feasible to obtain some idea of how far the client is amenable to considering other views of her situation, depending on whether she appears to have had a reasonable opportunity to explore other options in the past. Were there previous refusals to engage in therapy? Were there inpatient admissions, and what was the outcome of these?
- Has the client ever seen a dietitian? What kind of information or advice did the dietitian give? Was this merely a general information sheet approach, or was there an analysis of the client's current diet and some suggestions of change based on that together with reasons for the changes?
- How did any previous therapy or advice consultations end? Was this by mutual agreement, or did the client 'drop out', and if so, why was this?
- Most importantly, what are the client's current expectations of counselling? What would she like to achieve through counselling? On the basis of the information available to you, does this seem realistic?

The use of questionnaires in the assessment of eating disorder

In addition to an interview, a range of questionnaires can be used to clarify the nature of the client's problems. While responses to questionnaires may be helpful in describing certain psychological characteristics and behaviours of clients, they do not provide full explanations as to the causes of a disorder and can never take the place of a thorough interview.

However, they may be useful from several points of view. First, they may point to aspects which have been missed at interview, either because the counsellor forgot to ask, or because the client avoided responding to a particular line of questioning. Second, those which have been widely researched on people with eating disorders are useful as a means of assessing objective severity of a disorder. Some are useful in terms of offering a profile of clients across several dimensions and can identify or highlight areas where clients need particular help. Others may be useful as a 'shortcut' means of clarifying negative thinking or core beliefs, which might otherwise be elicited only after months of therapy. Using a questionnaire measure can be helpful as a means of measuring change over time or in response to therapy, and is particularly useful in small-scale projects where the therapist may wish to compare the outcome of groups of clients. Counsellors should, however, bear in mind that most of the measures have been used only with adult women and therefore may not be helpful when used with children or with men. Also, the person who tends to deny problems will be just as likely to do so in response to a questionnaire as in an interview.

There follows a list of some questionnaires relating to eating disorder, with a brief description of each. Some are available to purchase or online; others are available only in the original journal article or from the author, but are worth pursuing as ways to extend the counsellor's knowledge about ways to assess the person with an eating disorder and the kinds of question to ask. The list is by no means exhaustive (see also Crowther and Sherwood 1997).

- *Binge Eating Scale* (Gormally et al. 1982)
  A self-report scale designed to assess binge eating problems among obese people. The 16 scale items include eight describing feelings or cognitions such as guilt or preoccupation with attempts to control eating; and eight behavioural manifestations such as inability to stop eating voluntarily, and eating in secret.
- *Binge Scale Questionnaire* (Hawkins and Clement 1980)
  A self-report scale with nine items assessing the frequency of bingeing, the duration of each binge, the presence of purging, the degree of control experienced, and mood following the binge.
- *Bulimia Test – BULIT and BULIT-R* (Smith and Thelen 1984; Thelen et al. 1991)
  A 32-item self-report, multiple-choice scale designed to distinguish between people with bulimia and other eating disorders and between bulimics and people without eating disorder. It includes questions about purging, attitudes to eating and overeating, and the psychological effect on the person of disordered eating. The revised version of the questionnaire takes account of the changes in the diagnostic criteria for bulimia nervosa.
- *Bulimic Investigatory Test – BITE* (Henderson and Freeman 1987)
  This is a widely used self-report scale designed to detect binge eating and bulimia, and made up of two subscales: one consisting of 30 items relating to symptoms, behaviour and dieting; and a further subscale of six items measuring the severity of behaviour as defined by its frequency. The questions are simple to answer, being mainly 'yes/no' items.
- *Dieter's Inventory of Eating Temptations* (Schlundt and Zimmerig 1988)
  A self-report inventory designed to 'assess behavioural competence in six types of situations related to weight control: overeating, negative emotions, exercise, resisting temptation, positive social, and food choice'. Useful in the assessment of obese clients.
- *Eating Attitudes Test* (Garner and Garfinkel 1979)
  Known as the EAT-40 and the EAT-26 (brief version), this scale is said to measure the symptoms of anorexia nervosa and can be used to measure change in symptoms over time as recovered patients have normal scores. It has also been used to identify eating disturbances in non-clinical samples. It can indicate the presence of disturbed eating patterns but does not 'reveal the motivation or possible psychopathology underlying the manifest behaviour'.
- *Eating Disorder Examination – EDE(Q)* (Cooper, Cooper and Fairburn 1989)
  This is a very detailed and thoroughly researched structured interview schedule. It can be used to generate a diagnosis, and gives scores on four subscales: restraint; eating

concern; shape concern; and weight concern. It appears in full in Fairburn, Marcus and Wilson (1993: 333–356). There is, in addition, a written questionnaire version.
- *Eating Disorders Inventory* (Garner, Olmstead and Polivy 1983)
A 64-item scale designed to tap into specific psychological dimensions observed in anorexia nervosa and bulimia nervosa, and consists of eight subscales entitled: drive for thinness; bulimia; body dissatisfaction; ineffectiveness; perfectionism; interpersonal distrust; interoceptive awareness; and maturity fears. The more recent EDI-2 (Garner 1991) has three additional scales: asceticism; impulse regulation; and social insecurity. The scale is reliable and is widely used in both clinical and research settings as a before and after measure of change through treatment.
- *Slade Anorexic Behaviour Scale* (Slade 1973)
This is an observer rating scale, used to assess the severity of anorexic behaviour. Two observers, usually nurses on a ward, tick the presence or absence of 22 anorexic behaviours in three categories: resistance to eating (for example, 'begins by cutting up food into small pieces'); disposing of food; and 'overactivity' (for example, 'walks or runs about whenever possible').
- *Stirling Eating Disorder Scales – SEDS* (Williams and Power 1996)
A self-report questionnaire designed to measure the cognitive and behavioural aspects of bulimia nervosa and anorexia nervosa, and extract scores on four factors relevant to these disorders: external control; low assertiveness; low self-esteem; and self-directed hostility.
- *The Three-Factor Eating Questionnaire* (Stunkard and Messick 1985)
A 51-item questionnaire which measures three dimensions relating to eating behaviour: cognitive restraint (or the level of voluntary control over eating); disinhibition (or the tendency to lose control over eating when faced with external cues); and susceptibility to feelings of hunger. Most useful for overweight clients.

Questionnaires relating to underlying cognitions and schemas include the following:

- *Anorectic Cognitions Questionnaire – MAC-R* (Mizes et al. 2000)
A self-report scale consisting of 24 items which contribute to three factors: self-control and self esteem; the belief that eating and weight behaviour are the basis of approval from others; and rigid weight regulation and fear of weight gain. The authors claim good validity and the ability to discriminate between bulimics and anorexics. There are as yet no norms for the test.
- *Dysfunctional Attitude Scale – DAS* (Weissman and Beck 1978)
A self-report scale consisting of 100 items designed to assess clients' underlying assumptions and beliefs relating, for example, to approval (e.g. 'It's awful to be disapproved of by someone who is important to you'), achievement or perfectionism.
- *Eating Disorder Belief Questionnaire* (M.J. Cooper et al. 1997)
A self-report questionnaire designed to assess assumptions and beliefs associated with eating disorders. It claims to be able to assess assumptions in four areas: negative self-beliefs; weight and shape as a means to acceptance by others (for example, 'If I get fat I'll be less acceptable to others'); weight and shape as a means to self-acceptance; and control over eating.
- *Young–Rygh Avoidance Inventory – YRAI* (Young and Rygh 2003)
A 40-item self-rating scale that assesses the presence and degree of a variety of strategies that clients use to avoid experiencing pain: for example, withdrawal from people, distraction through activity, self-soothing by eating. The inventory is a clinical tool, with no norms or formal scoring instructions, but may be useful as means of helping clients to identify negative assumptions.

In addition to questionnaires relating to eating disorder *per se*, it may be useful to quantify or describe other problems experienced by the client. In particular it is useful to know to what extent the client may also be feeling depressed, as depression is often a symptom of eating disorder, and, in extreme cases, it is necessary to be aware of any suicidal thoughts or intent. In addition, there may be problems with body image and self-esteem, or trauma and abuse in childhood.

- *Beck Depression Inventory – BDI* (Beck 1972)
  A 21-item self-report questionnaire which yields a score for the severity of depression, and which is useful as a quick assessment tool to monitor improvements or deterioration of mood.
- *Beck Hopelessness Scale* (Beck et al. 1974)
  A 20-item self-administered scale, measuring clients' attitudes to their future, on which high scores are predictive of suicidal behaviour.
- *Body Shape Questionnaire – BSQ* (Cooper et al. 1987)
  A 51-item self-report questionnaire which measures concerns about body shape, in particular the experience of 'feeling fat'. It correlates with the total score on EAT and the Body Dissatisfaction subscale of the EDI. It is also associated with recovery from bulimia nervosa. Lowered scores on this questionnaire as well as symptomatic improvement may relate to a reduction in cognitive symptoms which is protective against relapse.
- *The Body Image Quality of Life Inventory – BIQLI* (Cash and Fleming 2002)
  A self-report scale designed to measure the effects of body image on 19 life domains, such as sense of self, social functioning, sexuality, emotional well-being, eating, exercise and appearance. Clients are asked to rate how far their attitude to their body impacts on each life domain on a five-point scale. It is said to be internally consistent and stable over a 2- to 3-week period and to be useful as an outcome measure of body image interventions.
- *The Situational Inventory of Body-Image Dysphoria – SIBID* (Cash 2002)
  A 48-item self-report measure of the frequency of negative body-image emotions across everyday life situations. The inventory asks respondents how often they experience body-image dysphoria or distress in each of 48 identified situations, including both social and non-social contexts and activities related to exercising, grooming, eating, intimacy, physical self-focus and appearance alterations. The authors have found that both this and the short form (SIBID-S), which has 20 items, are reliable and valid measures of body-image affect. (Both the SIBID and SIBID-S scales can be accessed on the author's website which also contains other information about his ongoing research into aspects of body image.)
- *Shape and Weight-Based Self-Esteem Inventory – SAWBS* (Geller, Johnston and Madsen 1997)
  This is a measure of the extent to which self-esteem is based on shape and weight as opposed to other self-esteem determinants, such as friendships, intimate relationships and competence at school or other activities. Clients select from a list of attributes those that are important to their sense of worth and divide a circle into pieces representing the proportion of each attribute in the total. The authors have found that lower shape- and weight-based self-esteem scores were associated with greater eating disorder symptoms, lower global and body esteem, and higher endorsement of societal ideals about shape and weight.
- *Child Abuse and Trauma Scale – CAT* (Sanders and Becker-Lausen 1995)
  A self-report scale which gives a quantitative index of the frequency and extent of certain negative experiences in childhood and adolescence.

- *Dissociation Questionnaire – DIS-Q* (Vanderlinden et al. 1992)
  A 63-item self-report questionnaire for the detection of dissociative disorders. The questionnaire is published in Vanderlinden and Vandereycken (1997), which gives a detailed discussion of traumatic and dissociative experiences in eating disorders.
- *Dissociative Experiences Scale – DES* (Bernstein and Putnam 1986)
  A 28-item self-report questionnaire in which clients make slashes along a 100 mm line for each question to demonstrate their level of agreement with each one. The authors have found that the scale measures three separate components: amnestic dissociation; depersonalisation and derealisation; and absorption and imaginative involvement.
- *Rosenberg Self-Esteem Scale – SES* (Rosenberg 1965)
  A 10-item self-report measure of global self-esteem. The higher a person's score, the higher his or her self-esteem.

Presenting the cognitive behavioural view and formulating the problem

It is important early on to present the cognitive behavioural view of eating disorder and at the same time to formulate clients' own problems in cognitive behavioural terms as a means of helping them to begin to see for themselves a way out of their disorder. This formulation will at first be fairly general. It may be possible to surmise from the history and current form of the client's disorder some aspects of the part the disorder plays in her life. However, any formulation will at the beginning of therapy be merely in 'draft' form, and must be presented to the client as such, as it is unlikely that core schemata would become apparent at this stage.

For example, Angela was living away from home for the first time and had just started a university course in Social Sciences. She was surrounded by many new people and had recently also become involved with a new boyfriend who wanted her to move in with him. She had begun dieting on arrival at college. She had always been slightly overweight and had tried dieting before but with little success. Unable to eat for the first three days, she had continued her non-eating behaviour into a strict diet, in an attempt to identify herself as one of the slim happy crowd of people she believed herself to be surrounded by. As the diet progressed, she became terrified of regaining her lost weight and the old unhappy self of her schooldays. But under stress caused by worries about doing assignments on time and her dilemma regarding her boyfriend, she began to binge eat on a regular basis and to follow this with vomiting, until she was doing it three or four times a week.

A preliminary formulation was as follows. Angela saw herself as having been socially unsuccessful prior to her arrival at university. She attributed her lack of success to her being overweight and attributed a great deal of importance to the ideal of being thin. She attributed her new-found social success to her improving waistline and believed that if she were to regain her lost weight she would lose her popularity and her boyfriend. She therefore dieted strictly and was in a continual state of mild deprivation. Therefore, liable to let go of her restraint under stress, she panicked whenever she felt that she had broken her diet. Failure at dieting compounded Angela's already low self-esteem and came to be linked with the idea of failure in all respects. In order to avoid this happening, Angela dieted even more strictly and found herself in a vicious circle of bingeing and more dieting and attempting to compensate for her behaviour by vomiting. This preliminary formulation was fed back to her and she was offered some sessions of cognitive behaviour therapy aimed at helping her to give up her bulimic behaviour and build up her self-esteem and social skills.

Often, in addition to a verbal presentation, it is helpful to present a formulation in diagrammatic form. Together with the client, the counsellor can make a list of predisposing factors (historical, environmental, physical), a list of triggers, a list of 'maintenance' factors and a list of strategies the client adopts in order to try to deal with the problem. These can be 'mapped' on a sheet of paper. The client may wish to take the formulation home in order to elaborate on it over the following week. In the case of Angela, the predisposing or vulnerability factors were low self-esteem, a tendency to overweight and having been bullied at school. Trigger factors were the arrival at university, which led simultaneously to dieting and to meeting her boyfriend. Angela's attempt to compensate for her diet lapses by purging could be depicted as a vicious circle where dieting and fear of failure led to purging which in turn led to bingeing and back to dieting, all of which were maintained by negative thoughts about her failure to diet and as a person (see Figure 4.1 on p. 59).

Assessment of motivational stage in people with an eating disorder

Not all clients are ready to change, however, and it can be useful to bear in mind the ideas of Prochaska and Di Clemente (1982) in this respect. All too often, when a client enters the consulting room, counsellors make the assumption that the person wishes unreservedly to change. We accept at face value the person's wish to 'get better'; often the more distressed the client, the more convinced we are of their motivation to change. It may take several months of missed appointments, forgotten homework assignments and general lack of progress before we suspect that a client might be ambivalent about, afraid, or even unwilling to change her behaviour. Prochaska and Di Clemente devised a model of change which suggested that people who are considering change go through six stages. These are: precontemplation, contemplation, determination, action, maintenance and relapse. Stages one through six can be described graphically on a wheel, which means that people can go from stage two round to stage six and back to stage two again. They can go through several cycles of these stages, from contemplation to relapse and back again, before finally coming out of the wheel. The task of the counsellor is to help clients to move through the stages, as expressed in Table 4.1.

At the precontemplation stage, the person has not yet considered the possibility of change, and is unlikely to have requested treatment. She may have been brought unwillingly to consult with a professional by a family member or friend. At the contemplation stage, the person is considering change but may not yet be entirely convinced of the need for it or may be ambivalent about giving up the problem behaviour. At the determination stage, the client is wanting to change, and is saying things like: 'I must do something about this. I can't spend the rest of

Table 4.1   Prochaska and Di Clemente's six stages of change

Precontemplation	Raise doubt – increase the client's perception of risks and problem behaviour
Contemplation	Tip the balance – evoke reasons for change, risks of not changing, strengthen client's self-efficacy for change
Determination	Help client to determine the best course of action to take in seeking change
Action	Help client to take steps towards change
Maintenance	Help client to identify and use relapse prevention strategies
Relapse	Help client to revisit earlier stages without becoming demoralized because of relapse

Source: Miller and Rollnick 1991: 18. Reprinted with the kind permission of the Guilford Press.

my life obsessed by food. What can I do?' According to Miller and Rollnick (1991), if at this time the client moves to the next stage, 'action', the change process continues. If not, however, the process may halt and the person will slip back into contemplation. After the action stage, 'the maintenance process' is vital in order to prevent relapse and in order to build up the skills needed to maintain and support the new behaviour. In the case of binge eating, for example, it is not enough merely to give up the behaviour for a few weeks. The sufferer will need to focus on areas of her life that were making the behaviour a rewarding way of coping. This might mean not only modifying her attitude to shape and weight, but also finding alternative ways of dealing with inevitable stress.

Where clients are ambivalent about change, the counsellor can help by suggesting that they draw up a balance sheet of possible strategies. They can ask: What are the advantages of staying the way you are? The disadvantages? The advantages of change, the disadvantages of change? Do any of the advantages of change outweigh the advantages of staying where you are? What are the aspects that will help you make the changes? What are the obstacles you will have to overcome?

Example: Wendy. Wendy was an overweight bulimic in the contemplation stage. She was asked to draw up a table of the advantages and disadvantages of her bulimia in order to begin work on deciding about whether or not she wished to commit herself to treatment. She had started her dieting and bingeing behaviour shortly after having been let down by her first boyfriend. Always conscious of her weight, she had begun a diet when he left her in the belief that she would have had more success with him if she were thinner. From the table (Table 4.2) it became clear that there were certain gains to be had from her bulimic behaviour. Though upset about her inability to resist the urge to binge, the bingeing and her overweight afforded her some protection from the stress of socialising with both women and men as she stayed at home whenever she was likely to binge. Before it became feasible to offer help with the bulimia, it was necessary to work with Wendy over several sessions on what she meant by her 'full potential' and how she would like to develop this, and on a more realistic appraisal of 'failure' and 'success' *vis-à-vis* relationships in her life.

Example: Sally. Sally had been anorexic for ten years, and was keen to give up her illness once and for all. She too was in the contemplation stage, but trying hard to determine that she would make changes. (See Table 4.3.)

Table 4.2   Wendy

Advantages of the way I am	Disadvantages of the way I am
I can eat a lot when bingeing	I am obsessed with food
I don't risk failure	I'm not developing my potential
I can't be hurt	I am always conscious of my body
There's no sexual competition	I remain lonely
	I continue to avoid people
Advantages of change	Disadvantages of change
I might start to be happier	I'd have to make an effort
I might want to see people	The future might be no better
I Would have time to develop my full potential	Then I'll be even sadder

Table 4.3   Sally

Disadvantages of having anorexia nervosa	Advantages of having anorexia nervosa
My life is restricted	I get support
I'm obsessed with thoughts of food and routine	I am 'special'
Physical weakness	I am good at something other people can't do
No stamina	
Disadvantages of change	Advantages of change
If I get to a healthy weight people will expect more of me	I'll be able to work all day without getting tired
I won't be special any more	I'll be able to eat more normal foods
I'll wonder why I didn't do it before	My family won't have to worry about me
	I'll be able to concentrate on my work

Questionnaires to help in the assessment of motivational stage

There are some assessment tools to aid the counsellor in establishing at what point a client is in the change process. These have been developed largely as research tools, but may be of interest as they detail several questions which may usefully be asked in order to glean information about the nature of a client's motivation to change.

- *The Readiness and Motivation Interview – RMI* (Geller and Drab 1999)
  This provides a standard format which may inform counsellors about the process of assessing readiness and motivation. The questions relate to the precontemplation, contemplation and action stages of change for each specific eating disorder symptom as described in the EDE (see page 64). The interview is a semi-structured, 45- to 75-minute interview in which the client is asked about how far specific symptoms are experienced as a problem and is guided through a series of further questions relating to desire and intention for change depending on their answers to previous questions. The potential advantage of using this format is that the information gathered can help with tailoring the treatment to the individual client, and the authors have found that ratings on the subscales predict future difficulty with making behavioural changes in the

week following the assessment. The RMI also provides scores on the extent to which work by the client on symptom change is for internal reasons (for the self) as opposed to external ones (for other people). The disadvantage of the interview is that it requires a considerable amount of time and training both to learn the procedure and to use the scoring format. Counsellors may prefer to use a self-administered questionnaire such as the Anorexia Nervosa Stages of Change Questionnaire.

- *Anorexia Nervosa Stages of Change Questionnaire – ANOSCQ* (Rieger, Touyz and Meumont 2002)
  This is a 20-item self-report questionnaire based on Prochaska and Di Clemente's (1982) stages of change model. Each item refers to a specific symptom and clients have a choice of agreeing with one or more of five statements, each of which represents one of the five stages of change. Hence it is quite a lengthy instrument for the client to read. The authors hold that the test is a reliable and valid instrument of client readiness to recover from anorexia nervosa. (Reliability: clients gave similar responses to the questionnaire at one week intervals, suggesting that the ideas it is testing are stable over time; validity: responses correlate with other measures such as of client engagement and attitudes to eating and are predictive of weight gain in treatment.)
- *Concerns about Change Scale CCS(R^2)* (Vitousek et al. 1995)
  This is a 112-item self-report questionnaire which measures the degree to which various concerns interfere with changing dysfunctional attitudes and behaviours. (for example, 'this problem is part of what makes me unique and special'). The scale has 17 subscales which reflect different themes relating to reasons for resisting change, and is particularly useful for working with anorexics as this group obtain significantly higher scores than do people in other eating disorder groups in four out of the eight scales related to resistance to change.

Another method commonly used in assessing the motivation of a client with an eating disorder is the use of letter writing. Clients are invited to write a letter to their bulimia nervosa or to their anorexia nervosa, first as a friend, and then as an enemy. The advantage of this exercise is that clients are given the opportunity to express positive as well as negative attitudes to their disorder. Lucy Serpell, researching at the Eating Disorders Unit of the Institute of Psychiatry in London, has investigated the themes raised in these letters. Nearly all bulimia nervosa patients described more cons than pros, as did anorexics, although the proportion of positive themes expressed was higher in anorexics. The most common benefit described by both groups was that of 'guardian', followed by the ability to avoid or manage emotions. Other common benefits described by the anorexia group include feeling in control and feeling special; and the benefits of bulimia nervosa include being able to eat and not get fat (see Serpell and Treasure 2002; Serpell et al. 1999). Any treatment offered must take into account the need to help clients find alternative means of enjoying these benefits if it is to have any effect. The letter task is given as 'homework' at an early stage in the treatment, and many clients are happy to tackle it. Some clients may find it difficult to complete the task, others 'forget', but however the client responds will provide information and material on which to base discussions about the future of their treatment.

Self-monitoring by the client

This involves clients initially in keeping a daily record of their eating habits and associated events, behaviours, and sometimes thoughts and feelings. Ideally, clients need to keep a record for around two weeks in order to have a representative record of their eating habits. Sometimes clients complain that the act of keeping a record itself alters their eating, making them behave either in a more 'normal' way than usual through reluctance to write down all the incidents which embarrass them, or forcing them to focus more on food and eating and hence eat even more. It is important at this stage to reassure clients that they are not being judged, and that the counsellor is quite accustomed to seeing records of people who have binged, purged or starved themselves to extreme degrees. Also, the effects of the record keeping itself on behaviour usually settle down after a few days and clients find that it need not intrude on their behaviour.

A typical eating record might include a column for the date or time; a column for food and drink taken; a column describing the situation (where, with whom, doing what); a column in which to record any attempts to counteract the effects of eating such as vomiting or taking laxatives or diuretics; and a column for describing any relevant thoughts or feelings at the time (see Table 4.4). All food taken should be listed, and binges should be distinguished from planned meals and snacks. For some clients, there might be an additional column detailing times at which the opportunity to eat was passed by (for example, when an anorexic misses a meal, or a binge eater declines to accept the offer of snack food).

Table 4.4   Daily record of food intake

Time	Food/ drink taken	Situation (Where, with whom, doing what)	Attempts to counteract effects of food	Thoughts/ feelings

Record keeping is probably one of the most abused pieces of behavioural advice ever given. Counsellors can expect to encounter many problems with asking clients to complete a record of their eating. At first, clients may either decline or forget to keep the record. Any instance of non-compliance should be used as a starting point for gathering further information. The client should be asked what difficulties she experienced with keeping the record, or what it was in particular that made her unwilling to complete all the columns.

Faith, who had suffered with bulimia for five years, had been asked at the end of her second session to keep a record of her eating and related events. The following exchange is taken from the beginning of the third session:

Counsellor: How did you get on with the record keeping?
Faith: I haven't done it … I didn't like to think about keeping the record. Someone might find it. [Her family for the most part apparently knew nothing of her problems.]
Counsellor: Do you have anywhere safe you could keep it when you are at home where you know no one would be likely to pry?
Faith: There are a couple of places, but I wouldn't really want to write all that stuff down for you to see. I can hardly bear to think about it myself. Once

Counsellor: I understand that you don't want to have to experience the upset of bingeing all over again. It's a bit like rubbing salt into a wound. Have you found
that by not thinking about it you can make it go away?

Faith: No, not at all. As soon as I've got rid of all the food I'm back to wonder-
ing what I can eat next.

Counsellor: So you can't just forget about it.

Faith: No way.

The counsellor was able to suggest to Faith that by focusing on her problems through keeping a written record she would be able to learn more about what kept the problems going and what might help them to improve.

It can be useful to bear in mind that this kind of problem can be pre-empted by careful preparation. When asking a client to try out a behavioural task, be it record keeping, or changing a specific behaviour, the counsellor can pursue the following line of questions:

- Can you think about when/how you might achieve this?
- Can you predict what difficulties you might have in keeping a record/completing this task?
- Can you predict what obstacles might get in the way of your doing this?

In providing the answers to these questions, the client prepares herself for the difficulties she will encounter and can be helped to consider solutions in advance.

A second aspect of record keeping that may pose problems is the timing of the record. Clients can often be seen in therapists' waiting rooms, frantically scribbling to complete a week of record forms. It is important to stress to the client that no record at all or just one or two days' records are more useful than a full record put together at the last minute. Such a record is produced from memory, and is extremely unlikely to give an accurate reflection of actual events in the client's life or of the client's true thoughts or feelings during the relevant time period. Hence it should be stressed that records must be kept immediately after the relevant events if at all possible, even if this requires the client carrying a notebook and pencil at all times!

A further consideration, once the hurdle of actually keeping a record has been overcome, is the importance of explaining the ABC (antecedents, behaviour and consequences) of behaviour to clients, to ensure that a full record is kept, rather than merely a list of everything they have consumed over the past week or two. This involves explaining to clients the way in which the things we do have certain consequences, depending also on the circumstances in which we do them. For example, if we are used to seeing and buying chocolate at the petrol station every time we go to get petrol for the car, we are more likely to do the same thing next time we go there, especially if we know that they sell our favourite brand. Hence, keeping a clear record can help us to break unhelpful patterns in the future.

Some clients master the skill of keeping a very full food intake record but find it more difficult when it comes to detailing thoughts and feelings experienced around the time of eating or purging. This aspect of record keeping will be dealt with in more detail in Chapter 6.

Setting the agenda for therapy

Many writers in the cognitive therapy field detail stages through which the therapy should pass. It is particularly appropriate to work in this way when the therapy is being conducted as part of a research trial. However, cognitive behavioural therapy is by its nature an individual process. Techniques which may be useful for one client are irrelevant to another. The therapy will no doubt move broadly from assessment through a stage characterised largely by practical educational and behavioural tasks, to a stage characterised more strongly by cognitive techniques. Beyond this, however, the specifics of what constitutes the passage through therapy for any one client must depend on the outcome of the assessment process. The idiosyncratic problem list for each client, together with that person's choice of areas on which he or she wishes to work, will itself define the direction of therapy and the order in which the relevant therapy techniques might be called upon. In practice, as outlined in Chapter 3, individual therapy will move between behavioural, educational and cognitive techniques, and from domains relating strictly to food to those relating to eating behaviour, to the social or to the intensely personal, and back again.

Psychoeducation

During the first stage of counselling, much of the material will of necessity be psychoeducational. The counsellor will spend a great deal of time in giving information about the disorder in order to help clients to understand both the cognitive view of how it might have been established and how it is being maintained. This will include information about the causes of the disorder, the sociocultural context of eating disorders and the pressures on women in particular to diet (see also Chapter 2 and Garner 1997). Clients can be given a handout relevant to the material covered in the session, for discussion next time. The material covered in Appendix 1 briefly defines the eating disorders and outlines some possible causes, as well as pointing to the dangers of excessive dieting and weight cycling and giving reasons why clients might want to give up purging. A variety of reading sources can also be recommended to the client who wishes to explore these ideas further (see Appendix 2).

As clients begin to understand the nature of their disorder, the counselling process will move naturally towards looking for ways to help them to make changes. Some of the behavioural and cognitive techniques available will be described in Chapters 6 and 7. However, counsellors also need to have an understanding of some of the physical aspects of eating disorders. For this reason, the following chapter sets out to describe the nutritional principles which might form the basis of the educational aspect of a treatment programme.

5 Nutritional Aspects of Helping the Eating-Disordered Client

The cognitive view of eating disorder encompasses the notion that disorders of undereating, overeating and purging are maintained in part by the effects of dieting and bingeing. Therefore, one of the most important aspects of counselling people with eating disorders is for both counsellors and clients to be able to understand and deal with the links between emotions and eating and misconceptions about weight loss and gain.

There is so much publicity given to the area of dieting and weight loss that it is easy to assume greater knowledge on the part of the eating-disordered client than she actually has. Many clients have spent several years worrying about dieting and some will have absorbed a great deal of apparently educative material – healthy eating pamphlets and cook books, magazines and articles devoted to slimming success stories and how to achieve a slim figure, in addition to numerous television programmes about obesity and dieting. Others have gained their information largely from discussions with other women – school friends, family, colleagues at work. Whether overweight, normal weight or underweight, all clients with eating disorders are likely to have mistaken beliefs and inadequate knowledge both about good nutrition, and about how weight is lost or gained.

Some counsellors hold the view that discussion of food issues is irrelevant to the client's problems, and that the desire on the part of the client to discuss details of weight and eating merely serves as a distraction from the 'real' issues, be they personal or interpersonal. There is therefore a strict division between the role of the psychotherapist or counsellor and the dietitian or nutritionist. In a cognitive therapy setting, however, there are no 'allowed' versus 'not allowed' topics. Thoughts about food and weight are central to the concerns of the eating-disordered client, not least because the processes of starvation and dieting themselves have an effect on emotional state and thinking behaviour (see Chapter 2), and as such must be addressed directly. If there are, indeed, other issues of importance, these will come to light as the more superficial issues are addressed and the layers of meaning around food and weight are uncovered and the client's underlying dysfunctional assumptions are voiced. This is not to say that the counsellor should necessarily take upon him- or herself the role of nutritional counsellor or that the nutritionist or dietitian can necessarily expect to be able to deal with all the psychological issues. Many clients with an eating disorder need to work both with a psychological counsellor and a dietary advisor. However, it is important both for the diet therapist working with a client to be aware of some of the psychological issues involved and for the counsellor to have some knowledge of nutrition. For example, one woman who had been anorexic for several years saw both a dietitian and a psychologist, ostensibly for help in overcoming her anorexia. With the dietitian she discussed in minutest detail how she might gradually increase her calorie intake and whether or not she could allow herself to include some sweet items in her diet. At the same time, with the psychologist, she admitted that because she viewed herself as having little worth, she believed that she did not deserve to eat enjoyable foods and was unlikely to be able to add to her diet the items discussed with the dietitian. Once, with her permission, the dietitian and psychologist had become aware of both aspects of the problem, it became possible to address the issue from both points of view in a more realistic and helpful way. The dietitian was able to introduce the sweet foods in a graded fashion, in the knowledge of the client's fear, while the psychologist was able to address the problem of 'deservingness' and monitor the client's changing perception of herself together with her ability to take an increasing range of sweet foods.

Where clients have contact both with a counsellor and a dietitian or nutritionist, it is of course essential for the two therapists to meet at least once, face to face, so that they can establish their respective roles and plan for continuing communication about the client's progress in treatment (see also Saloff-Coste, Hamburg and Herzog 1993).

Nutritional knowledge of eating-disordered clients

Clients may have a great many ideas about which foods should be avoided for health or to maintain a slim figure, but little knowledge of which foods make up a healthy normal diet or about the quantity of these foods that should be eaten. Thus, for example, many bulimics and anorexics believe that they require only 1000 calories per day to maintain their weight, when the correct figure for the average healthy woman is closer to 2000. Many people with an eating disorder believe that all fats are bad and should be avoided, and that carbohydrate foods such as bread, pasta and rice should be eaten in very small quantities or not at all. In line with these ideas, they may have developed unwritten lists of 'forbidden' foods. Any transgression of the strict limits she has set herself can result for an overweight woman in the collapse of a diet; for a bulimic, in a return to binge eating; and for a restricting anorexic, in very great difficulty in accepting a refeeding programme at all. For some clients, the list of forbidden foods is so long that it is easier to ascertain which foods are allowed than those which are not. The list of foods allowed is often extremely short, and for many people can consist of as few, for example, as the following items: salad vegetables, green vegetables, cottage cheese, and other low-fat protein foods such as tinned tuna fish and grilled or roast chicken.

The advantage, if any, of this bias in the knowledge of clients is perhaps held by the obese people, as it is for these people that knowing which foods to avoid is most important. The knowledge is, however, of no value to bulimics, who need to give up an abnormal eating pattern and develop regular eating habits, or to anorexics, who restrict themselves and cannot allow themselves to eat normally.

More clinically useful than the knowledge about which foods to avoid is the knowledge of foods, both type and quantity, which are positively conducive to good health. This knowledge appears to be lacking in most clients, partly perhaps because of the media attention given to what to avoid, and partly because of the lack of positive, as opposed to negative, nutritional information widely available. On questioning, some clients do have correct ideas about aspects of positive nutrition, and their inability to accept a varied diet has more to do with the irrational way they have come to see their own individual needs than with their knowledge about nutrition in general, which they are unable to apply to themselves.

For example, many clients, both bulimic and anorexic, accept that certain foods, such as pasta and pulses, are of value and should be eaten, but are unable to accept that they themselves might be included in the groups of people who should eat them.

Nutritional counselling

Nutritional counselling is an extremely important component of a cognitive behavioural therapy approach to eating disorders. There may indeed be a case for its being offered on its own as an effective short-term treatment for bulimia nervosa (Hsu, Holben and West 1992). The essential components of nutritional counselling include the following:

1 Teaching about the links between mood, cravings and binge eating.
2 The notion that bulimic behaviour is maintained by semi-starvation.
3 The notion that bulimic behaviour can be initiated by starvation or by other triggers, but either way it is self-perpetuating.
4 The notion that adequate nutritional knowledge will, in most cases, result in healthy eating behaviour.
5 Teaching in the principles of good nutrition.
6 Establishment and maintenance of a pattern of regular eating through meal planning.

It is useful for all clients to have at least one consultation with a dietitian for advice about how much and what kinds of food they should be consuming. Calorie counting has limited value for people with an eating disorder, as it tackles the question of quantity but not quality, and has no value in terms of teaching the person how to achieve a normal diet. It is extremely useful, however, for clients to receive some information about food groups, and about amounts of food they could reasonably take from these groups on a daily basis. If they find it useful also to count calories, they may do so, but the end result of using a diet based on food groups will be that they are taking foods from several food groups and that they are taking a well-balanced diet, conducive to health, rather than an idiosyncratically designed diet which may have little or no nutritional value.

Clients should be encouraged to select a variety of food from the following food groups: carbohydrate foods, including potatoes, bread and cereals; protein foods, including fish, meat, eggs and pulses; milk foods, including milk, cheese and yoghurt; fruit and vegetables; and fats and oils. Normal-weight and anorexic clients are always surprised when informed of the amounts of these foods that they should be taking. For example, the advice given by dietitians at Northwick Park Hospital is that they should take at least six portions per day of carbohydrate foods, where each portion constitutes, for example: one large slice of bread, 30 g (1 oz) breakfast cereal, or 115 g (4 oz), or two egg-size, potatoes. They should take at least two portions of protein foods per day, such as three tablespoons of cooked pulses, 120 g (4 oz) cooked fish, or 90 g (3 oz) lean meat. Milk products should include one pint (600 ml) of milk per day. (Alternatively, 1/3 pint [200 ml] of milk is equivalent to 1/4 pint [150 ml] yoghurt or 1 oz [30 g] hard cheese. Some dietitians allow equivalents of calcium-fortified soya milk for people who cannot tolerate cow's milk.) They should take at least three teaspoons of butter, margarine or oil daily, and at least two helpings of vegetables and three of fruit. (See Appendix 3 for sample handout for clients.)

Binge eaters will express horror at the thought of eating what seems to them a vast amount of food. However, if they have been keeping a daily food record, it can be pointed out that in terms of calories eaten, one day of keeping to this kind of regime will probably add up to fewer calories overall than a day of meal restriction combined with binge eating. Anorexics too will baulk at the thought of eating what appear to be such large amounts of food. They will assume, for example, that eating such amounts will lead to immediate large gains in weight and many will be unable to contemplate taking in anything like this amount of food.

The body's need for good nutrition

So many dieters and people with eating disorders have lost sight of the reasons for which our bodies need food that it can be useful to remind clients of the function of food for our bodies. Our bodies are living organisms and cannot thrive without food. All foods are made up of a combination of proteins, carbohydrates, fats, vitamins and minerals in varying quantities. Proteins, in the form of long chains of amino acids, are essential for the growth and repair of cells, and energy. Carbohydrates are broken down in the intestine into sugars which are used for energy. However, this does not mean that they are all 'bad'. Refined carbohydrates have been processed in some way from raw material. They include white and brown sugars, maple syrup and glucose, and are contained in manufactured foods such as biscuits and cakes. They are absorbed quickly in the blood stream and so provide energy more quickly than do unrefined sugars. Unrefined carbohydrates are found in a variety of foods such as wholewheat flour and bread, brown rice, potatoes and wholegrain cereals. These foods contain valuable vitamins and minerals and also contain dietary fibre which is vital for digestion and the working of the bowel. Fats are essential too as they consist of chains of fatty acids, including the fat-soluble vitamins A and D. Fats are essential for the proper structure and functioning of the brain. Unsaturated fats contained in fish, nuts, seeds and vegetable oils, are considered to be more healthy than the saturated fats; and one subdivision of these, the omega-3 fatty acid (alpha linoleic acid) and omega 6 (linoleic acid) are particularly important as they cannot be made by the body. They are believed to be important to heart health and are likely to be important for good emotional and mental health as they help to maintain the structure and functioning of brain cell membranes, nerve fibres and neurotransmitters. A deficit in omega-3 essential fats has recently been implicated in studies into the effect of nutrition on behavioural and learning difficulties in children. This underlines the importance of good nutrition for brain function and mental health in all of us.

Essential minerals

In addition to providing energy, foods provide minerals and vitamins essential for the maintenance of a healthy body. For example, our bones need calcium. We accumulate bone mass up until the age of 30, after which it declines. For many anorexics, who are in their teens or early 20s, the risk of osteoporosis in later life is high. Calcium is contained in many foods, but in order to obtain between 800 and 1000 mg of calcium per day, we need to take the equivalent of about a pint of milk. Uptake of calcium is said to be lower in women who are deprived of oestrogen (a consequence of amenorrhoea). Women with amenorrhoea can recover bone loss after short time periods of up to six months, but prolonged amenorrhoea of more than two or three years may lead to irreversible bone loss and osteoporosis in later life. Phosphorus, another mineral obtained from milk and milk products, bread and cereals, meat and fish, is essential for bone development and energy release from foods. Potassium, important for the health of nerves and muscles and vital for heart health, is obtained from grains, meats, dairy foods, fruits and vegetables. Other minerals contained in food are important for a variety of functions such as resistance to infection, the maintenance of healthy skin, hair, red blood cells, muscle and nerve conduction.

Essential vitamins

A range of vitamins is needed for normal metabolism and plays a protective role in immunity from disease and infection. Deficiency of vitamins, especially the B vitamins and vitamin C, can cause anaemia, mouth ulcers, sore gums and poor dentition. The B vitamins and folic acid are essential for the maintenance of the nervous system.

Knowledge about energy balance and weight regulation

Just as they have difficulty with the content of their diet, many clients also have great difficulty with the idea that they must plan to eat regular meals. One woman, Clare, claimed that she simply could not eat a meal, as then she was bound to get fat. When asked how this could possibly happen, she replied:

> I couldn't possibly eat a whole meal – I'd be like a balloon. My stomach gets bloated, I feel full up, I gain two or three pounds. And after that, I certainly couldn't eat breakfast the next day. I would have to make sure I didn't eat again for a day or two to make up for it.

I explained that in order to begin to overcome her eating disorder she would have to learn to eat regular meals and to cope with the feelings of fullness, as gradually she would learn that this was only temporary. For some considerable time, she was unable to hear my explanations, so overwhelming was her panic.

> I could probably eat one meal, on one evening. But no way could I continue to eat meals the next day and the day after. I'd put on two pounds at a time, and by the end of the week I'd be at least half a stone heavier than I am now.

At this point, it can be extremely useful to offer some explanation of how body weight is lost, gained and maintained, and of what happens to people with eating disorders when they binge, starve or attempt to purge themselves.

Our bodies are composed of a mixture of fat, a fat-free mass or lean tissue, and a glycogen store. All these constituents of our body are made up partly of water – in fact about 60 per cent of our body is water.

The fat or adipose tissue consists mainly of fat and a little water. The lean tissue is made up of protein, minerals and about 73 per cent water. Glycogen is a temporary energy store held mainly in the liver and muscle by a large amount of water.

When we stop eating, our stomach empties, the glycogen stores get used up and the water normally bound to the glycogen is lost. This explains the very large losses people sometimes have when they first go on a diet. Weight loss slows down after a few days, and real fat loss takes time. If you lose between one or two pounds or up to one kilogram in weight per week, then what you lose will consist mainly of fat; but if you lose weight faster, you are likely to be losing valuable lean tissue as well. This matters because metabolic rate depends mainly on lean tissue; the more lean tissue you lose, the lower your metabolic rate goes, and the less you need to eat. So, a weight loss of up to one kilogram (or between half a pound and two pounds) per week is best; if you lose weight faster, the more difficult it will be for you to keep the weight down.

Many people with eating disorders have deprived their bodies to the stage where they need very few calories to maintain their weight, and find that they are sustaining a higher average body weight than they did previously, while eating far less than ever they did before. Paradoxically, they may indeed need to find a way to eat more rather than less in order to arrive at a way to lose weight and maintain that loss permanently.

Thus, starvation is a particularly unhelpful way to lose weight. It results in a dramatic decrease in metabolic rate, and it therefore becomes quickly impossible to keep your weight down on anything but the tiniest intake. What is more, people who starve themselves soon have psychological difficulties such as loss of concentration and feeling irritable, and are prone to bouts of uncontrolled overeating when they stop their diet. Clients can at this point be given a handout outlining the results of the studies by Keys and colleagues in 1950 and drawing an analogy between experimental starvation and the symptoms experienced by anorexics and other eating-disordered clients (see Appendix 4).

Problems arise for the person with an eating disorder when, having restricted her food intake for some considerable time, she suddenly consumes a large amount of food. The stomach fills up, and the glycogen store is replaced, retaining with it the water which binds it. The person may feel immediately bloated and fatter, and believes that she has gained several pounds in weight, after perhaps only one or two days of eating or even only one large meal. Hence the belief 'I can gain two pounds in a night'. In fact, in order to gain one pound in weight, an additional 3500 calories is required over what is needed to keep weight stable. This is equivalent to the calorific value of ten Mars Bars or about 85 apples. Most people will agree, on hearing these figures, that they cannot possibly have gained more than one pound in fat in so short a time, however much they may have consumed.

Nevertheless, weight regain may be rapid, especially if the intake comprises mainly foods high in fats and sugars. Additional weight which is regained initially comprises a higher percentage of metabolically inactive fat than did the tissue originally lost, and only converts to lean tissue at a later stage. It has also been suggested, although not proven conclusively, that so-called 'yo-yo' dieting leads to a reduction in the metabolic rate of the remaining lean tissue, thus compromising further the person's ability to lose weight or maintain weight loss (see also Chapter 2, pp. 31–2). Hence the person who has lost and regained weight very fast may have an altered body composition, with the result that she may be more prone to putting on weight than previously or find it increasingly more difficult to lose weight in the first place.

Information about the specific effects of bingeing and purging

As a preliminary to advising eating-disordered clients to give up bingeing and purging, the counsellor needs to provide information about the damaging effects of these behaviours. Clients with eating disorders often have a variety of complaints, many of which may be a direct result either of their eating behaviour or of attempts to counter overeating such as vomiting or taking laxatives.

Bingeing

One negative effect of bingeing on high sugar foods is that they produce a sharp rise in blood sugar levels. The rise is followed by a low, some hours later, in both energy and mood when blood sugar drops again. In order to compensate for the resulting drop, we may then look for further foods which we know will satisfy a craving. Often, this leads to the consumption of more high sugar foods, with a consequent further swing in blood sugar level. It is useful for clients to have information about the 'glycaemic index' which is a ranking of carbohydrate/ starchy foods based on their immediate effect on blood sugar levels. Foods which have a lower glycaemic index have a lesser effect on blood sugar levels. Examples are: cereals such as porridge and muesli, wholegrain bread, potato and rice, pulses, low fat dairy products, fruit and vegetables. Examples of foods with a high glycaemic index are: cornflakes, sugar coated cereals, sweet biscuits, honey and French bread. One way to avoid the binge cycle is to maintain satiety levels with the help of low glycaemic index foods and regular meals and snacks throughout the day.

Another way to avoid binges is to take craving seriously as a sign that the body has a need for something and attempt to respond to them in a more appropriate way. The view that substances such as sugar and chocolate are addictive is controversial, but one suggestion is that some foods may increase levels of the pleasure-giving endorphins in the brain and that increasingly large amounts of these foods may be required to satisfy the same need. Certainly, many people note an immediate improvement if they are able to give up substances containing caffeine, including coffee, tea and chocolate. By the same token, many people find that improvements in the quality of the food they take lead to improvements in concentration and mood. (See also Geary (2001) for an interesting discussion of this aspect of nutrition.)

Vomiting and taking laxatives

The negative effects of purging may include tiredness, muscle weakness, feeling faint or dizzy, abdominal pains, sore throats, diarrhoea or constipation. Many bulimics in particular experience swelling of the salivary glands, possibly due either to bingeing or to vomiting, which enhances their feeling of being fat. Clients who vomit frequently and have done so for several years are likely to have dental problems, in particular erosion of tooth enamel of the upper teeth. The teeth may have increased sensitivity to temperature and be more prone to development of tooth decay. Clients are likely to suffer from dehydration as a result of vomiting or taking laxatives; this may partly explain feelings of dizziness, weakness and being light-headed. As a rebound effect, when they do allow themselves to eat and drink, they may experience fluid retention, which itself adds to the feelings of being fat and the belief that purging is necessary as a means of combating overeating.

Purging behaviour can lead to electrolyte imbalances caused by loss of essential minerals such as potassium, sodium, calcium, magnesium and chloride. These are reversed when purging stops, but can result in minor symptoms such as muscle weakness, and, at worst and rarely, can have serious medical consequences such as cardiac arrhythmias, even cardiac arrest or renal failure. In rare cases, bingeing itself can lead to acute gastric dilatation, even rupture; vomiting can cause tearing or rupture of the oesophagus.

Vomiting

Neither vomiting nor laxative abuse is an effective way of reversing the effects of binge eating. Vomiting may begin as a means of weight control, but can take on a life of its own. While a large proportion of calories taken in a binge may be ejected through vomiting, some are still absorbed, and the sufferer can still continue to gain weight. In fact, the knowledge that she has vomited can give the sufferer a false sense of security about having 'got rid of' a binge and hence lead to further eating. Feeling safe in the belief that she has apparently given herself a fresh start, the sufferer is free to begin overeating again, and binge eating is therefore to some extent justified and becomes more permissible. Also, some sufferers find it difficult to vomit unless they have consumed a large amount of food, so that they find themselves eating extra amounts of food in order to vomit. 'I shouldn't have eaten that so I might as well go the whole way as I am going to get rid of it anyway.' Hence, binges may become larger, with the result that the sufferer gains more weight and feels increasingly out of control and dependent on vomiting as her only means of controlling the binge eating.

Laxatives

Laxatives are equally ineffective as a means of weight control. They primarily affect the large intestine, whereas most nutrients are absorbed in the small intestine. In one study planned to investigate the effect of laxatives, Bo-Linn and his colleagues (1983) found that laxatives given to two normal and two bulimic women caused six litres of diarrhoea in a 24-hour period but reduced calorie absorption by only about 200 calories over the 1500 to 2000 taken in. The authors concluded that by the time the food and digestive juices have traversed the stomach and small intestine and reached the colon, almost all the ingested foods that will be absorbed have been absorbed already, and any apparent weight loss is through dehydration. Clients may experience an immediate sense of weight loss, but the reflex fluid and therefore weight gain leads to further laxative abuse. Unfortunately, tolerance to the laxatives develops and some clients may rapidly escalate from a normal dose of one or two tablets daily to 50 or 60 per day. As a consequence of laxative abuse, clients may have forgotten what it feels like to have a normal urge to have a bowel movement without the intense urgency produced by laxatives. At the same time, regular use of laxatives can lead to reduced bowel function. For many people, the problems of laxative abuse are compounded by resistance to drinking fluids for fear of causing water retention. Restricting fluid intake merely ensures that the stool is too dehydrated which itself contributes to constipation. Hence clients need to be encouraged to drink adequate amounts of fluid at the same time as giving up laxatives. (See Colton, Woodside and Kaplan (1999) for a detailed description of laxative withdrawal.)

It can be useful to give clients a handout summarising the foregoing paragraphs and the negative effects of bingeing and purging as described in Appendix 5. Appendix 7 outlines some ideas about how to give up vomiting.

Information about the effects of food and eating on metabolism

There are many similarities in the ways in which both anorexics and obese or normal-weight binge eaters need to re-establish a normal weight and a normal pattern of eating. These similarities have largely to do with changes in attitude, overall quality of foods eaten, ability to keep honest records, and ability to abandon the tendency to have lists of idiosyncratic rules about eating and not eating, the breaking of which may lead to immediate relapse into eating-disordered behaviour.

However, there are also very large differences, and these have to do with the quantities of food that need to be eaten by individuals to achieve and maintain a weight within normal limits.

Obese and normal-weight bulimics alike need to be advised about the possible metabolic effects of both dieting or starving and refeeding, and about possible ways of countering these effects in order to avoid continued weight gain. One means of maintaining weight loss, for example, or of countering the effects of rebound eating after a diet, is to take regular exercise, which is said to protect against reduction in resting metabolic rate. Certainly, in many studies in which obese people have been followed up after losing weight by means of dieting, taking exercise is a factor which correlates with continued weight loss or maintenance of weight loss after the end of the diet.

Exercise may be useful for more than the purely physical effects. In one study where exercise was offered as a treatment for binge eating disorder, women who increased their weekly exercise frequency were abstinent from bingeing at the end of treatment whereas those who did not increase the amount of exercise they took were still binge eating (Levine, Marcus and Moulton 1996). This may, of course, be merely an effect of compliance with treatment instructions, but at worst exercise may represent a useful activity, incompatible with eating.

What kind of diet?

There is a recent body of research that has investigated the question of the effect of the macronutrient content of food on satiety (see Latner and Wilson 2004 for a review). This work is relevant to people with eating disorders as it has implications for the kind of advice they need about how and what they need to eat.

We know that people who binge eat often derive a higher than normal percentage of their intake from fats and carbohydrates and a lower percentage from protein, especially on binge days. One line of investigation has suggested that foods high in fat have a lower satiety value than do foods high in carbohydrates, and the current practice is to encourage people to use carbohydrates as a major part of the diet. The evidence for the relative satiety value of carbohydrate versus high fat foods is as yet inconclusive (Rolls et al. 1994). However, while lean and obese men and women may consume similar numbers of calories overall, obese people appear to maintain their weight by means of a diet that is higher proportionally in fats and added sugars than that of lean people (Miller et al. 1994). Therefore, it may be helpful to suggest to both normal-weight and obese bulimics that while they may not need to diet indefinitely, they would be advised to keep to a diet as far as possible that is low in fat and sugar and high in fibre. Increasing the fibre content of the diet can be achieved simply by eating more raw vegetables, fresh fruits and wholegrain bread and cereal foods.

The idea of a diet low in fat and sugar and relatively high in fibre may be particularly important for some normal-weight bulimics who have become accustomed to taking a diet that is overall very low in calories and whose weight nevertheless appears to increase very rapidly with any attempt to eat normally. The digestion of food itself has an energy cost and it has been suggested that this is reduced in symptomatic bulimia nervosa clients, and that the magnitude of this 'thermic effect of food' also depends on the content of the food itself. Protein produces a response approximately three times greater than that seen following the consumption of carbohydrates, and fat consumption produces no thermic effect at all (Black, Davis and Kennedy 1993). In fact, the tendency of normal-weight bulimics to gain weight apparently easily normalises with treatment, and while bulimics often gain some weight, the gain stabilises as they achieve a normal eating pattern. In practice, there are indeed some eating-disordered people whose overall consumption of food has become very low. A binge for these people may consist of a mere couple of biscuits, or an occasional meal or handful of peanuts, small episodes of eating in a day where little else is consumed. Nevertheless, the so-called 'binge' may have been followed consistently by purging. Normalisation of such a diet may appear to involve a great increase in calories, and indeed the sufferer paradoxically appears to have to eat more in order to learn to achieve and maintain a normal weight and diet. In such cases, it is particularly important for the sufferer to have a consultation with a dietitian who can advise on a low-fat, high-fibre diet, in other words providing bulk without high calorific value, which can be modified gradually to include increasing amounts of carbohydrate, protein and fat. The sufferer may have to be warned of a possible initial weight gain, but with a subsequent plateau effect or even a loss, as her body becomes accustomed to taking a normal diet on a regular basis, without bingeing and purging.

In addition to the advantage held by carbohydrate over fats, several researchers have found that high protein meals produce stronger subsequent feelings of fullness than low protein meals and have a stronger effect on suppressing subsequent intake than high-carbohydrate meals. Latner and Wilson (2004) showed that supplementing the diets of binge eaters with protein reduced binge episodes over a two week period. On the basis of this and other findings with regard to the macronutient content of foods, they suggest that there is a case for ensuring that the diet of an eating disorder sufferer contains some protein at each meal as a possible protection against binge eating.

These considerations point to the need for clients to develop an awareness that the effects of what they eat, both physical and psychological, may play a role in the development and maintenance of an eating disorder; no less important perhaps, than the historical and emotional events which appear to drive their behaviour.

Eating regularly

Another factor for sufferers to bear in mind is the issue of eating at regular intervals throughout the day. Dieters and binge eaters, both obese and normal-weight, commonly eat little early in the day. Many begin their day by eating nothing at all, whence they may eat increasingly large amounts as they become more hungry and lose more of their dieting resolve later in the day. This behaviour could well have the effect of lowering metabolic rate: throughout most of the day, the body has to adapt to a lack of food and therefore available energy and may have to operate at a lower level of consumption. Then, when the energy is needed least, in the evening, there is a large intake of which the body has no immediate need, as it is about to go to sleep for the night.

It is necessary to advise clients that in order to avoid hunger and therefore excessive craving for snacks which could lead to a binge, they need to eat on a regular basis. A regime including three meals and two light snacks in between is usually recommended. 'I never eat breakfast' is a common remark of people with an eating disorder. Sometimes, the reason given has to do with practical issues such as time. More often it has something to do with clients' fear of losing control. If they can start off the day without eating at all, they may be able to continue that way. In practice, clients who do this often describe themselves as getting extremely hungry later in the day. Subsequent snacks and meals become increasingly higher in calories until the client might embark on a full-blown binge. However, in a review of the role of breakfast in the treatment of obesity, it has been suggested that in general people who eat breakfast regularly have more adequate micro-nutrient intakes, a lower percentage of calories from fat, and a higher intake of fibre, in particular in people who take prepared cereals (Schlundt et al. 1992). In a study by the same authors, dieters who took breakfast lost slightly more weight over a six-month period than did non-breakfast eaters, and were also less likely than non-breakfast eaters to take unplanned snacks later in the day and more likely to take snacks containing a lower amount of calories and fats.

Resistance to eating regularly is extremely common, and can be dealt with by the suggestion that the client try out her new regime for just one week, with weighing at the beginning and at the end of the week. She should keep a continuous record of what she eats and drinks during this time, so that the effects of eating in a different way can be carefully monitored. If there is a very great deal of resistance by binge eaters to eating regularly, it can be emphasised that when the client was binge eating, there were times when the total calorific value consumed during a binge day or over a period of say three days of alternate bingeing and starving would have been greater even than the calorific value of the food eaten during a period of eating regularly. Sometimes a client will refuse to attempt a regime which includes as many as three meals and two snacks. It can be helpful in this case to suggest a graded approach, where meals are at first very small, comprising only one course, and items such as fruit which might have been taken as a dessert perhaps can be taken as snacks in between meals.

Establishing a normal eating pattern with obese binge eaters: to diet or not?

For normal-weight bulimics, the primary goal is normalisation of eating and avoidance of binge eating. Obese binge eaters have weight loss as their main goal, with giving up binge eating an important but perhaps secondary goal. Nevertheless, it is just as important with this group to establish regular eating and reduce binge eating before weight loss can be achieved. Giving up dieting may seem contrary to the goals of obese clients, but it may be a necessary precondition for avoidance of binge eating and continued weight gain. Therefore the nutritional goals of treatment of obese binge eaters are similar to those of normal-weight bulimics. Normal-weight bulimics are more likely to have a larger range of forbidden foods and therefore a more restricted diet, and to use a wider range of strategies for dealing with the effects of binge eating. Obese binge eaters, however, are less likely to diet stringently in response to overeating; they are more likely to overeat in response to a binge or to succumb to the temptation of a forbidden food item when dieting. An important strategy, then, is to suggest, as with normal-weight bulimics, that the obese client learn to give up dieting and to increase the range of 'forbidden' foods allowed without perceiving these as inherently 'bad' or as a trigger for further overeating. In practice, this means that the overweight binge eater is encouraged not to eat larger amounts of forbidden foods than previously, but to conceive of it being normal to take these foods in moderation and hence to learn to control binges by reducing the range of foods seen as forbidden. For example, Rachel believed that chocolate was her downfall, and was unable to diet as she would eat large amounts of chocolate daily, hiding it from her family and escaping the house surreptitiously in order to maintain her supplies. She believed that she was 'addicted' to chocolate because once she started eating it she needed to finish her entire supply. In fact, however, her eating was driven less by desire or enjoyment, which decreased after the first taste, than by guilt about eating it and the need to remove the evidence. Once she was able to allow herself to conceive of eating chocolate as a normal thing to do, even for someone who is overweight, she was able to modify her furtive behaviour and allow herself to eat chocolate, still on a frequent basis, but in moderation. Once this goal had been achieved, it was an easy step for her to reduce her consumption of chocolate altogether, and as a consequence gain a degree of control over her eating in general and hence begin to lose some weight.

Behavioural self-control strategies may be as important a part of treatment as cognitive behavioural ones. In fact, Marcia Marcus (1995) has suggested that while both cognitive behavioural and behavioural treatments reduce binge eating in obese binge eaters, only behavioural treatment *per se* results in weight loss.

Establishing weight regain with anorexics

Anorexics have a lower resting metabolic rate than do other eating disorder clients. However, this does not result in a lower requirement for calorific intake.

Research by Kaye and his colleagues (1986) in the United States into the mechanics of weight gain in anorexics has suggested that while people of normal weight need on average an extra 7000 calories in order to gain one kilogram, anorexics may need on average 8301 calories extra, with a range of 4000 to 12 000 calories. The more activity the anorexic takes, the slower the gain. These findings are now supported by several research studies in which the resting energy expenditure (REE) of anorexics has been measured. (REE is the rate at which people burn energy while at rest.) REE has been found to be significantly lower in anorexic patients than in control subjects. During refeeding, however, REE increases disproportionately to weight gain and increases in lean tissue and cannot be explained by increased body mass alone (see also De Zwaan, Aslam and Mitchell 2002). In other words, the good news for anorexics is that while energy expenditure is very low when they are in a starved state, it quickly increases when they begin to eat more, and in many patients large amounts of extra calories are needed to achieve even small weight gains.

In the weight restoration programme of Kaye and colleagues (1986), they start anorexics on a daily diet of 30 calories per kilogram of current weight, which they have found is the average number of calories needed by normal-weight people for maintenance; but this is increased by 10 calories per kilogram per day every three to seven days, to more than 50 calories per kilogram per day, at which point weight gain starts to occur. They subsequently step their anorexics up to a maximum calorie intake of 80 to 100 cal/kg (4000–4500 calories per day), with the restricting anorexics needing and being offered about 15 per cent more calories than the bulimic anorexics, whose requirements appear to be lower both during and after weight recovery. It is extremely helpful to convey these figures to anorexic clients, as they are usually horrified by the apparently excessive diets they are offered. In fact, they often do not gain weight, or may do so only very slowly, on diets of as much as 3000 calories, and may be justifiably angry when told that they are 'just not trying hard enough'. They need to know that, perhaps contrary to what they have believed, their requirement for food is in fact greater at this point in time than that of people of normal weight, and that while they may find it helpful to use others as a model of how to eat normally, they actually need to eat more than these other people and need not feel guilty for wanting to do so.

Anorexics may, however, need considerable reassurance on two counts. The first of these is that as they continue to eat increasing amounts of food, they may feel bloated and uncomfortable, and consequently fat, a scenario which of course they fear the most! A bloated stomach is a common symptom of anorexia nervosa, and as the client gains weight in the initial stages of refeeding, this may appear to her to be accumulating mainly in her stomach. One reason for the bloating is that up to 15 kg of water may be accumulated in the early stages of refeeding (Treasure 1997), and it can take up to three months for normal fluid balance to be restored. Fluid may also collect around the eyes and ankles. Another reason for the bloating is that, on the one hand, the stomach is having to stretch and readapt to the unaccustomed food and, on the other, the gut of the anorexic is said to empty more slowly than normal. However, the anorexic client should be reassured that the discomfort will begin to subside after two weeks of normal eating and that weight will gradually redistribute itself around her body as she approaches a normal weight.

Another concern is that once the client has begun to eat normally, she will be unable to stop eating and will lose control and become fat. This concern may be fired by increasing hunger as she begins to allow herself to consume increasing quantities of food. Anorexic clients may become more hungry as their intake increases, leading to the fear that they will simply be unable to stop eating and will continue to overeat and get fat. In fact, as their weight approaches normal, this urge to eat will subside. In addition, it can be helpful to ask anorexic clients whether or not they have overweight parents. Having one overweight parent may increase the chances of the client being overweight at some point in life, and having two overweight parents increases the chances still further of being overweight. However, if there is no history of overweight in the family, there is no reason to believe that the client will get fat once she has given up her starvation behaviour.

Throughout this process of refeeding and weight gain, the low-weight anorexic is likely to be an inpatient and will be monitored for medical complications by both medical and dietetic staff. It will be important for each professional to provide ongoing reassurance and advice.

Meal planning

At the beginning of a programme, it is helpful for clients to be encouraged to plan meals in advance. If this is not done, even clients with the best of intentions may panic as a meal or snack time approaches and attempt to pare down the amount eaten or avoid eating at all. 'I did mean to try what you suggested,' said one client, 'but when it came to it, the amounts we talked about seemed far too much, and I just didn't get round to it.' Not only did she not 'get round to it', but as someone who lives alone, she had avoided buying most of the necessary ingredients for her meals lest she ate them all at once. In this case, it was necessary for the counsellor to discuss with the client in the sessions both the composition of the shopping list and what she was going to prepare for herself.

For some clients, both anorexic and bulimic, the daily diet has become so restricted that it is impossible for them to contemplate eating three meals and two snacks in a day. In this case, the therapist will need to outline with the client a sample day's eating, and develop some first steps on the way to building up towards eating the full amount. Hence, an initial programme may involve eating only a few items spread over the day, as a first step in eating regularly and increasing the food repertoire. Compliance with these first-step suggestions can be regarded as a sign of willingness to comply with continuing treatment, and the aim would be as quickly as possible to achieve a fuller and more varied daily intake.

Not only is it necessary to plan the content of the meal itself, but it is also useful to discuss the setting – such as the time of day, the situation in terms of who might be with the client, who might do the cooking, even who might serve the food out, and how far the client will allow herself to be 'served' by another person, or how far it might be appropriate for the client to prepare food for herself as opposed to eating food cooked by a close relative or friend. Garner and Bemis (1986) have suggested that meal planning should in the first instance be a mechanical process, that the anorexic or bulimic client be encouraged to eat a pre-set amount as a means of achieving a normal eating pattern, rather than attempting to rely prematurely on internal signals. The reasoning behind this is that the client does not have to make the choice between maintaining a 'diet' and eating previously forbidden foods and is not confronted continuously with choices about how much food she should be eating. Many clients find it helpful to have the responsibility of meal planning removed from them and some continue for months, even years, with only small modifications to their plan, made with the help of a dietitian or health professional.

It can be useful for a short while to use a dual recording system whereby clients record not only what they have eaten, but also, on a similar record sheet, what exactly they plan to buy, store and eat over the next couple of days. If the counsellor can go through this exercise with the client on at least one or two occasions, it may be possible to enhance the client's confidence in selecting an appropriate diet. It should also be possible to increase awareness of what the client's list of forbidden foods might include, with the aim of working towards helping the client to reduce this list by including some of them in a daily eating plan. Work at follow-up sessions can include a comparison of the two records, and if there are large discrepancies between what was planned and what was actually consumed, these discrepancies may become the subject for discussion, whereby the client's ideas and possible irrational thoughts about why the particular foods might have been avoided can be noted and alternative ideas about these foods elicited. Some clients may need to produce a 'hierarchy' of forbidden foods, listed in ascending order of difficulty of consumption. The therapist can then work with the client to introduce foods of increasing difficulty into the diet. Additional food eaten, and indeed specific 'forbidden' foods, can be redefined as 'treatment', even as 'prescribed medication', thus helping clients to assimilate the idea that eating a wide variety of foods is essential as a means to achieve a normal weight and eating pattern and to escape from the vicious circle in which they have found themselves.

The next chapter outlines ways in which clients can be helped to use the information given in this chapter by means of behavioural techniques, and thereby learn both to tailor the information to their own needs and acquire self-control over their eating habits.

6 Behavioural Techniques

Many counsellors are wary of using behavioural techniques, for fear of appearing to take a mechanistic approach to human problems. However, these techniques are an important aspect of successful cognitive behavioural therapy. For the most part, it is useful to regard these techniques as skills which can be taught to clients in order to help them to control their own behaviour and embark on the task of becoming their own counsellors. Problems have a way of evolving, and it is essential when clients reach the end of a treatment programme that they have the tools to solve any related problems that may arise in the future.

The separation of behavioural from cognitive techniques is, of course, entirely a false one as behaviour is often influenced by cognitions. For example, Garner and Bemis (1986) note that the food avoidance of the anorexic not only results from a fear of food, but is positively preferred by the sufferer because it helps her 'in the difficult task of oral self-restraint, despite voracious hunger'. In practice, cognitive techniques will need to be used alongside behavioural ones, and the two cannot really be separated. However, for the sake of simplicity, they are dealt with here in a separate chapter.

Self-monitoring

Self-monitoring of behaviour has already been dealt with in Chapter 4. It is just as important during the course of therapy as it is at the beginning, both for providing information about the nature of the problems and for monitoring changes in the way the person thinks and feels about them.

For the purposes of cognitive behavioural therapy, it is best if records take the form of headed columns, rather than passages of prose, unless there is a particular reason for the client to write a continuous passage. Headings can include time, place, food and drink taken, and something like 'what happened just before' or 'context' as a means of helping clients to establish the relationship between antecedents and consequences of their behaviour. Alternatively, clients may choose to use a column entitled for example: 'Did I achieve my target for today?' or 'Did I eat more/less than I had planned to today?' This way, on days when the work of the therapy goes well, they need write little down, and on days when things go less well, they can use additional columns to relate relevant factors which they can discuss in detail with the counsellor in order to assess the changes they need to make. Once the client is attempting to keep to a regular series of targets, it can be a good idea to add in an extra column asking the question 'Did I reward myself for achieving my target(s) today?' in order to help people to bear in mind the need for consistent use of self-reward.

As noted in Chapter 4, some clients master the skill of keeping a very full food intake record, but find it more difficult when it comes to detailing thoughts and feelings experienced around the time of eating or purging. In some instances, the request for information about thoughts and feelings is granted merely by the addition of a list of adjectives written alongside the food items, such as 'upset', 'angry', 'guilty'. At this point it may be necessary to coach clients to recognise the difference between thoughts and feelings. One way to do this is to present the client with a list on paper of thoughts and feelings and ask them to identify which is which. For example, 'I am anxious' (feeling); 'I am fed up' (feeling) 'I am a failure' (thought). Cooper, Todd and Wells have created a worksheet for this purpose (Cooper, Todd and Wells 2000: 233). Sometimes the client brings back a record where it is not clear what the thoughts were. This could include 'telegraphic' statements such as 'oh no, not again'. It is necessary to search for the meaning of these statements. For example is it 'I'm always bingeing?', 'I've let myself down', 'Bad things always happen to me'? The client may need help to express both the emotion – what they were feeling in each situation – and the thoughts.

Thoughts expressed as questions also need further investigation as they may mask automatic negative thoughts. For example, the meaning of 'Will I be able to manage?' may be 'I'll never be able to cope with this' and it is important to ascertain exactly what is meant by this. If the client is avoiding expression of the negative thoughts, she is not in a position to counter or work on them. Similarly, 'Why am I like this? could mean 'There is something wrong with me' ('I must be going mad'), 'I'm different from other people' or 'I shouldn't be like this'. Another difficulty that arises with the recording of negative thoughts is the tendency to distance the thought: 'I was thinking about' effectively distances the thought. It can be helpful to suggest that the client create a sentence in a speech bubble.

Sometimes it is necessary to explain to clients the need to listen to their self-talk in order to become more aware both of the things they say to themselves at times of stress and of feelings which may relate to eating behaviour. If clients have difficulty in focusing on or remembering their thinking, it can be useful to ask them to think back to particular episodes of binge eating.

For example: Faith had binged the day previously and in the 'thoughts and feelings' column of her record had written 'fed-up', but could not, when asked, expand this description. The counsellor asked her to think back to the time in question and describe exactly what had happened:

Faith:	It was suppertime and mum had called everyone to the kitchen. My brothers and sister were rowing about whose turn it was to wash up and dad got really angry with them. I wanted everyone to calm down so I said I'd do it, and then I felt angry with myself that I had got everyone to make peace at my expense again and would have to waste my time washing up when I had other things to do and it wasn't my turn anyway.
Counsellor:	So can you describe the actual thoughts that went through your mind at the time?
Faith:	I was thinking 'Why is it always me who has to sort everyone out? Why am I so stupid that I have to get involved?'
Counsellor:	It makes it easier to answer a negative thought and defuse the situation for yourself if you can phrase the thoughts you have as a statement rather than a question. For example, 'It's always me who has to sort everyone out. I am stupid to get involved.' Does that accurately reflect how you were feeling? You can then examine how realistic the statement is, and go on to think of alternative things you might have said to yourself.

Once clients are able to describe problematic situations in this kind of detail, the ground is prepared for the teaching of problem-solving techniques or, if relevant, for monitoring and dealing with negative automatic thoughts, which will be dealt with in more detail in the next chapter.

Target setting

In the initial stages of cognitive behavioural therapy for eating disorders there are certain targets which need to be set by the counsellor. For example, eating regular meals is necessary for restricting and bingeing anorexics, bulimics and obese binge eaters alike.

Eating on a regular basis reduces the need to binge and also encourages clients to return to or develop a more normal pattern of eating behaviour. In addition to eating regularly, clients often need to widen the range of foods eaten and reduce the number of items 'forbidden' on their daily diets. The task of the counsellor in the initial stages of therapy is often to negotiate with clients about just how many changes they are prepared to make and at what pace.

Some clients will be only too well practised at target setting: for example, the obese person who is habitually setting herself new and increasingly ambitious targets for weight loss, none of which she achieves; or the anorexic whose success at losing weight spurs her on to new and increasingly dangerous low targets. Both kinds of target have their origin in dysfunctional attitudes to weight and an attempt to bolster self-esteem through controlling weight. In these cases, some time will need to be spent in negotiating with the client completely different kinds of target. For the anorexic client, these will be based on helping clients to accept increasing weight gain, whereas for bulimics they will be based on helping clients to attribute less importance to the subject of weight and at the same time reducing the frequency of bingeing and compensatory behaviours.

It is useful to differentiate between short-term and long-term goals, be they behavioural or weight-related. For example, in the case of an anorexic client, it must be made clear that the ultimate goal is to eat regular meals which are adequate to maintain a normal weight. It may, however, be necessary to increase intake gradually, with the addition once a week, for example, of one item of previously 'forbidden' foods. Incidentally, some experts have found that rewarding anorexics for weight gain is more effective in helping them to achieve a normal weight than is rewarding them for changing their eating habits. It makes sense then to keep the focus of therapy on weight change as much as on behavioural change.

Liz had been bulimic for five years. She binged regularly and had no consistent meal pattern. Breakfast was a meal she simply could not contemplate. She could not envisage eating three meals a day, and in fact was in the habit of deciding only on a daily basis when she would allow herself to eat that day. However, she was persuaded by the idea of a regular meal plan and was able to agree an initial plan of four snacks per day, two of them at mealtimes. Targets were kept as manageable as possible. During the first week, Liz simply had to plan what snacks she would take the following day and was considered to have achieved her target on the days that she wrote down what she planned to eat the next day, even if she did not manage subsequently to stick to her plan. During the following week, the target was to eat at least two of the planned snacks every day, and so on. Gradually she was persuaded to enlarge the size of these snacks as she discovered that her desire to binge eat lessened, and within one month was eating three reasonably sized meals and two snacks per day. In this way, Liz was set up to succeed, rather than failing as she had done on nearly every previous occasion that she had attempted to change her eating habits.

Self-reward

Closely linked to the skill of setting and achieving targets is the skill of rewarding oneself. This is a skill that many people with eating disorders lack. Binge eaters often reward themselves with food, but this has its disadvantages. It raises the profile or importance of food in the person's life.

It is essential for the person with an eating disorder to learn that food is everyone's right, whether fat or thin, and it should not have to be earned. Madeleine was an anorexic who was doing her A' levels at sixth-form college. She regularly deprived herself of food in the evenings and sometimes at lunchtime, telling herself that when she had finished her work she could allow herself the time to eat. This also meant that she often had an excuse not to eat if she had not achieved some ambitious target with regard to the amount of work she had set herself to complete. It is therefore important to help clients to establish an alternative system of reward. It can be explained to clients that rewards need to be idiosyncratically planned. They should be agreed upon in advance of attempts to use them as part of treatment and can be used either in place of food rewards or in response to progress made in relation to eating more (anorexics), eating less or more appropriately (binge eating disorder and bulimia).

Rewards can be financial, for example the client rewards herself with coins collected in a jar, and saved up towards some desired item. Alternatively, she can buy herself some small item as a reward for appropriate behaviour. Rewards can also be to allow oneself an enjoyable activity, such as watching a favourite TV programme, reading a magazine, or soaking in the bath. Such activities can be useful too as alternative activities to over-exercising, overeating or purging. It should be stressed that rewards must be as immediate as possible in order to be effective, and should also, if they are activities, be as 'special' as possible in terms of being less available at other times, at least for the duration of the treatment.

Clients should be encouraged at the same time to learn to use self-reinforcing statements. For example, an anorexic could reward herself for eating with appropriate statements such as: 'Well, I managed to eat that whole meal. It was pretty difficult and I did really well to finish it.' Or a bulimic person: 'I ate a lot this evening, but I managed not to vomit. Every time I avoid purging, I am closer to overcoming my eating problems.' Or, 'I binged today, but I managed to eat the meals I had planned for myself and that's better than starving myself as I used to.' Few clients automatically produce these kinds of statements for themselves, and so it is worthwhile spending some time in discussing possible responses to various situations which clients can use when the occasion arises, and rehearsing them in the therapy session. While this may feel 'false' both to the client and to the counsellor, it does reinforce the idea that clients can eventually become their own therapists. Also, building the use of positive self-statements into treatment can help clients increase their confidence and enhance self-esteem.

Scheduling pleasant events

Slightly different from the idea of self-reward is the idea that clients broaden their repertoire of enjoyable or rewarding activities 'beyond the pleasures of weight loss and control' (Garner and Bemis 1982). In this way, they are preparing the ground for giving up anorexic or bulimic behaviour and strengthening themselves against future setbacks so that their problem behaviour is no longer the only conceivable way out. Clients may need help with listing possible activities, perhaps by describing those hobbies or activities they preferred before they developed an eating disorder or in which they would like to be involved in the future.

Behavioural techniques for controlling overeating (self-control)

Many of the techniques used to help people gain control over eating come from the obesity field. They come under the title of 'self-control', but this is not to be confused with the idea of stopping oneself from carrying out a particular behaviour merely by force of will or 'will-power'. Self-control techniques include 'stimulus control' techniques, these are based on the idea of sufferers controlling their environment so as to make it less likely that they will succumb to eating at inappropriate times or eating too much. Hence, eating can be restricted to certain times of day or places, or kept separate from certain other activities. Alternatively, clients can be encouraged to replace eating with other, incompatible behaviours such as swimming or pottery making. The behaviour of eating itself can be modified so that clients can practise eating more slowly, for example. Clients can be given a simple handout, along the lines of Appendix 6, which lists possible ways to acquire this control. The counsellor should review clients' food records in order to ascertain which of these techniques is likely to be the most useful at each stage of therapy.

There may be several strategies that are suggested on the basis of this list. The possible strategies should be listed in order of difficulty, with those that will present least problems at the top of the list. Clients can then attempt to work their way through the list, usually tackling only one or, at most, two tasks at a time. They should keep daily records of their success or otherwise with these tasks and in every session they should discuss progress with the counsellor. It is important to bear in mind that it is essential to have time for reflection and discussion with the counsellor, perhaps even after each attempt at record keeping.

The practice of vomiting after food can be tackled in a similar way. Clients can be encouraged to keep a record of situations where vomiting occurs and ascertain the behavioural 'chain' or pattern connecting the events surrounding vomiting. The aim is gradually to break the chain by means of either altering the pattern of triggers, or rearranging the situation so that the opportunity to vomit is less available. Simple techniques such as delaying or temporarily distracting oneself can be helpful in breaking the pattern. (See Appendix 7 for an example of information to give to clients about how to do this.)

Some clients are resistant to using behavioural self-control techniques or find them unhelpful as a means of resisting cravings for food or urges to binge or vomit. In this case, it can be useful to suggest that the client attempts something along the lines of learning to 'go with the feelings'.

Taking exercise

Taking exercise, either too much or too little, is a relevant aspect of eating disorder which should be exposed to scrutiny, as much as either overeating or under-eating. Many bulimics and obese binge eaters are inactive, and they should be advised to take regular exercise, as suggested by current health education initia-tives, in order both to encourage and to maintain weight loss. Exercise need not be particularly strenuous. Manoeuvres such as getting off the bus one stop earlier on the way to work, taking the stairs instead of the lift, making the effort to walk short distances rather than driving, or parking the car further away from one's destination, or building brief exercise slots (for swimming or sport) into one's life are all acceptable targets. People with binge eating disorder can be informed that maintenance of increased exercise is one of the main predictors of the ability to keep weight down in people who have dieted.

In anorexia nervosa, however, the question of exercise is more problematic. Some inpatient programmes deny their patients the possibility of taking exercise, or allow it contingent only on weight gain. This system is of course impossible to operate on an outpatient basis, but the counsellor should bear the issue in mind when assessing ongoing weight changes.

Practising 'normal' eating

Many eating disorder sufferers have become so accustomed to thinking about food and eating from an 'eating-disordered' perspective that they have forgotten what it is to eat in a normal, unrestrained fashion. Both anorexics and bulimics should be considering what it is to behave in a non-dieting fashion, and can be encouraged to practise mimicking the behaviour of people who are unconcerned about diet and eating. This temporarily relieves clients of the perpetual decision-making involved in maintaining dieting behaviour, with its exclusion of certain items of food or constituents of diet, and worry about whether they are keeping to the rules of their diets. One anorexic client, Anne, was able to make an inroad into giving up her rigid rules when she agreed to take a dieting 'holiday'. She took a brief holiday away from home and went to stay with friends in a different town. For a week she behaved as though she was not anorexic. She was able to pretend to herself that she was a person who eats what she likes, and she ate everything put in front of her. On arriving back home, the old stresses prevailed and she slipped back into rigid dieting; but she was able to recall her period of normal eating and, encouraged by the knowledge that it was possible, still managed to practise eating normally from time to time. Gradually, eating in a less rigid way became a part of her life; at the same time she was able to focus more clearly on the meaning in her life of the anorexic rules she had imposed on herself.

Eating normally in public is also something that the person with an eating disorder needs to learn. This gives practice both in avoiding forbidden foods and in the skill of eating without embarrassment about what others must be thinking about the size of that person's body.

Exposure

Exposure involves literally exposing the client to feared or avoided situations, usually in a gradual way. In the case of most people with eating disorders, this involves clients allowing themselves to be in the presence of, and to eat, an increasing variety of previously avoided or 'forbidden' foods. For the anorexic, this means enlarging the repertoire of foods allowed in the diet so as to approach a normal weight. For the binge eater, it means widening the repertoire of foods that can be taken without the client believing that her restraint has been broken and lapsing into bingeing behaviour.

Karen had been anorexic for two years and refused to go out with her school friends in the evenings because she did not want to have to sit and watch them while they ate. Janine, who was bulimic, could never visit her family at weekends around mealtimes because she could not trust herself to eat Sunday lunch without bingeing afterwards. Exposure to a greater variety of food was one of the targets of treatment for both women. In the case of Karen, this involved agreeing on a series of targets of eating a wider variety of foods and practice in eating in public. The latter task in itself required some coaching through the use of cognitive behavioural techniques as Karen's fear of eating in public stemmed from the belief that people would be watching her and thinking that she was too fat, and that she ate too much. In the case of Janine, there were other issues that needed to be tackled simultaneously, such as her poor relationship with her parents and the difficulties she experienced when they tried to force food on her. Her programme involved exposing herself to greater varieties of food when alone in her flat, so that she could repeat the experience of eating them without necessarily bingeing when she went out. She also had to learn to be assertive about what exactly she wanted and did not want to eat when in the company of her immediate family. Having learned to make a clearer choice of what she wanted to eat when she saw her family at the weekend, she then had to practise following up her visits to family with evenings where she ate a little without bingeing.

Modifying negative attitudes to weight and shape

Exposure to feared situations also involves, for people at all weights, confronting situations which they would previously have avoided. This includes weight- and shape-related situations. For example, it includes learning to cope with situations where one's appearance and shape can be exposed to public scrutiny, such as going swimming or to the beach and wearing a swimming costume. It includes learning to think about weighing or not weighing with equanimity. Some women may be weighing themselves excessively, and a part of their programme could be to reduce the number of times they weigh themselves (a form of reassurance seeking which is unhelpful). Others avoid the scales to an almost phobic degree, and may need to be encouraged to be weighed or to weigh themselves at regular intervals in order to learn that minor weight fluctuations do not represent real weight gain or loss over time. It also includes being prepared to try on clothes in shops and buying clothes at the person's current size in order to make the best of the shape she is in the present. Many people with eating disorder typically buy clothes one or two sizes too small in the vain hope that they will be able to grow into them – 'when I get thinner'. Clients should be encouraged to buy and enjoy clothes at their current size as one more way to improve their attitudes to their weight and shape and hence build up confidence in their body as it is now rather than as it might be in some future time.

A more specific task for helping clients to improve body image is a desensitisation task. The desensitisation technique is described in very clear detail for clients in *The Body Image Workbook* (Cash 1997), and clients with marked body-image problems can be encouraged to refer to this book alongside their therapy sessions. Desensitisation is a process whereby a client is gradually exposed, in a stepwise fashion, to a series of feared situations while in a relaxed state (see below for instructions about relaxation for clients). The theory behind this is that the relaxation and fear responses, because they are opposites, cannot both be active at the same time. If a person who is relaxed is presented with a stimulus she habitually fears, she will learn to attach less fear to it. There is some debate in the psychology literature as to the necessity of relaxation as an accompaniment to exposure, but in terms of acceptability, relaxation does play a role in making treatment with exposure more acceptable to clients.

With regard to body image, the client is asked to make a list of her body parts, including at least one with which she is reasonably satisfied, and organise them in order with the most liked at the bottom of the list and the least liked at the top. She is then asked to use the relaxation techniques she has learned to become as relaxed as possible before viewing herself in the mirror. She starts with the part of her body with which she feels most comfortable (the bottom of the hierarchy). In as relaxed a state as possible, she looks at this part in the mirror for a short time. She can either move on to looking at the body part for increasing lengths of time or to looking at the next part on the list. Each period of exposure is followed by a few minutes of relaxation, and each session ends with relaxation. Each subsequent session begins with the last item from the previous session with which the client felt comfortable. As the treatment progresses, the client should be able to confront her body parts with increasing ease. 'Mirror confrontation' can produce significant improvements in body image (see also Key et al. 2002). Counsellors should, however, exercise extreme care when introducing these ideas to clients. There are some clients for whom even talk of body-image problems engenders very great anxiety, and Adrienne Key and her colleagues advise extreme caution with people who have a strong reaction to this kind of work and in particular with people who have been sexually abused. While this work is behavioural, it is by no means a simple task to be taken lightly. It requires a good therapeutic relationship and a degree of trust between client and counsellor, as the issues involved are almost always deeply personal.

Assertiveness around food

The area of learning to be assertive around food and about one's personal needs for food is a crucial one in relation to eating disorder. There is often a great deal of confusion in the minds both of people who are restricting themselves and of those who are overeating about exactly what they are 'allowed' to eat. In both cases, they may have spent many years following (often hidden) self-prescribed rules about which foods are acceptable and which are not. In addition, because of the general 'diet' culture pervading society, many people with an eating disorder feel that they are not entitled to certain foods. Some obese women, for example, will not admit to preferring a high-fat dessert for fear of criticism. Hence, many people with bulimia or binge eating disorder are unable to follow their natural preference for certain foods when in public, feeling as they do that they are entitled to choose only the salad and fruit dishes as opposed to the cream sauce and the puddings. The outcome of this is that they make the 'correct' choices in public and binge in secret, a pattern which cannot be broken unless they can learn to allow themselves a truly unfettered choice whatever the social situation.

A similar problem can occur for anorexics too. Mary was a university student who was extremely motivated to overcome her anorexia. During one session we were discussing her difficulty with eating in front of her college friends:

Mary: Sometimes what I'd really like is a tuna mayonnaise sandwich. But I can't possibly have one when everyone is watching me so I always have the salad one or just an apple.
Counsellor: Why is that?
Mary: Because they know I'm anorexic.
Counsellor: Can you explain that a bit more?
Mary: It means they know I've made myself thin by dieting and that I'm very good at it. If they see me eating the tuna sandwich they'll think I've stopped being anorexic and I don't have a problem any more.
Counsellor: And how is that a problem to you?
Mary: Then they'll think they can keep offering me fattening food and I couldn't cope with that.

We agreed that one of the tasks Mary had to achieve in therapy was to learn to be more assertive about saying what she wanted in relation to food regardless of what others might think of her. This involved learning that she had the right to make choices for herself, independently of the opinions, real or imagined, of others. If clients are to benefit from therapy, it is important that they are able to make free choices both to eat and to not eat. Thus, for example, if a client with bulimia chooses either to eat 'fattening' foods or to restrict herself to a salad when she is with other people, she must feel that she has made a free choice and need not be answerable to or made to feel guilty by her companions. By the same token, there may be some situations where, if an anorexic client wishes to choose a salad rather than chips, she must feel that she has the right to do so. In many cases of eating disorder, the sufferer has felt driven by the need to escape the controlling influence of other people in her life and has lost track of how far her eating or not eating is representative of a struggle for independence. Therefore she needs to establish, perhaps for the first time, the notion that it is she alone who chooses and controls whether she eats or not, starves or binges.

I have used the suggestion to read a 'Bill of Rights' handout as a homework task. The list is adapted from a list of basic rights described by Ann Dickson in her book *A Woman in Your Own Right* (1982) (see Appendix 8). Clients should be asked to read the list and be prepared to talk about where they agree or disagree with the ideas expressed in the list. Many clients have felt somehow emancipated after reading this list and delight in the realisation that they no longer need to behave in the way apparently expected of dieters.

Relaxation and stress management

It is not known how far training in relaxation and stress management is useful in the treatment of eating disorder. However, it makes sense from the point of view of many clients to include some training in these ideas in the treatment programme. Many people who overeat will admit to doing so at times of stress and when feeling tense, although there is no evidence that eating is indeed relaxing; in fact it can often have the opposite effect of making the sufferer feel guilty and hence worse than before. One client with binge eating disorder was a busy deputy head teacher who was constantly called on to deal with a myriad of problems in her school and take the place of absentee teachers. She felt constantly under stress and kept supplies of snack food in her desk drawer to eat whenever she found herself alone. She was encouraged to learn relaxation techniques, and instead of eating was taught to use a card in her desk drawer as a cue to practising a quick relaxation technique whenever she opened the drawer.

Another client, Anne, with anorexia nervosa, experienced intense anxiety whenever she attempted to increase her food intake or eat something previously avoided. She was, however, keen to overcome her problems and willing to learn relaxation techniques as an aid to treatment. She found it helpful to spend a few minutes relaxing before a meal and was also able to use the techniques if she found herself in a difficult social situation where there was an expectation that she should eat as much as the other people at the table. My own preference is to use the progressive relaxation method of Jacobson (1974). I lend clients a tape, on one side of which is recorded the progressive relaxation instructions and on the other side are instructions for differential relaxation (relaxing one part of the body while another part is at work, for example working at a desk or walking). I also discuss with clients alternative methods of brief relaxation, including the use of a shortened relaxation schedule, concentrating on diaphragmatic breathing, or using a specific cue or cues such as a card or specific item to stimulate recall of the relaxed state.

The phrase 'stress management' covers most aspects of treatment, including becoming more assertive, dealing with problems, countering negative self-talk, and creating solutions to everyday problems such as managing time and setting priorities. Which of these specific aspects are covered will depend on what issues have arisen in the initial assessment and on clients' self-monitoring forms. Clients can be referred to books for further reading, which should complement the work they are doing within the sessions. For example, *The Relaxation and Stress Reduction*

Workbook (Davis, McKay and Robbins Eshelman 1995) provides detailed self-help instructions for a variety of stress management techniques.

Conclusion

This chapter has reviewed the practical aspects of cognitive behavioural counselling for eating disorder, in which the client is offered a combination of information and advice and moves towards learning techniques for self-control and for monitoring her own behaviour, thoughts and feelings.

As counsellor and client move through the practical aspects of record keeping, information giving, target setting and achievement, the client's beliefs, ideas and emotions with regard to her problems will become increasingly salient, if they have not been apparent previously. In the next chapter, the emphasis moves on to the use of cognitive techniques. In practice, the distinction between behavioural and cognitive techniques may feel somewhat uncomfortable. In most cases, the counsellor will already be using cognitive techniques and addressing thoughts, feelings and emotions and questioning clients further in these areas to inform the work of counselling, often without stating this formally to the client. However, the techniques are addressed in separate chapters here as a way of helping the counsellor to focus on them as specific skills.

7 Cognitive Techniques

Identifying negative thoughts

As clients begin to keep full records of problems related to eating and not eating, it should become feasible to help them to recognise negative patterns of thinking associated with their behaviour and to make a start with countering the negative thoughts.

In the treatment of depression and anxiety, helping people to recognise their negative thoughts often has the function of breaking the links between dysfunctional attitudes and negative feelings. While this is also the case in relation to the eating disorders, helping people to recognise negative automatic thoughts has the additional, more immediate, effect of helping to break the links between dysfunctional attitudes and behaviour.

For example, Ann was in the process of recovering from her anorexia and was struggling to increase the number of daily calories she was taking and push her weight closer to the expected weight for her height. Every time she added something extra into her diet she was overcome with fear and recognised a series of negative thoughts such as: 'I've eaten too much.' 'I've had too many calories.' 'I am too full.' 'I'll put on weight.' She recognised that these thoughts had the direct effect of stopping her from increasing her intake and were the motivation behind her tendency to skip meals. As she was already aware of the link between her thoughts and her behaviour, the aim of counselling at this point was to help her to question the validity of the thoughts and look for alternative, more helpful, ways of rephrasing them.

If clients are not already recording their thoughts together with the amount they are eating, as in the previous chapter, they can be taught to keep a record focusing on upsetting thoughts, identifying the cognitive distortions on which the thoughts are based, and listing possible alternative more rational (helpful) responses.

In the process of identifying negative thoughts, it is helpful to show clients how the thoughts fall into categories along the lines of Beck's original categorisation. Garner and Bemis (1982) have given some typical examples of thinking errors made by anorexics. Table 7.1 is adapted from their description, and this is supplemented in Table 7.2 with the addition of errors made by clients who binge eat or are overweight.

Negative thoughts of people with eating disorders may fall into any one of five general categories.

1 *Client evaluation of own progress*
   This includes negative thoughts about behaviour and its control, or lack of it. For example, it includes thoughts about having lapsed from good behaviour or having acted against good intentions. It also includes thinking errors such as labelling ('I'm such a pig', 'I'm a failure') or catastrophising ('I've eaten one chocolate, this is the end of the diet').

Table 7.1   Typical anorexic thinking errors

Faulty thinking	Example
Selective abstraction, or basing a conclusion on isolated details while ignoring contradictory evidence	The only way I can be in control is through eating I am so weak
Overgeneralisation or extracting a rule on the basis of one event and applying it to other dissimilar situations	I was unhappy when I was overweight so if I gain weight again I'll feel bad When I used to eat carbohydrates I was fat so I mustn't have them now or I'll be fat again
All-or-nothing reasoning	If I gain one pound in weight I'll carry on gaining and won't be able to stop I must never eat chocolate/butter/bread
Self-reference/personalisation	When I see someone who is overweight I worry that I will be like her I can't eat in public as I know that people are watching me and noticing what I eat They are thinking how fat/greedy I am
Superstitious thinking, or believing in a cause–effect relationship between unconnected events	If I eat a sweet it will be converted instantly into stomach fat I can't eat anything with fat in it as it goes to fat in the stomach I can't relax and enjoy myself because something bad always happens to me when I do

Source: Adapted from Garner and Bemis 1982: 137, with the kind permission of the authors and Plenum Publishing Corporation.

2   *Attitudes to food and eating*
   This has to do with attitudes, sometimes erroneous, towards food and eating. It includes thoughts about the mechanics of weight gain and loss ('If I eat that slice of bread I'll put on a pound'); the dichotomy between 'good' and 'bad' foods, food avoidance, skipping meals, or eating too little; eliminating dieting; fasting versus feasting; and fears of weight gain. It includes examples of all-or-nothing thinking ('If I eat one apple I'll gain weight and be fat') and magical thinking ('If I look at food I'll be fat').

3   *Attitudes around the importance of weight and shape*
   This category encompasses attitudes to weight and shape, in relation to self-worth, in other people, in society. It includes thoughts comparing the self to other people, for example a tendency to feel unattractive in comparison to people in magazines, people met socially or in impersonal public situations such as on the beach or at the swimming pool. It also includes thoughts attributing negative events or interpersonal difficulties to one's size or appearance (Thomas Cash (1997) calls this the 'Blame Game').

4   *'Feeling fat' as metaphor*
   This category of negative thoughts is more elusive. The client may describe feeling fat on some days and not others, where there is no obvious trigger. On further questioning

Table 7.2   Typical dieter/overeater thinking errors

Faulty thinking	Example
Shoulds	I should be able to keep to my diet
	I have to be in control
	I must never eat pasta
Discounting the positive	So what if I lost a pound this week, I should have lost six by now
Catastrophising	If someone comments on my size, I will die
Do-nothingism	There's nothing I can do
Selective abstraction	I've failed at my diet, so I'm a complete failure
Overgeneralisation	If I eat a meal, I'll totally lost control
	If I lapse from my diet, I'm a total failure
All-or-nothing thinking	I've totally ruined my diet with that cake. I might as well carry on eating
	I must never eat chocolate
Labelling	Why am I such a pig?
	I'm a failure
Wishful thinking	If only I could lose 30 pounds by the summer
Fortune telling (predicting the future)	I'll never be any thinner I'll never be able to control my eating

it may be possible to ascertain that the feeling is linked to behavioural or environ-mental triggers and that it leads to bingeing or starving as a mechanism for coping. For example, Adrienne had suffered a great deal of emotional abuse as a child. Her response was to want to make herself as invisible as possible. Whenever under stress she literally felt fat and had the thought 'Everything will be okay if I can get/stay thin'.

5   *Thoughts about the self and relationships*
Other thoughts may be linked to interpersonal difficulties not directly related to weight or eating, and are comparable to the kinds of thought experienced by clients who are depressed or have low self-esteem. For example, clients may have thoughts about acceptability ('No one will like me') or about worth ('I am useless').

Many of these thoughts may also be underlying assumptions or core beliefs. However, for the purposes of beginning therapy, it is reasonable to treat them as thoughts, if that is how they are presented; and it may be appropriate to work with them at a deeper level at a later stage.

Answering negative thoughts

The traditional way to question negative automatic thoughts (NATs) is by means of Socratic questioning. This involves asking questions in such a way that the client is able to work out answers for herself based on information she already has. It encourages clients to work out for themselves a different way of looking at their situation. First, the counsellor will need to ask the client questions about specifics: what? when? where? how did you feel? what did you do? and so on. The next stage is to ask a series of questions along the following lines:

- Can you think of any evidence for/against the idea (thought)? i.e. how far is it true?
- What is the advantage/disadvantage of thinking in this way? i.e. how helpful is it to think like this?
- Is there an alternative way to look at the situation?
- What would be the advantages/disadvantages of looking at things in this different way?
- How might someone else in your situation view this?
- How might you have looked at it before you became ill/had the current problems?

The counsellor cannot assume that the client is mistaken in the way she views her situation. The process of modifying negative automatic thoughts involves a combination of collaboration between counsellor and client and Socratic questioning (as illustrated here) to guide the client towards new ways to see the situation. Other questions are:

- What if ... happened?
- What does/would this mean to you?
- What would other people think about you if this were true?

The counsellor will need to tailor the questions used to each individual case, and on some occasions it may be necessary to take a more didactic approach and to supply information to help counter the thoughts. For example, immediately after a meal Mandy would say to herself: 'I'll put on weight.' Her counsellor countered this negative thought with the following factual information:

Eating one large meal does not lead a person to gain weight. You put on weight over time, when the number of calories you take in exceeds the energy you use up.

However, putting on weight was one of the primary aims of Mandy's therapy, so it was necessary to engage her in an attempt to see putting on weight as a positive, rather than a negative, outcome of therapy.

Counsellor: We agreed at the beginning of the therapy that the purpose of our sessions was to help you to gain 5 kilograms in weight as an initial target. Can you say what it is about the thought that is so upsetting? What does the thought mean to you?

Mandy: It means I'll get fat.

At this point it was possible for the counsellor to pursue some of the above questions, aimed at answering NATs, which led Mandy to explore her problem in more detail and come to a slightly different conclusion.

Counsellor: How likely is it that you will get fat after one meal?

Mandy: Not really likely. But if I carry on eating more than I need, and so much more than I was doing before, then I am bound to put on weight eventually.

Counsellor:	Yes, you will put on some weight. Does that mean you'll get fat?
Mandy:	Logically, I suppose not. Come to think of it, it is the word 'weight' that's the problem.
Counsellor:	I can see that. You have spent a long time, along with other women, avoiding something called 'weight gain'. Can you think of some other way of phrasing it to yourself that might be more helpful to you?
Mandy:	Well, I know that other people won't regard me as fat. I am so used to being super-thin that any ounce of flesh on my body will make me feel fat. I guess I will have to try and live with the idea until I can get used to it.
Counsellor:	So, can you think of another more helpful thought to replace the negative thought?
Mandy:	Well, next time I find myself saying 'I'll put on weight' I could try to remember that putting on some weight does not have to mean getting fat – not immediately, anyway! It could just mean getting more healthy. And this is what I am working towards.

Erica was a bulimic, at the beginning of her treatment. She was battling with the suggestion that she eat three meals and two snacks per day, and had recognised that she regularly had the thought 'I have to starve' prior to her binges. The following passage illustrates the use of Socratic questioning to investigate this thought and help Erica to look for alternatives. Note how the counsellor also uses the example to illustrate for Erica the cognitive view of the link between dieting and bingeing.

Erica:	I can't eat three meals a day. I'll gain weight. I need to lose weight first. I just want to starve for three weeks. Then I'll be the weight I want to be and I can start again.
Counsellor:	What happened last time you tried that?
Erica:	I ate something I hadn't planned for and then I binged. That's always the problem. Either I'm bingeing or I'm starving. But I couldn't eat three meals and all those snacks. I'd just think I was bingeing and I wouldn't be able to stop eating. … Eating any of the normal snack things, such as a bag of crisps, would make me feel so guilty. If I ate one packet I wouldn't be able to stop.
Counsellor:	OK. What if you were allowed a packet of crisps every day? What if you didn't have to feel guilty about eating crisps but knew that they were a permitted part of your diet?
Erica:	That might make a difference. Whenever I've been on a diet in the past I've said to myself 'I'll eat today, because tomorrow I'm going on a diet.' Then I just eat everything I can get hold of. Packets of crisps, loads of chocolate, biscuits, sandwiches. My boyfriend can't understand it. 'If you are going on a diet tomorrow, why can't you just eat normally until then? Instead of that, you eat even more than usual, as if you are never going to eat again!' It's crazy, I know, but that's exactly how I feel.
Counsellor:	So the very thought of going on a diet, or having the intention to diet, results in your eating even more than usual, even overeating or bingeing?
Erica:	Yes, I suppose it does.
Counsellor:	If you didn't have to diet but could eat whatever you wanted whenever you felt like it, would the same thing happen?
Erica:	No, I suppose it wouldn't. I might eat less.

Counsellor:	It seems to me from what you have said that the more you have starved yourself or even thought about starving or dieting, the more you have actually eaten at times.
Erica:	Yes, that's true. And then I've had to go back on the diet again. But it never lasts. I might eat just one thing I'm not supposed to have and then I lose control.
Counsellor:	So all in all, you have been on and off diets for many years.
Erica:	Yes, and I've got to do something about it because I'm fatter now than ever.
Counsellor:	What do you mean by that?
Erica:	Well, when I think about it, I was only about 10 stone when I started. Actually I wasn't fat at all. But now I'm about 14 stone. I'm fatter now than when I started dieting!
Counsellor:	To summarise then: you go for low-fat, low-calorie options; you avoid many foods; and you are often on a diet or trying to starve yourself to lose weight. Your diet gets broken if you eat something you feel is not allowed on your diet, and once this has happened you go to the other extreme: you eat vast amounts of food, high-fat, high-carbohydrate food in particular. The more you tell yourself you'll go back on the diet, the more you eat in preparation for the time when you will have to stop eating. Even if you try to follow a sensible diet plan, the thought 'I have to starve' leads you back into the vicious circle of bingeing and dieting. You have no in-between way of eating. You never allow yourself what other people would consider a normal spread of meals through the day.
Erica:	That's right. And even when I do eat a bit extra, even if it's only a little, I tell myself it's alright, I can get rid of it. But then in order to vomit, I have to eat even more, and sometimes I literally force myself to eat a large amount of food so that I can be sure I'll vomit.

In order to give up her constant thoughts about the need to starve, Erica needed to replace them with a more rational alternative idea about the connection between regular eating and her rehabilitation. Merely thinking this would be inadequate, and she had to develop alternative self-talk to replace the admonition to starve herself. At the same time, she had to try out the behavioural experiment of eating regularly in order to convince herself that the suggestion made sense in order to break the binge–purge cycle.

Patricia had a specific body image problem. She believed that her hips and thighs were especially large. She was not worried about the size of the rest of her body but dieted and binged in response to the need to reduce her thighs.

Patricia:	People notice them. I have to hide them. I couldn't possibly wear shorts as everyone can see how fat they are.
Counsellor:	First, let's clarify exactly what the negative thoughts are here. Am I right in thinking that there are two ideas causing a problem? One is something like 'I have fat thighs.' The other is 'Everyone notices my fat thighs.'
Patricia:	Yes.

The counsellor needs to be aware of the possible beliefs underlying the client's thoughts for discussion at a later stage. In this case, the first idea (I have fat thighs) was likely to be connected to the client's overvaluation of the importance of being thin and to her poor body image and overestimation of her size. Therefore it was less likely to be amenable to change than was the second idea, on which the counsellor therefore focuses.

Counsellor: Let us look at the thought that people are looking at your fat thighs. Can you think of any particular evidence that people are thinking you are fat?

Patricia: People have commented on my bottom in the past, so I know they notice. Once a boy in the pub said something about me fitting on the bench.

Counsellor: Perhaps people have commented in the past. Do you think that the comments of one boy in the pub are likely to represent those of people in general?

Patricia: They might do.

Counsellor: Who was this boy? Was he someone whose opinion you'd respect? Would you want his good opinion?

Patricia: Not especially. But other people must be thinking it too. Even a girlfriend once said something – we were thinking of swapping some clothes for a party and she said 'You'll never get into my jeans.'

Patricia's thoughts had a powerful effect on her behaviour. The task of the counsellor was to help her to answer her negative thoughts and hence to decrease their power over her behaviour. However, attacking negative thoughts directly, as can be seen from this example, does not always bring the magical switch in thinking that the counsellor might be looking for. In this case, the counsellor was in danger of being drawn into a no-win situation about the number of people who may or may not have noticed whether the client had fat thighs.

At this point, it is often helpful, rather than looking for evidence for the belief, to develop an understanding with the client of what the thought means to her.

Counsellor: It seems there are at least two issues here. One is the question of whether you do indeed have an objectively fatter behind than other women. Another is that of what it means to you if you do and the effect that has on your behaviour.

Patricia: I can't feel relaxed when I chat to boys – they must be thinking 'Who does she think she is, with a behind like that?' Even if anyone asks me out, I always say 'no'. If someone touched me there I'd die of embarrassment. They'd find out how fat I am, so it's better not to go.

Counsellor: The first question is one that we cannot really answer. You will always find people who are thinner or fatter than you in a variety of ways and so looking for evidence is not helpful to you. The second is a question that we will need to address at a later stage in therapy. However, given that there may indeed be women with slimmer behinds than you, it is important to ask yourself how helpful it is to you to measure yourself and other people in this way. What are the advantages to you of thinking in this way? What are the disadvantages? Realistically, is there anything you can do to change the situation? How would someone else in your situation view this? What alternatives do you have?

One possible difficulty that counsellors may encounter with regard to helping people to reassess negative thinking is the tendency to get stuck in a position where the client has learned to produce many negative thoughts but is unable to move on to looking at her situation in a different way. This is sometimes quite noticeable in people who come to therapy having received previous treatment with a cognitive behavioural approach, where, for a variety of reasons, treatment ended before the person was able to feel an improvement in her symptoms. When asked about the previous treatment she reports: 'Oh, it was all about my negative thoughts and I was supposed to try to think more positively … but it didn't help me feel any better.' One reason for this is that it is often easier to elicit negative thoughts than to find ways to help clients to create change. It can be helpful to address one aspect of a problem initially in order to consolidate some small change, rather than asking clients to keep extensive records on the totality of their experience with eating disorder on a regular basis.

Another useful approach to change is to use language with a positive construc-tive focus. For example, the counsellor could ask Patricia 'How would you like it to be?' or 'how would you like to be?' and 'can you imagine a way to think about this which would help you feel better?' This involves the use of constructive lan-guage to elicit positive thinking and 'foster optimism' (Padesky 2002). The focus then becomes less 'problem'-oriented, and the client is often able to engage with the therapist in a more creative, experimental enterprise.

Patricia was not able immediately to cast off her concerns about the shape of her body, but she was able to develop an alternative view to repeat to herself when-ever she found herself reciting the old pattern of thoughts.

> I may have a fatter behind than … but I am thinner in other places and can wear clothes that my friends can't get into. I may hate having a large behind but not everyone else sees it in the same way. In any case, I'm not likely to be able to change it, so I have to live with it. I have to try to make the best of my other features so that I can forget about it and get on with my life.

In practice, the process of reaching this point can be quite drawn out, depend-ing on how quickly the idea of monitoring negative thoughts and attempting to answer them makes sense to the client. In this particular case, several conversa-tions over four sessions have been collapsed into one. In real life, there was much repetition and backtracking before Patricia was finally able to reach the conclusion described here.

Homework

In addition to the discussion in the sessions, clients can be asked to fill out a negative-thought record on a daily basis in order to practise countering negative automatic thoughts. The term 'negative thought' is often substituted with the phrase 'hot thought' or 'upsetting thought'. The record could have columns for date or time; situation (what, where, with whom); automatic thought; emotion(s); alternative, more rational (adaptive) response; and outcome (i.e. How do you feel now?/What can you do now?). Some cognitive behavioural therapists ask clients to specify their percentage belief in the thought (i.e. between 0 and 100 per cent) both in the 'automatic thought' column and in the 'outcome' column, as a meas-ure of improvement in mood. The theory is that a client's belief in the thought will be measurably reduced after practice at modifying thoughts, using the records.

(See also Aaron Beck et al. 1976 and Judith Beck 1995: 125–135 for further descriptions of dysfunctional thought records. I have also found it helpful to suggest that clients read Melanie Fennell's handout on 'How to Deal with Negative Thoughts' between sessions [Fennell 1989: 218–34].)

Identifying and dealing with dysfunctional assumptions and core beliefs

Sometimes the process of identifying and modifying negative automatic thoughts can itself lead to identifying either core beliefs or dysfunctional attitudes or assumptions. Core beliefs are deep, usually longstanding, beliefs, established in childhood, about the self. In the case of an eating or other psychological disorder, these are usually negative, and may be related to competence, such as 'I am inadequate', or to do with self-worth, for example, 'I am unlovable', 'I am worthless'. Connecting these beliefs to the person's behaviour are often a series of dysfunctional attitudes or assumptions (see Table 7.3). For example, 'If I am fat, no one can love me.' 'If I do not shine at every thing I do, people will know how worthless I am.' 'If I am seen as weak and ill, no one will know how inadequate I am.' These ideas can themselves produce expectations about the self, or rules, which help to maintain disorder. For example: 'I must always be seen to be dieting.' 'I have to do everything to perfection.' 'I need to remain weak and ill so that nothing can be expected of me. I cannot compete, and therefore I cannot fail.'

These beliefs and assumptions are not immediately apparent. They may never surface at all. In contrast, for some clients the process of defining them may occur very naturally. Thus, the answer to the question 'What does the thought mean to you?' can itself lead directly to a core belief which the person holds about herself. For example, Angela, a bulimic, had the negative automatic thoughts: 'I'm a failure'; 'I'll never keep to my diet'. When asked about the meaning of these thoughts, one of her replies was 'I'm inadequate'. She expressed the attitude that if only she could keep to her diet she could continue to keep her friends and be successful; and that people would not like her if they knew what she was really like. It was necessary for the counsellor to work with her on the core belief that she was inadequate, among others, together with the ideas she had about how she might protect herself from her believed inadequacy by her attempts to be thin.

Sally had just broken up with her boyfriend, who was always critical of her figure. He had told her that she 'could do with losing a bit of weight'. Sally already had low self-esteem and had developed the assumptions from an early age that people could only love her if she did what they wanted, and the way

Table 7.3   Negative assumptions of people with eating disorder

I've got to be thin to be loved
Unless I do something perfectly, there's no point in doing it at all
I can't respect/love myself unless I look good (i.e. thin)
The way a person looks is the most important thing in his or her life
No one could like/love me if they knew what I was really like

someone looks is the most important thing about them. Not surprisingly, the break-up with her boyfriend led to the activation of her negative assumptions, and she began dieting as a way to feel better about herself.

Another way to identify dysfunctional assumptions and core beliefs is to use the 'downward arrow technique' (see also Burns 1980: 270). The counsellor (or the client herself) repeatedly asks the question 'What would/does that mean to you/to me?' or 'What does that/would that mean about you?' 'What is the worst it could mean/say about you?' or 'What do you think other people would think about you?'

For example, Mandy was battling with the idea of giving up her anorexia nervosa, and every time she tried to add a previously prohibited food to her diet, she found herself thinking: 'I don't need this. It's just pure greed.' The counsellor had explained the notion of core beliefs to Mandy and she had agreed that, as part of the attempt to remove blocks to giving up her anorexia nervosa, they would spend some time in exploring the nature of the assumptions or beliefs underlying her behaviour and symptoms.

Counsellor: What does it mean to you to be greedy?
Mandy: It's horrible.
Counsellor: What is horrible about it?
Mandy: It means I'm not a nice person.
Counsellor: What does that mean to you – 'not a nice person'?
Mandy: It means other people won't like you. They think you are worthless.

It transpired that Mandy had a sister, Clare, with whom there had always been conflict. Her sister had always been the golden girl of the family, in Mandy's eyes spoilt and pretty, while she herself was considered sensible and trustworthy. Clare had a tendency to plumpness, and had never been able to diet successfully. Dieting was the one thing Mandy saw herself as being able to compete with, and had become her sole source of self-esteem in what she believed was a continuing comparison between herself and her sister. In order not to be seen as 'worthless', and to prove her superiority over Clare, Mandy felt driven to continue her ascetic pursuit of thinness and self-control.

Modifying assumptions and core beliefs

Dysfunctional assumptions and core beliefs can be challenged in the same way as negative thoughts: asking for evidence, looking for alternative views, examining the advantages and disadvantages of holding a certain belief. Other questions might be:

- What is another way of looking at these facts? Is this true for other people too? Think of an example of a friend of yours. Do you apply the same rules? What would you say to a friend who had this experience? What would your best friend say if you told her about it? Why should you apply different standards to yourself? What are the advantages/disadvantages for you of holding this belief?

Using these techniques, Mandy was able very quickly to appreciate that there are in fact very few people who would actively dislike a woman who indulged herself; that a person's worth is not necessarily defined by his or her ability to follow a rigid self-imposed regime of dieting; and that she herself possibly had positive attributes other than perfect good looks.

Sally drove herself to be perfect not only in her ability to diet but also in her work. For the first time since being out of hospital, she had acquired a part-time job as an art teacher, and worked late in the night to prepare her lessons. 'If my work isn't up to scratch, they'll find me out', she believed. She had been brought up by a mother who revered academic learning above all things. Mother herself, however, had been unable to pursue her education because she was the oldest of six children and had to leave school to help look after her younger brothers and sisters because her own mother suffered badly with depression. Sally had chosen to take up art but had always felt guilty that she had been unable to fulfil her mother's more academic ambitions for her.

Counsellor: It is difficult for you to work so hard when you are also battling so with hunger.
Sally: Yes, it is. But I can't bring myself to eat more.
Counsellor: If you could eat more, how would that affect your work?
Sally: I could work much harder. And I wouldn't be so tired, so I'd get more done.
Counsellor: So if you fear that your work is not good enough, what is it that stops you from letting go a little more of the dieting?
Sally: I couldn't do that, because then I'd be so much stronger, and people would expect so much more of me. I suppose now I have an excuse. I'm weak and ill, and people feel sorry for me. But if I weighed more, I wouldn't have an excuse for not doing better.

In this example, Sally's belief that she was inadequate (to her job, academically, in the eyes of her mother, perhaps) was supported by her negative assumption that if she was weak and ill, less would be expected of her. Hence she did not have to deal with her feelings of inadequacy and the belief that she had let her mother down by not doing better academically.

This is one example of a situation where examining the history of an assumption or a belief can help clients to reinterpret their meaning, through understanding how they came to be. The client can be asked to recall herself from a very early age, and think about when she first came to hold the belief. Once the client is able to put unhelpful beliefs in context, she is more able to understand how the beliefs were established and reinterpret the past based on the information she holds as a grown adult rather than as a child.

An alternative to identifying beliefs in a 'deconstructive' way is to use 'constructive' language (Padesky 2001). The focus of this approach is a positive frame. 'Deconstructive' language uses problem-focused language: 'How is that a problem for you?' 'What are the disadvantages of thinking in this way?' Constructive language, however, focuses on the possibility of the positive. It uses questions like 'How would you like it to be?' 'How would you like to be?' 'What rules/beliefs would you want to use to reach your goal?'

The next stage in the counselling must then be for the client to experiment with creating new beliefs and using them to drive her behaviour. In Sally's case, the aim of further counselling sessions became to help her to modify her beliefs about her felt inadequacy and to ask for help when she needed it. She chose to work on the principle that if asked to do something by her mother or at work, she could say 'no' rather than continuing to use her illness as a mask to hide behind.

Another useful way to weaken the strength of negative core beliefs is to build new ones with the help of a 'continuum'. This is a technique described by Padesky (1994, 2001) which relies on graphic representation rather than the use of language alone. It involves eliciting from the client a belief which is either opposite to an existing negative core belief or, more usually, enough at a tangent to it to be acceptable to the client and believable.

For example, Adrienne had the belief that she had no worth as a person and did not deserve to do nice things for herself, such as buying herself a treat. This belief also had implications for her inability to feed herself appropriately. Adrienne agreed that she would like to be able to believe the idea 'I have some worth'. We drew a continuum for this belief. This involves drawing a line and marking the far right-hand end with the extreme of the belief, in this case 'I have some worth'. At the other end of the line was the opposite of the belief: 'I have no worth'. Adrienne marked the point along the line which she believed represented her degree of worth.

The next stage is to break down the components of the belief in order to find ways to begin to modify it. Adrienne was asked to list all the characteristics that a friend might have which would be evidence that the friend had worth. We then drew a continuum for each of the characteristics Adrienne had described (see Figure 7.1). Next, Adrienne was asked to rate some of her friends along these new continua. She also had to rate herself on them. In this way, the construct of worthwhileness was broken down into specific behavioural characteristics, and Adrienne could not help but rate herself more positively than she had done on the original continuum. Finally, Adrienne was asked to re-rate herself on the continuum 'I have some worth'. She was surprised to find that having done the work on breaking down the idea into its component parts, she now rated herself slightly more highly than previously and was able to see that she might be able to learn to see herself in a more positive light.

Figure 7.1   Changing negative core beliefs with a 'continuum': Adrienne

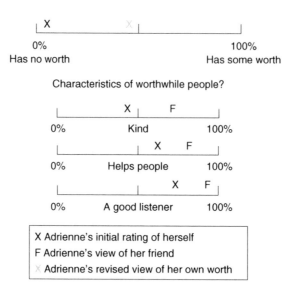

It should be stressed that this kind of work must not be embarked on lightly. It may not be feasible to consider schema or belief change methods where, for example, a client has had difficulty in engaging with initial work at the level of negative automatic thoughts, and in particular if she has had difficulty in generating alternative, more helpful ways of thinking. There should always be space towards the end of a session which looks at belief change, for 'debriefing': for assessing the impact of the session on the client, for getting feedback, both positive and negative, and for addressing any upsetting sequelae. The potential dangers are expressed in a comment by teachers of cognitive therapy from Newcastle University

> Working at the level of core beliefs can sometimes produce great emotional and cognitive shifts for the patient. ... In such circumstances, the patient's destabilised state may lead him/her to make dramatic life-changing decisions (i.e. to separate from a partner, to leave a job, to confront an abuser) and some of these decisions may be made prematurely. (James and Barton 2004)

Exploring the meaning of eating disorder symptoms

Both for bulimics, who are normal weight but fear weight gain, and for anorexics, who fear weight gain but need to be encouraged to gain weight as a goal of therapy, it is important to modify underlying assumptions about weight, shape and thinness as major defining attributes of self-worth. While anorexics need to be persuaded to cope with considerable weight gain, normal-weight bulimics can for the most part be reassured that weight gain during their treatment will be minimal: that as soon as they are eating in a regular fashion, their weight will stabilise within a range of about seven pounds.

Clients with binge eating disorder, however, need to appreciate that treatment will not necessarily help them to lose weight, at least in the first instance. One of the aims of therapy for them is to come to terms with their weight as it is in the present, rather than looking always towards some far-off point in the future when they might achieve a slim body.

The need to reduce the importance that the concepts of weight and shape hold for clients is the same in all cases. Clients can be asked if they would expect others to conform to their own standards of beauty and slimness before they could like or admire them. They can be asked to compile lists of their own achievements and non-physical attributes. They can be asked about other aspects of their lives that are important for them, and so on. They can be encouraged to read for themselves some of the feminist literature which points to the objectification and de-sexualisation of women through unrealistic expectations about shape, weight and beauty. (See Appendix 2 for a list of reading for clients.) They can be asked to identify other women, both normal and overweight, whom they see as attractive or interesting despite being large.

As the counselling proceeds, clients may reach a stage where, through their attempt to identify negative automatic thoughts, and through arriving at negative assumptions and core beliefs about themselves, they find themselves also exploring the personal meaning of their symptoms. Some clients will move directly to this stage before they are ready to make behavioural changes and without having learned to monitor or change negative automatic thoughts.

With regard to the binge itself, clients have described it as fulfilling a pressing need experienced at that time. They may be unaware of any relevant thoughts or even of concurrent moods. This need has been described variously as having to 'fill a big hole'; 'to give myself comfort'; or, as one woman put it: 'There's this need for something, and I have to fill it with food: a great yawning chasm that can't be filled.' It can be very useful to explore further with the client what the meaning of this can be, and this meaning is different for different clients. A range of questions can be asked at this point:

- What does this mean to you?
- Can you recall what you were doing when you began to eat/first noticed the urge to overeat/first had the craving? How were you feeling? What was going through your mind?

It is also useful to ask about previous, similar experiences:

- Can you remember other times when you have felt this way/this has happened?
- Do these times have anything in common?

The counselling does not have to be purely verbal at this stage. Some workers integrate the use of imagery into the cognitive behavioural programme. For example, the client can be asked to close her eyes and describe a previous binge episode as if it were happening in the present. She begins by describing the situation, her feelings, the surroundings. She then describes the events leading up to the binge and is asked at each stage to check on her thoughts and feelings.

One very common response to questioning about bingeing is as follows: 'Yes, it's always when I'm alone and there's no one to stop me. Then I lose control.' It is important in this case to investigate further – what does it mean to the person to be alone, does this have something to do with being, apart from the absence of controlling others? Is being alone merely a state which has negative connotations for the sufferer? Some have described bingeing as a defiant act, or as an act of despair. Consider the case of Carla. Carla came from a very close-knit, Italian family. Her father was a pastry chef and mother was always cooking. The family was extremely strict and maintained a tight control over their children's social lives, which were highly circumscribed. While food at home was always plentiful, mother feared that the children would become overweight and often laid down limits as to how much the children were allowed to eat. In defiance, Carla began to eat secretly in her room, and gradually became increasingly overweight.

In other cases, notably in some overweight people with binge eating disorder, the binge eating began prior to dieting, often as a means of deriving comfort. Philippa was the middle child of a single mother who herself had immense social and personal problems. Mother had little time for the children, working as she did full-time. Philippa recalled raiding the larder as a child, often at the end of an evening when mother had not got around to cooking. She would grab as many chocolates and crisps as she could find and demolish them in the privacy of her room, after which she would put herself to bed and cry. Overeating had become for her an escape mechanism whenever she was under stress and pressure or wanted to ignore issues needing her attention. Her understanding of the meaning of food and bingeing to her was derived from sessions in which she described recent negative emotions and was able to recall times in the past when she had felt a similar way. It then became possible to work on the negative assumption: 'If I eat I don't have to feel so powerless'.

The links between past or present events, feelings and behaviour and bingeing are often difficult to establish. Consider the example of Christina, who described the very first time she had a binge:

> I was on my first date, if you could call it that. I sat in the back row of the cinema with the boy who had asked me out. I was very nervous, and suddenly the boy and I were kissing. I had never been this close to someone of the opposite sex before and I was so worried about this – what did he think of me, how did I feel about it? – that I couldn't wait to get home. As soon as I got there I ran to the fridge and started to eat slice after slice of bread and butter. I ate the whole loaf.

It can be extremely difficult to explain the link between precipitating events and bingeing without recourse to interpretative guesswork, a practice with which most cognitive behavioural therapists feel distinctly uncomfortable. A common response to questioning runs something like: 'I don't know, it's this terrible urge, and it just takes over. My mind is dead, and I'm not thinking about anything.' This is where the temptation both for client and for the counsellor to avoid any further explanation and rely on purely practical behavioural techniques is very strong indeed.

The difficulty is that often, the bingeing, and also purging behaviours, appear to have a strong dissociative element. There is no apparent connection between the bingeing itself and the behaviour or events immediately prior to it. Attention is removed from the immediate environment, and the sufferer is temporarily less able to process incoming information while she focuses her attention on a binge. It has been suggested that this refocusing allows a reduction in negative affect or a general reduction in self-awareness (Heatherton and Baumeister 1991). Dissociative experiences may also relate to a high incidence of a history of traumatic experiences such as physical and/or sexual abuse. Indeed, in some cases, the dissociative experience, linked to eating pathology, may have started as a means of survival to escape from the damage of overwhelming trauma. Where there is no history of severe trauma, counsellors may feel able to discuss with clients how they might begin to develop strategies for becoming more aware of themselves in the here and now as an alternative to allowing food to distract them. However, in cases where there has been a history of trauma, there is a case for further detailed assessment and even consultation with other colleagues. Vanderlinden and Vandereycken (1990) have suggested that hypnotherapeutic methods may be useful aids to assessment and treatment of clients for whom dissociation is a major part of their problem. Purging, also, has a symbolic meaning for some people. For example, it has been described as 'getting rid of, starting again', 'as if it never happened', a kind of wiping the slate clean.

Diane came to counselling with the aim of getting over her bulimia 'once and for all'. She talked of her bulimia almost as if it were a live part of her. 'It's been with me as long as I can remember. I'm sick of it, but I don't know how to cope without it.' Near the beginning of her treatment, she had started to record her episodes of bingeing and vomiting. In her determination to give up the disorder, she had stopped vomiting but felt that this meant making a huge effort.

Diane:	I'm so tired of having to fight it. And I hate the feeling of not being in control.
Counsellor:	Now that you have given up vomiting, in what way are you 'not in control'?
Diane:	It was my control, it was what I did to feel in control.
Counsellor:	What does the vomiting mean to you?
Diane:	I feel good afterwards, empty.
Counsellor:	And what does that mean to you, to feel empty?
Diane:	Cleaned out, the emotion has gone. I can start again with a clean slate.

The vomiting had become Diane's way of dealing with her feelings. Whether she felt sad, bad, angry or nervous, the vomiting would give her the, albeit false, feeling that she had done away with her emotions and hence did not have to deal with them or with their consequences. It hardly mattered any more what Diane ate prior to vomiting, and she had begun to use the knowledge that she intended to vomit as an excuse to eat all manner of junk food. Eating too much of the 'wrong' food became, in turn, Diane's excuse to vomit. Very much wanting to be thinner, she had become confused as to what the real nature of her disorder was. Her relationship with food had become complex and distorted.

At this stage, it is necessary to work with clients to address the emotional and interpersonal problems they may be facing, much as the counsellor would work in a cognitive behavioural way with a client who is depressed. In Diane's case, now that she was no longer vomiting, she was able to identify situations when she felt upset. For example, she was becoming increasingly aware of her need to be more assertive with her very demanding family, and the counsellor was able to help her prepare herself for occasions when she had to confront them.

Many clients are also able at this stage to address the meaning of being or becoming fat, or of the act of eating itself.

Most obese women will claim that there is nothing that they want more than to be slim. However, in arriving at dysfunctional assumptions underlying their behaviour, it often transpires that there is a great deal of ambivalence around this idea. For example, Edith had been in teaching for many years and was battling with being overweight for almost as many. In considering the advantages and disadvantages of her weight, she recognised that to some extent she felt cocooned inside her body; her weight gave her a feeling of power and of being protected – from insult ('they wouldn't dare'), from competition with the other teachers in the staff room ('I can't discuss clothes and I don't go on dates so I can hold myself aloof'). Getting thin would mean rewriting her relationships with friends and colleagues and finding new ways of bolstering her self-esteem both at work and at home.

Similarly, Madeleine, a young anorexic woman, described her ambivalence about finally giving up her disorder, as she recognised that it gave her considerable status and attention at college. She held the dysfunctional attitude that 'being anorexic makes me special'. This was related to the core belief: 'I have no personality', and together with the considerable attention she was receiving at home from a worried family, the star status her illness gave her at college rendered it extremely difficult for her to make a consistent attempt to dispense with it. Part of this star status, of course, derives from a general background ideology about the desirability of beauty and slimness for women in general. At some point in the treatment of any eating disorder, and often at several times, it becomes necessary for the counsellor to explore the relevance of these attributes to the client and develop ways to ensure that they become less salient as characteristics of the self.

Further counselling sessions centred on the following topics: making and keeping friends, and what makes a friend someone you want to be with; what thinness and dieting mean to people in general and at college – and how acceptable it is to wear and shop for average-sized clothes rather than needing the smallest on the rail; and giving up childhood but still retaining parental love and attention and not being afraid to let parents know when you need their help.

Sometimes it is necessary to 'chip away' at dysfunctional assumptions over a period of time. For example, Sally's belief in the need for her to be perfect was extremely resistant to change. She could see that it was reasonable for other people to be kind to themselves, to eat a reasonable amount of food, and to give up diets. As far as she was concerned, however, if she could not remain perfect, which included starving herself perfectly, she believed that other areas of her life too would begin to slip.

It would not be reasonable to expect clients to dismiss the beliefs of a lifetime in response to a single counselling session. However, the process can be reinforced with the help of homework assignments. For example, clients can be asked to draw up lists of advantages and disadvantages of assumptions, and, with the help of the counsellor, can compose descriptions of how negative assumptions were arrived at together with examples of alternative modified beliefs (see J.S. Beck 1995). They can be asked to take these lists of revised assumptions home with them for rereading and further modifying.

For example, one of Sally's negative assumptions was 'I have to be perfect in everything I do' (or else people will know that I am inadequate). She took home with her the modified assumption 'It is important to do the best I can. Making mistakes is part of being human.'

She continued to attend counselling sessions for over a year, with increasing gaps in between sessions towards the end. During this time, she was able to push her weight up by between seven and ten pounds. Whenever she was under stress, however, she would return to her bad habits of before. At follow-up sessions she would reiterate some of her old negative assumptions and ask to be reminded of how she modified them previously. There are some people for whom core maladaptive beliefs or schemas (combinations of interconnecting beliefs) are so firmly entrenched that it may require several repetitions of session material before the client can incorporate the new material. This is where written homework is very useful, and often giving the client a tape of the sessions to take home and listen to again can also pay dividends in terms of time saved.

Getting 'stuck'

There are times in the therapy when the counsellor may feel that despite his or her best efforts, nothing that he or she does seems to help. One common problem is that clients may refuse or simply 'forget' to do homework tasks. In an early work of Beck's, he outlined some common excuses in a questionnaire which he devised together with David Burns. The questionnaire was presented to patients when they did not do their homework (Beck et al. 1976: 408). I would not necessarily recommend using a questionnaire as my own clients have described this as feeling quite punitive. However, it may be helpful to bear in mind some self-statements of which to be aware. For example:

- Nothing can help me so there's no point in trying.
- I keep forgetting.
- I don't have time, I've too much to do.
- I feel too bad to think about it.
- I was okay this week so didn't want to spoil it.
- My therapist is trying to control me.

Eliciting reasons for not doing homework tasks can provide useful information about fears the client may have about change, fears of the therapy process, and even the transference.

Theoretically, client and therapist are involved on a joint enterprise. This requires that both feel able to give continuous feedback about the progress of sessions, that both client and counsellor have a shared formulation of the problem and that the client understands and believes in the tasks the counsellor is asking her to do.

When the therapist suggests homework tasks, he or she should ideally ask motivational questions:

- Is there anything that will make this difficult for you in the coming week?
- How will you find time?
- What might make it easier for you?
- How have you felt about today's session? What have you found most helpful/least helpful about today's session?
- How would you like it to be different next time?
- What would you find more helpful?

Another reason for difficulties in the progress of therapy is that the therapist is trying to treat the wrong problem. For example, a reconceptualisation of a case may point to the possibility that the client's problems arise from, or are being maintained by, an issue not previously covered, such as a previous abuse experience or an as yet hidden family issue.

A further, sometimes awkward, issue is the question of the relationship between counsellor and client. Both client and counsellor bring with them a history of relationships with other people, expectations about people, particular ways of relating to people. The counsellor and the client have assumptions and core beliefs which may interfere with the therapy process. While this aspect is not a part of the treatment as it is in psychoanalytical therapy, it is important to keep in mind the fact that the relationship between counsellor and client can affect the therapy and is bound to affect the nature of the collaborative effort.

One example of a difficulty that may arise is a situation when a counsellor holds similar core beliefs or assumptions as the client. To take an extreme case, for example, if a client's negative assumption 'I cannot be perfect unless I am thin' were reflected in that of the counsellor, this could make it difficult for the counsellor to explore alternative views with the client.

Another difficulty can arise if, when a therapy programme is not going well, the counsellor's beliefs about his or her own role in the situation get in the way of his or her being able to think creatively about an alternative strategy. For example, it is not uncommon for counsellors to become 'seduced' by the idea of being able to help a client. Thoughts such as 'No one else can help', 'I cannot let my client down', 'I am the best therapist for this client', 'I must carry on however difficult this is', may be unwittingly reinforced by a client who has perhaps talked about her problems in detail for the first time. Underlying such thoughts, counsellors may hold the assumption 'If I fail everyone will know what a bad therapist I am' or 'to give up is a sign of failure or incompetence'.

These issues raise the importance for counsellors of ongoing training and development and regular supervision. Learning can be through many different media – from one-to-one or group supervision, to using video- and audio-tapes, reading and possibly even Internet or telephone supervision.

Conclusion

This chapter has reviewed the use of cognitive techniques in eating disorders. It is important to keep a balance between following the lead of clients in terms of where they are in the change process and taking the initiative in showing them how to question and change maladaptive thinking and recognise underlying negative assumptions and core beliefs. In this way, clients can be helped towards making gradual changes in their behaviour and in their belief systems, in relation both to sociocultural demands about beauty and slimness and to clients' attitudes to the inner self.

Not all clients respond well to (cognitive behavioural) treatment, and the next chapter will discuss some of the difficulties. It will also discuss issues around teaching people to cope when they cannot get relief from symptoms or give up their eating disordered behaviour; working in tandem with other disciplines; and discharging clients.

8 Adapting to Complex Situations and Dealing with Endings

Cognitive behaviour therapy methods need to be adapted in various ways for many people with an eating disorder, especially in cases where the difficulties are longstanding and when there is comorbidity. This chapter will address the issues raised by difficulties encountered in the counselling process and by the end of counselling, whether it comes from a mutual decision or from an individual decision, by either the counsellor or the client. It will also address the issues involved in counselling clients in other than a one-to-one situation, such as working in groups and involving family members.

Working with severe and complex cases

Studies which have attempted to predict the outcome of therapy for bulimia nervosa have concluded that poor outcome relates to a high degree of personality disturbance, alcohol abuse, high impulsivity (including suicidal behaviour) and low self-esteem (see Herzog et al. 1991). Hence, although CBT fares well in comparison with other treatments, there are several situations where cognitive behavioural counselling aimed specifically at the eating disorder alone is only partially effective or needs to be adapted.

Chronic anorexia nervosa

One such case is that of chronic anorexia nervosa, where the counsellor's role may be one of 'holding' the client's difficulties, of being a sounding board for gradual attempts to change or a mirror for the reflection of thoughts and feelings. The relationship between counsellor and client may be stretched to the limit with some clients, who appear never to change, never to be able to benefit from therapy and yet unable to leave it. For example, some people with chronic anorexia nervosa remain in close touch with mental health services, sometimes with great reluctance. They may appear to both need and want the time of the counsellor, but to resist any suggestion of change and to show continuing ambivalence about the need for it. For them, the advantages of the illness far outweigh the dangers of giving it up. Michael Strober, an American professor specialising in the treatment of eating disorders, has put the counsellor's dilemma most eloquently: '[The counsellor can be] discouraged by a lack of measurable progress, struggling with feelings of ineffectiveness, wavering inconsistently ... between aggressively confrontational or passive approaches, and weighed down by paralysing countertransference' (Strober 2004: 246). He comments on the need for therapists who treat, or rather manage, chronically ill patients with eating disorders to have the ability to tolerate sameness; and a professional identity which 'does not require successes measured by patient progress'. On the contrary, the therapist needs to be able to work creatively with the chronicity. He or she needs to be 'there' for patients in terms of being ready to discuss and encourage whatever small changes they are able to make, and yet to show sensitivity in his or her own emotional response. For example, the counsellor should avoid putting pressure on patients by showing too much excitement should they decide to venture a change in their diet or nutrition.

Working with clients who have been abused

Another case is where the client has suffered childhood sexual or physical abuse. There is as yet no clear evidence that clients with eating disorder are any more likely to have suffered physical or sexual abuse than have other clients (see also Chapter 2). However, where abuse does exist, treatment needs to take this into account. Often, survivors of abuse experience the symptoms of their eating disorder as a means of escaping from or masking painful feelings. The feelings themselves may have been engendered by memories of the abuse or by clients' current experience in relationships which remind them in some way of past abusive relationships. In this case, the counsellor needs to take account of the abuse in the counselling process. Clients may not offer full information about abuse in an initial assessment, and the nature of the abuse may come to light only in subsequent sessions. It is important that the counsellor recognises the strength of feeling voiced by clients, who may be battling with anger, guilt, despair, engendered by their understanding of the link between their eating behaviour and past experiences, and is able to allow the client to focus on the abuse. Where other eating-disorder clients are concerned, improvement may be possible without attitude change and without ever working on core beliefs. However, in the case of clients who have been abused, it is more often necessary to tackle attitudes to other people, and core beliefs such as those of worthlessness and unlovability. Cognitive behavioural therapy has been used successfully as a treatment for people who have suffered abuse and trauma, sometimes in combination with other methods, including guided imagery (see also Fallon and Wonderlich 1997) or an 'imagery rescripting' approach (see Ohanian 2002). The counsellor needs constantly to be aware of the general context in which client's problems are set in order to avoid the trap of offering packaged approaches to treatment.

Working with impulsive behaviour

Another situation where CBT has been described in the literature as only partially effective for eating disorders is that where clients are also abusing other substances, such as alcohol or street drugs. These other disorders need to be addressed, either prior to the eating disorder or in tandem, if only because the use of drugs and alcohol alters clients' behaviour, memory for new material and receptivity to new ideas. One group of clients who present particular difficulties are those whose behaviour is often impulsive and out of control: for example they may steal, initially to support an overeating habit; they may also abuse other substances, and they may harm themselves in other more direct ways, such as cutting themselves (self-mutilation) or even making suicidal attempts. These clients may come from the group described as having a 'personality disorder', and they may also be characterised by chaotic relationships and extremes of mood, such as depression, anxiety or anger. Treatment of these clients is likely to be protracted and complicated, and the eating disorder cannot be treated in isolation (see Beck, Freeman and Associates 1990; Linehan 1993a).

In order to deal with this kind of difficulty, some specialists have drawn from dialectical behaviour therapy to teach mindfulness skills to clients. In practice, this method teaches clients to accept negative feeling states rather than working to change them in the first instance. However, this can be a helpful tool as a means of helping to reduce risk and empower clients who are feeling out of control of impulsive behaviour, as a first step towards change.

Clients are taught the distinction between the 'emotional mind' and the 'reasonable mind', and the potential for the two to be integrated in 'wise mind'. The theory behind this is that we cannot expect to overcome emotions with reason, but we can go within ourselves and integrate the two with wise mind, which is similar to intuition. Clients are taught 'mindfulness skills' to deal with extremes of emotion. This involves learning first to observe emotion without getting caught up in the experience. Clients are asked to practise this in their everyday lives with simple actions such as walking, doing household chores, etc. The key is to be attentive but not to try to push away thoughts or focus on them: simply to watch them as if they were clouds in the sky. The second task is to describe the emotion or thought and put it into words, in a non-judgemental way. In order to learn the skill of mindfulness, clients are advised to practise concentrating on doing one thing at a time; for example, when eating, only to eat; when walking, walk; when working, work; when planning, plan. They can then apply this approach to the way they deal with thoughts and feelings. A binge eater might observe: 'I am having the urge to binge'. The client must use her wise mind to participate fully in the experience, and then to let go of it. (see Linehan 1993b).

Tanya used a similar approach to cope with urges to self-harm and binge eat. She learned to observe the feelings and put them aside while listening to favourite pieces of music. She would focus on an urge by choosing a piece of music to put in her personal stereo that reflected her current mood: angry if she was feeling angry, sad if she was feeling sad. She used the music to help her focus on and observe the feeling, and then let go of it. In this way she was able gradually to reduce her tendency to act on impulse.

However, counsellors should never have to be in the position of working with problems of this nature and complexity entirely alone or unsupported, and decisions about the nature and intensity of treatment should always be shared.

The end of the counselling relationship

Counselling may come to an end for a variety of reasons. The most desirable outcome is one where the client has improved and client and counsellor agree that now is the time for the client to put her improvement to the test. A course of treatment is usually between 12 and 20 weeks for bulimics, at the end of which time many clients are binge- and purge-free. With regard to binge eating disorder, the course of treatment may be longer, between three and six months. The client may not necessarily expect to have reached a target weight within the normal range, as the chief goal of treatment is eating in a controlled and 'normal' fashion, without bingeing. This involves treading a fine line between avoidance of strict dieting (which can exacerbate bingeing) and avoidance of overeating.

Similarly, the course of treatment for a recovering anorexic can be up to a year or even two, as decisions about making the necessary changes are often slower and the process of actual change may occur over a longer period than with other clients. Towards the end of counselling, or in the case of anorexics, where change can be slow, counsellor and client might agree to set sessions with longer intervals between them, say a fortnight to even a month. It is important, however, to ensure that the decision to do this is open to renegotiation, and has not been made purely for the sake of expediency (for example, the counsellor has a busy schedule, or the client does not like to take time off work). The disadvantage of setting sessions with long time intervals in between is that if a client is ambivalent about change, there is time between sessions for her to slip back into old habits, or to give up a new target for change, with no opportunity to reinforce the material and the decisions of the previous session. The advantage of longer intervals between sessions is that it gives people who are recovering an opportunity to test new behaviours and discuss any problems or relapse with the counsellor, and in the case of clients who are still by their own admission very ambivalent about change, it gives them the opportunity (anorexics in particular) to maintain contact with the counsellor without being pressured on a regular basis to make changes they do not feel ready for.

Another reason for counselling to come to an end is, of course, that clients simply 'drop out' or stop coming to their sessions before the treatment has come to an end. This is an issue which is not widely emphasised in the treatment and research literature. However, the numbers of people not completing treatment are fairly substantial, and it is important for counsellors to be aware of the figures in order to be prepared, if only to avoid attributing blame to themselves for treatment failures. About 14 per cent of clients simply fail to engage in therapy in the first place, and between 17 and 30 per cent of bulimic clients do not complete therapy once they have started (Waller 1997). By the nature of the cognitive therapy process, with its goal of collaboration between counsellor and client, it should be possible to predict this, as the counsellor is continually checking back with the client about her level of understanding and satisfaction. For example, at the end of every session, the counsellor should ideally summarise the content of the session and ask if the client has any questions or has been unduly upset by anything that has been said in the session. However, counsellors and therapists cannot always recognise or deal with clients' ambivalence, clients themselves are often reluctant to voice their dissatisfaction or simply do not recognise it until they have had time to go home and think about it, and people stop attending without warning however hard the counsellor may have worked to keep communication channels clear.

In one research study, women who did not complete their treatment scored higher than completers on two measures of psychopathology: perceived severity of bulimic symptoms and borderline personality (Waller 1997). This finding is in line with those about the outcome of therapy for bulimia nervosa, which suggest that poor outcome in general relates to a high degree of personality disturbance, alcohol abuse, high impulsivity (including suicidal behaviour) and low self-esteem (see Herzog et al. 1991).

One client, Sylvia, a dancer, stopped attending her sessions after a very short period of time but was then re-referred to the same counsellor one year later. When asked what it was that had led her to stop coming the time previously, she reported that she had felt that there was no point in coming, as she could not imagine ever wanting to give up her purging behaviour. Bingeing and vomiting were, for her, a part of her life. She could barely remember a time when she had not used them, and she did not feel that she would be able to do without them. One year on, she was feeling weak and ill, she had a new boyfriend who had noticed that something was amiss and she wanted to get better so that she could live a more normal life with him. In fact, she also had many other problems, including low self-esteem, poor family relationships and long-term emotional and interpersonal problems for which she subsequently needed a long period of ongoing therapy.

Another stage at which clients fail to attend is after a period of time when they have managed to give up bingeing. Some normal-weight bulimics and obese people with binge eating disorder react in a catastrophic way to a lapse in their eating behaviour and often, despite careful preparation, will relapse completely, and simply stop attending sessions if on one occasion they binge. This is where efforts to prevent relapse are particularly important.

Preventing relapse

There are many techniques used for the prevention of relapse in eating disorders, and more specifically in relation to treatment of obesity. The most important is for clients to be prepared for the possibility of relapse and to have available plans to deal with it. About half of diet slips or 'lapses' are triggered by negative feelings which come from within a person, such as fear, anxiety, feeling pain, frustration or depression, or simply having an 'urge' to eat. General stress can trigger overeating in many people, and just feeling that one has overeaten can lead to more eating. So it is not only the relapse itself that is important, but also what it means to the person to have slipped up. Another half of diet slips are triggered by interpersonal events, such as social pressure, or being upset by someone. Some are caused by social pressure, for example someone offering food. Some are caused by conflict with other people. It is important to let sufferers know that sooner or later everyone who tries to make changes 'relapses', in other words returns to their old way of eating. Some people are able to put themselves back on track very quickly, but for many this is the beginning of the end. Relapse is more likely to happen to clients who have put themselves on a strict regime than to those who are making gradual changes, and so people with eating disorders, who by their very nature are strict with themselves, are especially vulnerable.

Therefore there are certain suggestions which can be made to people with eating disorders to prepare them for relapse, or possibly to help them to avoid it altogether. The first is to suggest that the client attempts to be reasonable in her expectations of success, in terms of not expecting to make too many changes at once, or too quickly. Once a diet or eating change is under way, however, it is important to accept that there will be times when new habits will be difficult to keep up and that the times of most difficulty cannot be overcome without some careful planning. The second step, therefore, is for the client to recognise in which situations she is at the most risk. 'To be forewarned is to be forearmed.' This is where careful record keeping can help. The third step is to devise some strategies for dealing with the situations. For example, Wendy had begun to take control of her bulimia and had managed with the help of a dietitian to increase the amount of food she was eating on a regular basis. From eating very little at irregular intervals and bingeing sporadically, she had graduated to eating low-fat meals with a great deal of vegetables and a reasonable amount of carbohydrate foods. Her weight, which at the beginning of counselling went up slightly as she began to eat more in terms both of amount and of variety, had now stabilised, and she was losing weight gradually. One day, she was confronted with a sudden celebration at work. She was hungry, but there was little choice of foods. She ate what she felt were a great many crisps and other snack foods. On her way home, she bought a large amount of food and binged. At her next session, she described feeling angry with herself and hopeless about returning to the plan she had devised for herself with the help of the dietitian.

Wendy:	Once I'd had those crisps instead of the sandwich I had in my desk drawer, there was no stopping me. It's useless. I might as well give up the whole thing.
Counsellor:	You remember that we've talked a lot recently about negative thoughts and trying to replace them with more helpful ones. Can you spot one in the things you just said?
Wendy:	Oh, alright. Perhaps I was being a bit drastic. Of course I'm not going to give up now. It's just that it's so hard.
Counsellor:	I know that. Perhaps we can try to think about some ways you can be more prepared for events like the work party.
Wendy:	What sort of things?
Counsellor:	Can you think of some?
Wendy:	Well, if I'd known what was going to happen, I could have stayed at home that day. Or I could have gone back to collect my sandwiches and sat with everyone eating my own stuff – but that would have looked silly.
Counsellor:	Well, that would be for you to decide. Remember that for some people with specific food allergies or problems with certain foods, they might just have to do that, and it would be OK. What you need to decide is how far you want to make an issue of sticking to your plan, or whether you want to find a way to bend your rules sometimes without feeling that you have ruined the progress you have made.
Wendy:	I could try to make sure I always ate on my own, and I could tell everyone I never eat at parties. But really I'd rather be like everyone else.
Counsellor:	In that case, can you think of a way you could eat 'forbidden' things and still keep to your plan?
Wendy:	I could do it if it didn't make me feel so deprived the rest of the time, and if I didn't feel so guilty.

The rest of the session was taken up with Wendy considering how she could avoid feeling guilty. She worked out that this would mean focusing on her negative thoughts about lapsing from the diet and thinking of statements to say to herself such as: 'There is no harm in eating crisps on one day. I can go back to my healthy eating plan later today. This one party isn't going to make me fat unless I let it be the end of my eating plan.'

Often, the temptation to lapse into old habits arises from emotional rather than food triggers. For example, Peggy was recovering from bulimia nervosa when she had a row with her flatmates and found herself alone and angry. Both being alone and feeling angry and isolated were for her important triggers of bingeing and she had made a trip to the all-night garage for a basket full of binge items before she had time to realise what she was doing. The key here was for her to learn to be prepared to deal with emotional upset and, failing that, to use behavioural self-control tactics to delay buying food or bingeing until she was feeling stronger.

Emotional triggers can be important too in relation to recovering anorexics. Sally was repeatedly in conflict with her sister over how best to dispose of the family business, which their father had recently left them in his will. Any renewal of their disagreements led to Sally returning to starving herself, and on one occasion she lost seven pounds in the fortnight before her follow-up session. The work of this and subsequent sessions, therefore, had to be geared towards helping her to deal with the emotional and financial problems without resorting to starvation as a means of coping with stress and hence 'opting out' of further conflict.

Involving family members in the counselling

Although this book is written essentially for the counsellor working with individual clients, there is often a place for involving family members or even close friends in interviews with clients. The family can help to alter the client's home environment in order to foster change and may also be able to help the client to overcome the difficulties she faces both with regard to managing a change in her behaviour and with regard to cognitive change.

In the case of clients with anorexia nervosa, family treatment has been shown to be the most effective for clients of 18 years and under (see also Chapter 2). Therefore, if younger clients are living at home, family therapy should be offered wherever possible. However, family sessions can be effective for a wide range of clients (see Dare and Eisler 1997).

In the case of clients with bulimia nervosa and binge eating disorder, just as with anorexia nervosa, there may be a great deal of tension at home surrounding the issue of food, and possibly also of purging and vomiting. Often, a parent or sibling has recently discovered the existence of vomiting and is on permanent alert for further occurrences. Some clients are grateful for the opportunity to bring a significant other to a session for discussion of their problems and to hear how best to help them. The relative may wish to see the counsellor in private but, preferably, should be persuaded to voice his or her concerns in front of the client, so that the issues can be addressed honestly and without the counsellor having to develop separate allegiances or hold secrets from one or other party.

The client may already have informed the counsellor how much her relative or friend knows about her problem already, but the counsellor may wish to start by ascertaining just how much the relative knows about the problem or, with the permission of the client, informing him or her about the problem and about the strategies the client is using in an attempt to make changes. It is important to avoid the scenario where the relative becomes accuser or persecutor whenever it is apparent that the client is experiencing problems, for example refusing to eat in the case of an anorexic, or vomiting in the case of a bulimic. There can, however, be previously agreed strategies for helping. For example, the mother of an anorexic can be informed about the nature of the client's targets for eating in any particular period of time, and there can be rules about how far each is allowed to make demands on the other. Mandy, when she was at home for meals, inspected the contents of her mother's saucepans and argued about the ingredients of the cooking. Meanwhile, mother, determined that her daughter should eat more, piled food on her plate and became very upset when she refused to eat. Together with the counsellor, mother and daughter were able to agree on portion sizes and Mandy was able to agree not to inspect the saucepans and demand to know exactly what was in them at every mealtime.

Madeleine had admitted in individual sessions with the counsellor that one of the reasons for her reluctance about giving up her anorexia nervosa was her fear that she would have to grow up too quickly and that her parents would see her not as a little girl but as an adult who no longer needed their help. She relished the attention her illness brought her and knew no other way to ask for it. She was subsequently able in a family session to express her fears with the help of the counsellor, and she and her parents were able to agree ways in which they might continue to support her even when she no longer needed help with the anorexia.

Susannah's boyfriend was aware of the times when she vomited after meals and was keen to help her in her attempt to overcome the bulimia nervosa. At a point in the counselling where Susannah had her bingeing partly under control, and was attempting to stop vomiting altogether, she was able to bring her boyfriend to a session. The couple agreed that in the evenings, Susannah's boyfriend would keep her company for an hour after dinner, and that she would attempt to avoid the urge to go to the bathroom. If, however, Susannah did vomit, her boyfriend agreed that he would make no comment except to remind her that she would feel better about the meal she had eaten if she could hang on to it until the morning and that she was keeping her weight stable.

James Lock, an American psychiatrist, has collaborated with workers from the Maudsley Group in the United Kingdom to devise a manualised approach to family therapy for anorexia nervosa (see Lock et al. 2001). Following on from the success of this approach, Lock has more recently developed a manual for the treatment of adolescent bulimia nervosa. The manual is a modified version of Fairburn's original method and involves parents in a three-stage approach. In the first stage, parents are asked to help ensure that the client attends sessions, to provide mealtime structure, and to assist the client in avoiding binge eating and purging. In the second stage, parents help with the reintroduction of feared and avoided foods and with addressing common triggers for binge eating. In the third stage, they help with setting up realistic expectations and devising relapse prevention strategies. The author has claimed success similar to that of individual CBT in preliminary studies (see Lock 2002). This approach addresses the eating disorder at a largely behavioural level. It may be more complex, although theoretically not impossible, to address the disorder at the more schematic level.

Working with groups

Much of the research into the efficacy of CBT for eating disorders has been in a group setting, and hence it is known that treating people in groups is effective. Researchers in Sydney compared the outcome of individual CBT and group CBT in a randomised control trial. Both treatments were effective in reducing bingeing and vomiting. The group treatment was more cost-effective and had a superior effect on anxiety levels and social functioning. However, the group condition was less effective at producing abstinence from bulimic behaviours after treatment and the authors suggest that this might be a disadvantage of not having individual discussions with clients (Chen et al. 2003).

Working in a clinical setting rarely mirrors the research setting. Clients cannot be selected, and given that they are referred at varying times, the expectation from both clients and referrers is more often than not that they are treated on an individual basis. Nevertheless, it is sometimes more appropriate for clients to be placed in groups, especially where there are large numbers and therapy time is limited. Groups have been found to be extremely effective at producing general improvements in bulimia nervosa symptoms even when the purpose of the group has been specifically for teaching purposes as opposed to counselling *per se* (see Davis et al. 1997). The educational aspects of treatment can easily be put across in a group, and there may in fact be some advantages to treating people in groups for this purpose even if they are also offered individual counselling for the more personal aspects of their problems (see also McKisack and Waller 1997). The direction of flow of information is mainly from the counsellor to the client(s), but groups are also a more appropriate vehicle than are individual sessions for wide-ranging discussions, particularly about the cultural aspects of eating disorders and the pressures on women in society.

There is a great deal of opportunity in a group setting for evolving creative solutions to individual problems through a kind of brainstorming process that can occur in response to the problems of one or other member of the group. For example, in one group led by the author, a client with binge eating disorder was unable to resolve the question of how she could avoid bingeing at the annual family reunion on the occasion of her parents' wedding anniversary. Food and eating were of great importance to her family, and food was always in great abundance at any family gathering.

'I have to eat chocolates because it's part of the fun,' said Carla. The group offered suggestions as to behavioural solutions to this problem, ranging from asking the family to refrain from presenting their usual display, to suggesting that Carla refuse to go home unless the food was removed, and providing an alternative display of 'goodies', including a colourful display of fruit and vegetables. Carla's reluctance to take up any of these suggestions was met with a series of questions which led to an exploration of her motivation to make changes in her habitual response to food situations and to a discussion of the meaning to her of saying 'no' to her family or behaving differently from them. While these same issues could well have been covered in individual sessions, it would not have been appropriate for the counsellor to offer a series of suggestions. These would have had to come from the client. The group situation allowed the discussion to move on more quickly, and helped Carla to arrive at an appreciation of her assumptions about the food and its meaning in her family life. It also provided support for her while she explored the options, knowing that the suggestions being made and questions being raised came from people who themselves were facing similar problems and who therefore were a credible source of usable ideas.

In this way, groups can be exciting for both therapists and clients, who can see change evolving visibly in front of them. They can provide a forum for clients who know only too well how easy it is to help others while they might find it impossible to help themselves.

One other apparent advantage of group work is that it is more economical of time. If six to eight people can be treated in an hour and a half as an alternative to all these people being offered individual sessions, then the saving is superficially 45 hours over a period of ten sessions. The arithmetic is not quite so simple in practice. Clients do not necessarily benefit personally from discussions about other group members, and, unless there is great homogeneity of problems, may feel after some sessions that their problems have not been addressed at all. Where homogeneity does exist, cognitive behaviour therapy administered in small groups has been found to be an effective treatment (for example, Telch and her colleagues [1990] reported a 94 per cent reduction in binge eating in a group of non-purging bulimics after a ten-week programme).

The question of homogeneity versus heterogeneity of membership of groups can be a difficult one. Unless the counsellor is operating in a very large catchment area for people with eating disorders, it is unlikely that there will be much similarity among group members, in terms of diagnosis, of type or severity of symptoms, or even of age. Counsellors need to bear in mind the possibility that obese clients will envy those with anorexia nervosa or bulimia ('At least they're not fat'), while binge eaters and purgers may envy those with restricting anorexia ('They have self-control'). The cognitive behavioural work that each of these groups need to do in order to pursue alternative solutions to their eating problems is similar, but it can take several weeks for the realisation of this fact to sink in, and the experience of other group members as 'different from me' can be given as a reason for dropping out of therapy.

There are also some limitations in terms of the need to exclude certain clients from groups: those who are extremely depressed or suicidal, or extremely underweight and in need of inpatient care (unless the group is being run in a medical inpatient facility). One other critical disadvantage of group work is the tendency for drop-out from treatment to be even higher than in individual treatment, and for many clients to attend erratically. Several counsellors and therapists report that when establishing groups, they interview and offer places to at least ten clients in order to be left with a group of six or seven or even as few as four or five members who go on to complete the course. (See also McKisack and Waller 1996 for a further discussion of the characteristics of women who drop out from group therapy for bulimia.)

Working in parallel with other treatments

There are some clients who may be referred simultaneously to more than one therapist or to more than one setting. This is the case if a client is an inpatient on a psychiatric ward and suffering from eating disorder together with other difficulties, or a patient in a daycare facility. The difficulty here is that other treatments being offered are unlikely to be cognitive behavioural and there is a great deal of potential for confusion both about the client's needs and about the client's own understanding of the aims of treatment and the differences between different professionals she is meeting on a daily basis. The only solution here is for the counsellor to meet continuously with the other professionals involved in the client's care and to be aware constantly of differences in approach in order to be able to explain and highlight them to the client.

There are times also when the counselling process may break down as a result of the need for clients to be treated elsewhere. For example, when an anorexic client drops to below a body mass index of 17, an outpatient programme can become untenable and the client may have to be admitted to hospital. In practice, the recommendation is that most anorexics be treated as outpatients, and admission will not usually be considered until weight is at or below BMI 14 or 15. The figure will differ from one area to another and the criteria for admission are usually also based on other factors, such as the degree of social support available to the client and the degree to which she is considered to be at risk of either self-neglect or self harm. One important issue here is that counsellors need to have clear limits in their own minds as to what are the margins of acceptable weight loss and what are the limits of their expertise and sphere of responsibility. In other words, they need to have stipulated openly to the client a pre-agreed lower limit of weight for each client, below which they will not feel comfortable working with that client. This lower limit will vary from one treatment setting to another and will depend very much on the availability of specialised treatment and the speed with which the decision to hospitalise can be made (see also Crisp and McLelland 1996: 56–57 for a discussion of this issue). Unless she is on a ward which specialises in the treatment of anorexia nervosa, it may be difficult to continue with the client with discussions along cognitive behavioural lines, at least until she is discharged. In any case, much of the content of sessions has to do with establishing self-control of eating, and while the person needs both to accommodate to increasing weight and to prepare herself for self-care at home, she may not be in a position to make real choices until she has been discharged from hospital.

A similar issue arises when an overweight client with binge eating disorder is offered anorexiant drugs, a spell of inpatient care, or even a medical intervention such as stomach stapling or gastroplasty (see the review article by Kellum, De Maria and Sugerman 1998; and Kral 1995). In such cases, the potential and motivation for the client to control her own eating behaviour is reduced, and a cognitive behavioural therapy intervention becomes less feasible, at least in relation to the overeating *per se*. The client can be offered a series of sessions aimed at preparing her for a return to self-control at the end of the proposed intervention. This can work well if supported and encouraged, and even made a condition of treatment offered by all the professionals involved, but in practice it can be problematic as the client often believes, erroneously, that once the medical treatment is completed, she will (magically) be better able to deal with her eating problem.

Conclusion

Many of the clients seen by counsellors on a day-to-day basis exhibit some of the characteristics of the special cases described in this chapter. For example, those clients who have asked for or been referred for help most frequently in the past are often also those who have abused other substances, mutilated themselves, made suicidal attempts, and had the most problematic relationships. Others seem to be constantly at risk, or always in treatment but never seeming to move forward. In practice, counselling people with eating disorders is rarely straightforward and does not necessarily follow a predictable course. Therefore the skills needed for counselling people for eating disorder *per se* need to be combined on a fairly regular basis with other, more general skills in addition to the ability to recognise when it becomes necessary to ask for help, or refer to an alternative facility or for a different form of therapy.

Conclusion

This book has been an introduction to using a cognitive behavioural and educational approach to counselling people with eating disorders. There are many practical skills the counsellor can bring to working with this group of clients: from assessment to practical behavioural advice about self-control; to the use of cognitive techniques to help clients to make changes in the way they think and feel about their problems. The counselling process moves from the realms of the practical to the creative as counsellor and client begin to address underlying attitudes to eating, weight and shape and move on to developing an understanding of the meaning of eating disorder to clients and sometimes to an appreciation of clients' core beliefs about themselves.

There is a potential danger inherent in writing any book which purports to tell counsellors 'how to do it'. Counsellors will find many similarities between people with similar eating disorder types. However, each client's expression of disorder is individual. My hope is that, using some of the ideas described here, readers will be able to help clients to develop and unfold their own personal solutions.

Appendix 1   Eating Disorders and
Their Effects

Binge eating is experienced by large numbers of people, perhaps up to 20 per cent of young women. In some groups, for example college students, the numbers are even higher, with up to 90 per cent admitting to binge eating at some time or another. So, on its own, binge eating is not considered a serious disabling problem.

Bulimia nervosa is a more serious problem. It includes attempts by sufferers to rid themselves of unwanted calories, for example by vomiting or taking laxatives, and is more likely to need medical or psychological treatment. It affects about one in a hundred adolescent and young adult women. Binge eating disorder, which is also characterised by feelings of loss of control and distress about binge eating but not purging, probably affects about two in every hundred people and about four in every hundred obese people. Anorexia nervosa affects less than one in a hundred women. Sufferers starve themselves to the point of emaciation, losing at least 15 per cent of their normal body weight.

What causes eating disorders?

Many different reasons have been put forward for why people develop eating disorders. It is now clear that there is no one cause, but that the disorder can appear as a result of a combination of influences in a person's life. Some of these influences have to do with background factors such as relationships with family, feelings about childhood and about one's self. Others have more to do with current situations such as whether or not the person goes on a diet, or what kinds of stresses she or he is subject to.

The effects of deprivation itself

Some people have suggested that the actual deprivation of a diet is partly to blame for the problems and certainly has a powerful effect on maintaining them. Dieting itself, or at least starvation, appears to make some people more vulnerable to bingeing behaviour or behave in a strange, obsessive way around food. A very powerful example of this comes from the results of an experiment set up just after the Second World War. Thirty-four conscientious objectors in America were put on half rations for a period of three months in order to study the effects of starvation and find out more about how to help ex-prisoners of war. What happened to these men was astounding. They had perfectly normal personalities and behaviour prior to the experiment but under conditions of starvation they became irritable, they thought about and talked constantly of food, they stole food, they binged occasionally and then felt guilty. While eating, some of them played with their food, cut it up into tiny pieces, and hoarded it. Even after a period of refeeding when the experiment was over, some of them continued to eat when full, and alternately dieted and binge ate in an uncontrolled way. Some of them continued to be interested in food and weight and three of the men even went on to become chefs!

This all fits in too with what we know about another negative effect of dieting. Dieters in general have described themselves as experiencing a changed relationship with food, such as powerful urges to eat or excessive preoccupation with food and feelings of being out of control around food. So, many of the symptoms of people with eating disorders are likely to stem from natural, physical, causes.

The effects of cycles of dieting ('yo-yo' dieting)

Some people argue that repeated cycles of dieting can make matters even worse, in that people may have to eat even less and for longer to lose the same amount of weight.

For example, some athletes who have to keep within a particular weight class from one season to the next complain that they have to diet more strictly and that it takes them longer each time.

In 1989 an American researcher followed up over 1000 patients who had joined a very low-calorie diet programme at least twice during nine years, and who had regained at least 20 per cent of their initial weight loss in the intervening time. Weight loss in the second cycle was significantly less than in the first cycle.

Restrained eaters or 'platewatchers'

Another theory suggests that strict dieting can lead to problems with a person's attitude to food and weight, leading to erratic behaviour with food. Researchers have found that people who are concerned about their weight and who are often dieting tend to have their normal restraint broken if they think they have broken their diet. Habitual dieters often eat more after they have just eaten something fattening than after something non-fattening; and they will eat more if they are simply led to believe that they have just had something fattening, even if they haven't. (For example, in one experiment dieters overate ice cream following a milk-shake but dieters who were given a mixture of cottage cheese and fruit salad equivalent in calories to the milk-shake didn't overeat. In other words, in the mind of the dieter a bowl of cottage cheese and salad doesn't break a diet, however many calories it may contain, but ice cream does!)

Research has also found that dieters eat more if made anxious, or think they are about to be given something fattening, and even if they think they have just had alcohol (a substance people know to be disinhibiting!).

In other words, what we think about what we have eaten or are about to eat has an important influence on what we eat subsequently.

Society's obsession with thinness

Thinking about food and worrying about weight is a phenomenon strongly reinforced by society. There is a powerful current emphasis in society on thinness which makes women, and young women in particular, especially vulnerable to the temptation to diet and worry about eating and weight, and sometimes as a consequence to attribute many difficulties to problems with weight and body image. Some Canadian researchers studied the pictures of *Playboy* magazine centrefold girls and of winners of the Miss America pageant from 1959 to 1978. They noticed that the ideal female shape, as demonstrated by the measurements of the women in the pictures, became increasingly thinner over the years. At the same time, there was a significant increase in the proportion of space given to material about diet and slimming in six major women's magazines. Yet during this time, paradoxically, the weights of both women and men were on the increase. This trend still continues today, and while we are all getting fatter, many people diet and exercise in an attempt to get thinner. Even people who are not fat believe they need to lose weight. For example, a survey of dietary and body shape concerns in a group of British schoolgirls found that whereas 4 per cent were overweight, over 40 per cent considered themselves so, and about half of them wanted to lose weight.

Eating disorder as a vicious circle

Dieting on its own does not, of course, lead to eating disorder. There is an idea that some people may become trapped in a vicious circle partly in an attempt to get out of impossible emotional turmoil. The behaviour of dieting, started as a way to avoid being fat, may take over as the sufferer begins to feel satisfaction about being in control. Bingeing, if it happens, can make the person feel bloated, uncomfortable, out of control. As a result, the person takes to dieting, starving or purging themselves, and these behaviours can become extremely rewarding as a consequence. Hence the sufferer is in a vicious circle from which she cannot escape. Strict dieting too can take on a life of its own, as it does in anorexia nervosa, with the sufferer getting great satisfaction out of the feeling of success and becoming increasingly determined never to put on weight again.

What happens to people who diet?

One of the chief triggers (though not the main cause) for an eating disorder is dieting itself. In order to understand this it is important to understand something about how our bodies store and use energy and what happens if we try to change our weight by dieting.

Our bodies are composed of a mixture of fat, a fat-free mass or lean tissue, and a glycogen store. The fat or adipose tissue consists mainly of fat and a little water. The lean tissue is made up of protein, minerals and about 73 per cent water. Glycogen is a temporary energy store held mainly in the liver and muscle by a large amount of water. In fact about 60 per cent of our body is water.

One of the ways in which we use energy is through our basal metabolic rate. This is the rate at which the body uses up energy when we are at rest. If we use more energy than we put in, we lose weight; if we use less than we put in, we gain weight. The bigger the person, the higher the metabolic rate. Taller people generally have higher metabolic rates than shorter people, and metabolic rate is also slightly higher on average in fat people than in lean people of similar height. In other words, the amount of energy (or food) you need to live depends to a large extent on your size.

Some overweight people believe that the fault of their extra fat lies in a lower than normal metabolic rate. This is usually not the case. There are, of course, differences between individual people of similar weight in the amount of energy they need; but everyone can lose weight given the correct energy intake.

The less you eat, the more weight you will lose. As you lose weight, your metabolic rate goes down along with your size, and you need less food to keep you going than you did at the beginning of the diet. In order to keep the weight down, you will need to cut down permanently on what you eat. If you go back to eating as you did before the diet started, your weight will gradually creep up to its original level.

How fast can you lose weight?

When we stop eating, our stomach empties, the glycogen stores get used up and the water normally bound to the glycogen is lost. This explains the very large losses people sometimes have when they first go on a diet. Weight loss slows down after a few days. Fat loss takes time. If you lose between one or two pounds or up to one kilogram in weight per week, then what you lose will consist mainly of fat; but if you lose weight faster, you will lose valuable lean tissue as well. This matters because metabolic rate depends mainly on lean tissue: the more lean tissue you lose, the lower your metabolic rate goes, and the less you need to eat.

What is wrong with starvation or very strict diets?

Starvation is a particularly unhelpful way to lose weight. It results in a dramatic decrease in metabolic rate, and it therefore quickly becomes impossible to keep your weight down on anything but the smallest intake. What is more, people who starve themselves soon have psychological difficulties such as loss of concentration and feeling irritable, and are prone to bouts of uncontrolled overeating when they stop their diet.

So, for the person who needs to lose weight, a less strict reduction in food intake is best, with a target weight loss of between half a pound and two pounds per week.

What is wrong with vomiting or taking laxatives to lose weight?

Vomiting is a very ineffective way of emptying the stomach. It removes only some of the food eaten, so that the sufferer soon feels hungry again. Also, the habit of vomiting serves only to lock sufferers into their cycle of bingeing and purging. This is because the knowledge that she can vomit when she has overeaten often serves to reassure a bulimic that she can undo the harm she has done. Knowing that she intends to vomit, a bulimic can then decide that in order to make vomiting worthwhile she may as well eat a large amount of food. Some sufferers will go ahead and fill up on a range of normally forbidden items, in many cases needing to reach a certain degree of fullness before they are able to vomit. This serves only to keep the binge cycle going and leads ultimately to increased weight gain.

Besides its ineffectiveness as a means of weight control, vomiting is physically dangerous. Repeated vomiting upsets the body's fluid balance and depletes the body of electrolytes such as potassium and sodium, causing a range of unpleasant symptoms such as muscle weakness and even heart arrhythmias.

Taking large quantities of laxatives produces similar symptoms to vomiting and is also an ineffective way of controlling weight. Laxatives work on the lower part of the gut, whereas most of the food has already been absorbed higher up in the stomach and intestines. The laxatives cause diarrhoea, which produces a large loss of water. This makes the sufferer feel thinner but only because she has become temporarily dehydrated. As soon as she eats or drinks again the loss is made up. In fact the body stores water in an attempt to return itself to normal, with the result that someone who abuses laxatives often feels bloated. This leads her back into taking laxatives, so that she becomes trapped in a vicious circle. In addition, long-term laxative abuse can also have nasty long-term effects. The muscles in the colon can become less effective and the sufferer may as a result occasionally lose control altogether and be prone to 'accidents'.

Appendix 2 Eating Problems: Resources for Clients

Many people with an eating disorder are helped by reading. There follows a list of books which offer self-help advice or information about problems related to eating disorder.

Eating disorder self-help books

Kim Chernin (1994) *The Hungry Self: Women, Eating and Identity*. New York: Harper Perennial.

Myra Cooper, Gillian Todd and Adrian Wells (2000) *Bulimia Nervosa: A Cognitive Therapy Programme for Clients*. London and New York: Jessica Kingsley.

Peter Cooper (1993) *Bulimia Nervosa: A Guide to Recovery* [including a self-help manual for sufferers]. London: Robinson.

Arthur Crisp, Neil Joughin, Christine Halek and Carol Bowyer (1996) *Anorexia Nervosa and the Wish to Change* (2nd edn). Hove: Psychology Press.

Christopher Fairburn (1995) *Overcoming Binge Eating*. New York: Guilford Press.

Christopher Freeman (2000) *Overcoming Anorexia Nervosa*. London: Robinson.

Ulrike Schmidt and Janet Treasure (1993) *Getting Better Bit(e) By Bit(e)*. Hove: Psychology Press.

Help for families

Bryan Lask and Rachel Bryant-Waugh (2004) *Eating Disorders: A Parents' Guide*. London: Brunner Routledge.

Roberta Trattner Sherman and Ron A. Thompson (1997) *Bulimia: A Guide for Family and Friends*. San Francisco: Jossey-Bass. (Useful as an adjunct to CBT.)

Michele Siegel, Judith Brisman and Margot Weinshel (1997) *Surviving an Eating Disorder: Strategies for Family and Friends*. New York: Harper Perennial.

Janet Treasure (1997) *Breaking Free from Anorexia Nervosa: A Survival Guide for Families, Friends and Sufferers*. Hove: Psychology Press.

Self-help for emotional difficulties

Lorraine Bell (2003) *Managing Intense Emotions and Overcoming Self-destructive Habits: A Self-help Manual*. London: Brunner Routledge.

David Burns (1999) *Feeling Good: The New Mood Therapy*. New York: Avon Books.

David Burns (2000) *The Feeling Good Handbook*. Harmondsworth: Penguin.

Paul Gilbert (1997) *Overcoming Depression: A Self-help Guide Using Cognitive Behavioural Techniques*. London: Robinson.

Dennis Greenberger and Christine Padesky (1995) *Mind Over Mood: A Cognitive Therapy Treatment Manual for Clients*. New York: Guilford Press.

Helen Kennerly (1997) *Overcoming Anxiety: A Self-help Guide Using Cognitive Behavioural Techniques*. London: Constable and Robinson.

Self-esteem and relationships

David Burns (1999) *Ten Days to Self-esteem*. New York: William Morrow.

Melanie Fennell (1999) *Overcoming Low Self-esteem: Self-help Guide Using Cognitive Behavioural Techniques*. London: Constable and Robinson.

Gillian Butler (2001) *Overcoming Anxiety and Shyness: A Self-help Guide Using Cognitive Behavioural Techniques*. New York: New York University Press.

Thomas Cash (1997) *The Body Image Workbook: An 8-Step Program for Learning to Like Your Looks*. Oakland, CA: New Harbinger Publications.

Anne Dickson (1982) *A Woman in Your Own Right: Assertiveness and You*. London: Quartet Books.

Robin Skynner and John Cleese (1983) *Families and How to Survive Them*. London: Methuen.

Childhood abuse

Susan Forward (1989) *Toxic Parents: Overcoming the Legacy of Parental Abuse*. London: Bantam Press.

Eliana Gil (1983) *Outgrowing the Pain*. New York: Bantam Dell.

Helen Kennerly (2000) *Overcoming Childhood Trauma: A Self-help Guide Using Cognitive Behavioural Techniques*. New York: New York University Press.

Penny Parks (1990) *Rescuing the Inner Child: Therapy for Adults Sexually Abused as Children*. London: Souvenir.

Some useful websites

www.edauk.com – the website of the Eating Disorders Association in the UK, a voluntary body which aims to offer information and advice to sufferers.

www.nice.org.uk – follow the links to eating disorders to see NICE guidelines (for the UK).

http://edr.org.uk – Eating Disorders Resources (EDR) is run by Lucy Serpell, a clinical and research psychologist based in London, UK. The website 'aims to be a clearing house for the latest eating disorder information and research, specifically relevant to the UK and Europe'.

www.nationaleatingdisorders.org – website of the National Eating Disorders Association – a 'non-profit organisation in the United States working to eliminate eating disorders' which has a clinical and advisory council comprising many of the published academic names in eating disorders in the US. The website includes an alphabetical list of information for sufferers and families.

www.nedic.ca – National Eating Disorder Information Centre – a Toronto based non-profit organisation which provides information and resources on eating disorders and weight preoccupation.

www.anred.com – Anorexia Nervosa and Related Eating Disorders, Inc (ANRED). A non-profit organisation in the US providing information about eating disorders including about 50 documents covering definition, statistics, warning signs, causes, treatment and self-help suggestions.

Appendix 3   Guidelines for Normal Healthy Eating

Eating a variety of foods at regular intervals is important for good health. This will provide the energy and range of nutrients you need. It *is* possible to maintain a normal body weight by choosing from the different food groups.

Choose foods from each of the following groups every day:

- bread and cereals
- fish, meat, eggs, pulses and nuts
- milk, cheese and yogurt
- fruit and vegetables
- fats and oils

Bread, cereals and potatoes

(include wholegrain varieties of rice, pasta and breakfast cereals)

Include starchy foods at each meal. Aim to eat a minimum of **6 portions** each day.
NB: tbs = rounded serving spoon

1 portion equals 1 slice bread from large loaf
1 small roll
½ small pitta bread
1 small chappati
4 tbs (3 oz/9 g) boiled rice or pasta
2 egg-size potatoes
1 oz/30 g breakfast cereal
1 Weetabix or Shredded Wheat
3 crispbread (e.g. Ryvita)
1 digestive biscuit or 2 plain biscuits

Meat, fish and alternatives

Include at least **2 portions** from this list every day

1 portion equals 2–3 slices (3 oz/90 g) lean cooked meat
4 oz/120 g cooked fish
1 oz/30 g hard cheese
1½ oz/40 g medium fat cheese, e.g. Edam, Brie, Camembert
3 tbs (4 oz/120 g) cottage cheese or fromage frais

1–2 eggs
3 tbs (4 oz/120 g) cooked pulses – peas, beans and lentils
4 tbs (5 oz/140 g) baked beans
Nuts (2 oz/60 g) peanuts, almonds, brazil

Combining pulses (peas, beans and lentils) with cereals such as bread, rice or pasta, e.g. beans on toast or bean casserole and rice, provides a good source of protein.

Milk and yogurt

Include **1 pint (600 ml) of milk** per day – some can be swapped for yogurt or cheese

1 cup ($\frac{1}{3}$ pint/200 ml) = 150 ml carton yogurt
= 1 portion cheese

Fruit and vegetables

Fruit – at least **3 helpings** a day

Include citrus fruit, e.g. oranges, grapefruit and their juices, as these are a good source of vitamin C. Other types of fresh, cooked, dried and tinned fruit in natural juice are also useful.

Vegetables – at least **2 helpings** a day

Include dark green varieties, e.g. cabbage or broccoli, as well as salad vegetables, e.g. tomatoes, carrots, celery and sweet peppers.
    Frozen vegetables are just as nutritious as fresh ones. Do not overcook vegetables as this reduces their vitamin content. Steam or cook in a small amount of boiling water for the shortest possible time.

Fats and oils

Some fat is needed for good health. At least **3 teaspoons** of butter, margarine or oil should be used daily.

Suitable snacks

Fresh fruit	Sandwiches	Toast
Plain biscuits	Fruit loaf	Dried fruit & nuts
Scones	Yogurt	

It is important to drink enough fluid each day: 6–8 cups of water, fruit juice, tea or milk, rather than coffee, cola or diet drinks.

Suggested meal plan

Breakfast: Fruit juice or fresh fruit
                 Breakfast cereal or porridge and/or bread
                 or toast with butter or margarine
                 Tea/coffee
Mid-morning: Drink of choice
                 Snack, if desired
Lunch: Bread, potatoes, rice or pasta
                 Meat, fish, cheese, eggs or beans
                 Cooked vegetables or salad
                 Fruit, yogurt or dessert
Mid-afternoon: Drink of choice
                 Fruit/snack, if desired
Evening meal: Potatoes, rice, pasta or bread
                 Meat, fish, cheese, eggs or beans
                 Vegetables or salad
                 Fruit, yogurt or dessert
Bedtime: Milky drink
                 Snack, if desired

Reproduced with the kind permission of the Nutrition and Dietetic Department of Northwick Park and St Mark's NHS Trust.

Appendix 4   The Effects of Strict Dieting and Starvation and of Giving Them Up

Strict dieting is one of the chief triggers (though not the main cause) of eating disorders. Being a habitual dieter is also itself what makes it so difficult for some people to give up an eating disorder. In order to understand this it is important to understand something about how our bodies store and use energy and what happens if we try to change our weight by dieting.

What happens when we lose weight

Our bodies are composed of a mixture of fat, a fat-free mass or lean tissue, and a glycogen store.

The fat or adipose tissue consists mainly of fat and a little water. The lean tissue is made up of protein, minerals and about 73 per cent water. Glycogen is a temporary energy store held mainly in the liver and muscle by a large amount of water. In fact about 60 per cent of our body is water. When we stop eating, our stomach empties, the glycogen stores get used up and the water normally bound to the glycogen is lost. This explains the very large weight losses people sometimes have when they first go on a diet. Weight loss slows down after a few days. If you lose between one or two pounds or up to one kilogram in weight per week, then what you lose will consist mainly of fat; but if you lose weight faster, you will lose valuable lean tissue as well. You will also lose lean tissue if you continue to lose weight beyond the lower weight limit that is normal for your height.

The effects of starvation

Starvation is a particularly unhelpful way to lose weight. It results in a dramatic decrease in metabolic rate, and it therefore quickly becomes impossible to keep your weight down on anything but the tiniest intake. What is more, people who starve themselves soon have psychological difficulties such as loss of concentration and feeling irritable, and are prone to bouts of uncontrolled overeating when they stop their diet.

Some people have suggested that the actual deprivation of a diet is partly to blame for the problems of people with eating disorders. Dieting itself, or at least starvation, appears to make some people more vulnerable to bingeing behaviour and other food-related psychological problems.

The psychological as well as physical effects of drastically reducing our food intake were graphically illustrated in a series of experiments conducted on 34 young healthy male conscientious objectors as an alternative to military duties during the Second World War. The aim of the experiments was to gather information about the effects of starvation under abnormal conditions such as those in prisoner of war camps. The men ate normally during the first three months of the experiment while their behaviour, eating patterns and personality were studied. They were then put on a strict diet where their normal intakes were cut by half for a period of three months. Afterwards, they went through a three-month period of 'rehabilitation' when they were reintroduced to eating normal amounts of food. What happened in the experiment suggests that the effects of severely reducing one's intake are far-reaching. Food became the main topic of conversation, reading and daydreams for almost all of the men. Men who had previously had no particular interest in food and cooking became fascinated by cookery and menus. About half-way through the semi-starvation period 13 of the men expressed an interest in taking up cooking after the experiment was over. A few of them even planned to become chefs! Many of the men found it impossible to keep to the diet. They ate secretly on impulse and felt guilty afterwards. Psychologically they began worrying and became prone to feeling depressed, they had difficulty in concentrating, and they began to withdraw from other people and become less sociable.

At the end of the semi-starvation period, the men's personalities reverted to normal. However, very many of them continued to have problems with eating. They were now allowed to eat whatever they liked but they continued to want more than they were given and to be preoccupied with food and how they would eat it. Some of them reported that their hunger pangs were even worse than before. Some had cravings for certain foods: mainly sweets, dairy products and nuts. Three weeks after the special diet had ended, at least four of the men found themselves unable to feel full up after eating and wanted to eat more, even though their stomachs were full to bursting; and many of them snacked between meals. Another four weeks later, 10 of the 15 men who were still in touch with the researchers had become so concerned about their weight that they had put themselves on a reducing diet. A few were continuing to eat 'prodigious' quantities of food and had gained weight. Three months after the end of the starvation phase, food was still a major concern of 15 out of 24 men. Moreover, the concern continued to be a problem for up to eight months after the 'diet' was over.

These effects of starvation are fairly powerful. Of course, because this was an experiment, the circumstances surrounding it were very abnormal. However, the calorie allowance was not dissimilar from that of many very strict diets; and the experiment is of particular interest because it described the experience of men, who are not usually greatly concerned about dieting and weight. These men experienced thoughts and feelings remarkably similar to those of people who feel deprived on a slimming diet, and their behaviour, particularly in the starvation phase, was not dissimilar to that of many anorexics – with the concern about food, hoarding food, playing with food on their plates. What is more, the experience of dieting itself engendered in these men a concern about weight and diet which they had not felt previously. In other words, very strict dieting, if not dieting in general, may itself cause dieters to develop a concern about weight and diet which they have not experienced before.

Weight loss and energy balance

The less you eat, the more weight you will lose. As you lose weight, your metabolic rate goes down along with your size, and you need less food to keep you going than you did at the beginning of the diet.

Metabolic rate is the rate at which a person uses energy. In general, the more you weigh, the higher your metabolic rate. The taller you are, the higher your metabolic rate, and the shorter you are, the lower it is. Fatter people have higher metabolic rates than thin people, but lean tissue uses more energy than fat. This means that if you continue to lose weight for a long time, the more lean tissue you lose, the lower your metabolic rate goes, and the less you need to eat.

So anorexics often find themselves surviving on a very small amount of food compared with other people. This makes it easy to believe that if you ate just a bit more, you would gain weight very fast and become fat. This belief may seem to be confirmed when, after eating very little for weeks on end, you suddenly eat a large amount of food. Your stomach fills up, the glycogen store is replaced, retaining with it the water which binds it. You may feel immediately bloated and fatter, and believe that you have gained several pounds in weight, after perhaps only one or two days of eating or even only one large meal. So, many anorexics hold beliefs such as 'I can gain two pounds in a night,' and are determined to continue to keep their weight down. Eating just a little more can make them feel quite out of control – as if the pounds are going to pile on immediately, and they will get fatter and fatter.

The mechanics of weight gain

In fact, in order to gain one pound in weight, an additional 3500 calories is required *over* what is needed to keep weight stable. This is equivalent to the calorific value of 10 Mars Bars or about 85 apples! Most people will agree, on hearing these figures, that they cannot possibly have gained more than one pound in fat in so short a time, however much they may have eaten.

Anorexics also fear that if they do start to regain their weight, they will gain very fast, they will lose control over their eating, and quickly become fat. In fact, anorexics do have a lower resting metabolic rate than do other eating disorder clients, but this does not result in needing fewer calories once their intake increases. As soon as an anorexic begins to eat normally, it is as if the body suddenly goes into overdrive and begins to use up the calories faster, to make up for all the nutrients it has been lacking for so long.

Research in the United States into the mechanics of weight gain in anorexics has shown that anorexics need more extra calories to gain weight than do people of normal weight. In fact, anorexics often do not gain weight, or may do so only very slowly, on diets of as much as 3000 calories. In many programmes, anorexics can gain only a pound or two, or a kilogram per week, on diets of upwards of 4000 or 5000 calories.

People with eating disorders often compare themselves with other people, watching what they eat and trying not to eat more than they do. However, it is pointless at this time for someone with anorexia nervosa to compare herself to a person of normal weight. Once you have started to gain weight, you will need a great deal more food than that other person. So, while you might find it helpful to use others as a model of how to eat normally, how not to worry about food and how to allow yourself the occasional luxury, you have to remember that you actually need to eat more than these other people and must not feel guilty for wanting to do so.

As you eat increasing amounts of food, you may feel bloated and uncomfortable, and consequently fat. In the space of a few hours, that first step towards trying to eat normally again can turn into the nightmare scenario you most feared. This bloated feeling is normal, and very common. A bloated stomach is a well-known symptom of anorexia nervosa, and as you gain weight, especially in the initial stages of refeeding, this may appear to be accumulating mainly in your stomach. One possible reason for it is that the stomach of an anorexic takes longer to empty after a meal than that of a normal-weight person, perhaps a part of the body's attempt to compensate for being starved. However, your stomach will empty, and any fat that you gain around your stomach will gradually redistribute itself as lean tissue around your body to replace what you have lost as you approach a normal weight. If you find this hard to believe, ask yourself how many people you have seen of normal weight or even overweight whose weight sits mainly on their stomachs and nowhere else!

Another worry you may have is that once you have begun to eat normally, you will be unable to stop eating and will lose control and become fat. This worry might be made worse by increasing hunger as you begin to allow yourself to eat increasing quantities of food. You fear that you will simply be unable to stop eating and will continue to overeat and get fat. In fact, as your weight approaches normal and your body is once again getting the nutrients it needs, this urge to eat will subside.

Appendix 5   Medical and Physical Problems Caused by the Symptoms of Eating Disorders

Binge eating

The stomach can become bloated or distended, sometimes even to the extent of being very painful. In very rare extreme cases, the stomach wall can become so stretched that it is damaged or even tears. This is a very serious situation needing urgent medical attention.

Starvation

If energy intake is inadequate, the body has to use its own stores, especially of protein, such as muscle or blood protein, to supply the shortfall. This leads to muscle wastage and depletion of blood proteins. All the muscles of the body can be weakened, including the heart, lungs and limb muscles.

The body lowers its metabolic rate to conserve energy. This causes a drop in body temperature, poor circulation, feelings of tiredness, depression, and poor concentration.

Dizziness and fainting
Extreme undereating can lead to decreased heart rate and blood pressure, resulting in dizziness and fainting.

Feeling cold
Anorexics often have a lowered body temperature and cannot tolerate the cold, and tend to stay wrapped up in extra layers of clothing even in the summer.

Poor resistance to infection
Protein is needed to produce antibodies to fight infection. As a result of eating low amounts of protein and the body having to break down protein to compensate for low energy intake, sufferers may become more prone to disease.

Skin and hair changes
Lower levels of body protein slow skin and hair renewal. Hair becomes brittle and is lost more quickly, and both hair and skin become thinner.

Constipation

Eating very little also slows down the activity of the gut, causing constipation. This can worsen the feeling of having a distended stomach, and make the person feel fat, even though she may in fact be emaciated.

Amenorrhoea

Strict dieting can also affect menstruation. Our bodies are composed of a mixture of fat, a fat-free mass or lean tissue, and a glycogen store. It is normal and indeed necessary for everyone to have a certain amount of fat in their bodies. A woman needs to have at least 22 per cent of her body weight as fat in order to have regular periods. Many women with anorexia nervosa do not have periods for this reason. However, having regular periods also relies on body hormones. Body hormones can be affected by dieting and weight loss, so even when she has enough body fat, a woman's periods may become irregular or stop. Sleep patterns also change, body hair is lost, and the problems are compounded as appetite actually goes down.

Infertility

There is an association between eating disorder and infertility. This is the case both for anorexics, many of whom do not menstruate, and for bulimics. The exact nature of the link is not yet known. It is possible that the chief culprits are dieting and weight loss, and for some people, therefore, the effects may be reversible.

Bone density problems

Anorexia nervosa sufferers often have a decreased bone density owing to lack of calcium in their diet. This can result in osteoporosis or brittle bones, and sufferers are often more prone than the average person to breaking bones in later life. These problems are also associated with low levels of oestrogen, which is why they affect post-menopausal women.

Vomiting

Vomiting is in fact an ineffective way of emptying the stomach. It makes the sufferer feel hungry again as it removes some but not all of the food eaten. At the same time, the knowledge that she can vomit often gives the sufferer permission to eat more both before and after vomiting. This serves only to keep the binge cycle going and leads ultimately to increased weight gain. Also, vomiting frequently over a long period of time can cause serious physical damage.

Dental problems

Vomit contains hydrochloric acid, which is produced by the stomach to digest food, and which normally does not travel to the mouth. The presence of vomit and therefore acid in the mouth gradually damages the teeth by eroding away tooth enamel. Once sufferers stop vomiting, the teeth are no longer damaged, but tooth enamel cannot be replaced.

Swollen parotid glands

Some of the saliva-producing glands around the face gradually swell in people who induce vomiting. One of these glands is the parotid gland. When this gland is swollen, it gives the face a rounder appearance, and many people see themselves as having a fat face, which of course simply increases their worry about looking fat and being overweight.

Sore throat

Most people who induce vomiting have to force themselves to do so, sometimes by putting a finger or an object down the back of their throat. Some complain of a sore throat, and being hoarse. In addition, some people who habitually use a finger or a hand to induce vomiting suffer damage to the skin as a result, often a tell-tale sign of bulimia.

Heartburn

Frequent vomiting can also lead to problems with reflux (partly digested food coming back up from the stomach and causing heartburn).

Electrolyte and fluid imbalance

Repeated vomiting upsets the body's fluid balance and depletes the body of electrolytes such as potassium and sodium. Low potassium can cause muscular cramps and weakness, kidney damage, heart arrhythmias and even sudden cardiac arrest. As soon as vomiting is stopped, however, these irregularities return to normal.

Laxatives

Taking large quantities of laxatives produces symptoms similar to vomiting. However, at the same time it is an ineffective way of controlling weight. Laxatives work on the lower part of the gut, whereas most of the food has already been absorbed higher up in the stomach and intestines. The laxatives cause diarrhoea, which produces a large loss of water. This makes the sufferer feel thinner, but only because she has become temporarily dehydrated. As soon as she eats or drinks again, the loss is made up. In fact the body stores water in an attempt to return itself to normal, with the result that someone who abuses laxatives often feels bloated. This leads her back into taking laxatives again, so that she becomes trapped in a vicious circle. This can be made worse by the fact that people who take laxatives come to need larger numbers to have the same effect, and can end up taking large doses. Laxative abuse can also have nasty long-term effects. The muscles in the colon can become less effective and the sufferer may as a result occasionally lose control altogether and be prone to 'accidents'.

Diuretics

Some women take diuretics, particularly in the time prior to menstruation, in an attempt to overcome the feeling of bloating due to water retention. However, taking diuretics results in dehydration. This can lead to a lack of sodium and potassium, which creates an electrolyte imbalance. Sufferers can experience muscle weakness, numbness and, at worst, paralysis.

The combined effects of purging by means of vomiting, taking laxatives or taking diuretics also cause more damage through the psychological effect on the sufferer. The sufferer feels that she has rid herself of unwanted calories, but unfortunately this is untrue, as a large amount of the loss is of fluid. The person feels thinner, although many of the calories are still absorbed, and feels permitted to eat more or binge again as a result. To stop taking either diuretics or laxatives can result in fluid retention, and it is tempting to go back to taking them again.

Appendix 6   Controlling What You Eat

Altering your surroundings to make food less important

If you are someone who eats when you see food, when you see other people eating, or even because you are thinking about food, some of the following suggestions might help you to plan for change:

1. Eat only in one place
If you are someone who eats in several rooms in the house, or wanders around idly munching, it may be helpful to you to decide to eat in one place only, preferably sitting down, at a table.

2. Do nothing else while eating
Perhaps you eat while watching the TV or reading a book. The more able you are to make eating a 'pure' experience, the less inclined you will be to eat just out of habit, because that is usually what you do when the TV is on, while you are reading, or because you happen to see food lying around. Some people have suggested that you are very rigid about this, eating always in the same place. This means, for example, that if you are in the lounge watching the TV and you fancy a piece of cheese you have to go to the kitchen, eat, and return to the TV when you have finished. If you want another piece, you have to go back, cut another piece, eat it there and return to the TV again; the idea is not to bring the whole cheese into the TV room with you.

3. Eat only with a knife and fork
Another technique is to eat everything with a knife and fork, on a plate; this goes for anything, apples, even chocolate. The reasoning behind this is that you therefore restrict the surroundings in which you eat, which may as a consequence help you to eat less, particularly of snack food.

4. Make eating extra snacks and helpings more difficult
Do you find it hard to resist eating when you see food? For example, you may eat because other people are eating, or polish off leftovers ('It's not worth leaving that little bit').

- Try keeping snack foods in opaque containers, out of impulse range in a cupboard.
- Get the family to prepare and fetch their own snacks.
- Have low-calorie snacks available to eat while other people are nibbling.

- Don't leave the serving dishes on the table. Make it more difficult to go for 'seconds'.
- Practise throwing away leftover food. This is something that many of us find very difficult; but there is no point in leaving it sitting in the fridge to tempt you if you are going to spend half an hour soul searching and end up eating it anyway. It is quite reasonable to exercise control by making leftover food unavailable in the waste-bin. Perhaps at a later stage in your programme you will be better able to resist food that is on show, but if you cannot at first, there is no point in struggling. Throwing away leftover food is no more wasteful than eating it yourself if you have no need for it, in which case, it can do a great deal of harm to you and your self-esteem and no good whatsoever to the starving masses.

5. Shop with a list

Keep problem/high-fat, high-sugar food out of the house if possible or try to avoid situations where you might buy it out of habit. An obvious example is to shop with a list, so as to avoid buying calorific treats or special offers at the supermarket check-out. You might make it a target not to buy biscuits or snack foods 'for the children' or 'for when my friends come'. (Will there really be any left for the children? The visitors might get some, but will you have eaten twice as much before they arrive?) If you cannot walk past the patisserie or the confectioner's without going in, try walking round the shops or home from work in a different direction.

6. Avoid extreme hunger or boredom

Being hungry or bored or tired can only make you more vulnerable to 'impulse' eating, if the food is there.

Thoughts about food

If you are trying to change an eating habit, you are even more likely than usual to find yourself thinking about food. Try to decide whether you really are hungry or not. This is not easy, but you may perhaps have just eaten; you may be particularly vulnerable to thinking about food when bored or miserable or perhaps just seeing and thinking about food makes you want it. If you have decided that you have no reason for physical hunger, you might try distracting yourself from the thought of food by doing something else, perhaps taking some exercise.

Is the way you eat a problem?

If you eat very fast, sometimes perhaps without realising how much you have eaten, it may help to take some practical steps to alter the way you eat.

Try eating more slowly. You could practise chewing your food more slowly, keeping the food in your mouth for longer intervals before swallowing. In order to slow the pace of eating even further, you might try pausing between mouthfuls, putting your knife and fork down while you swallow, and picking them up again when your mouth is empty. You might practise making the intervals between mouthfuls longer by counting to a higher number each time.

Tackle problems gradually

Changing old habits takes time. Before you can say that a habit has changed, you will have had several false starts; you will simply have forgotten your intentions on some occasions; you will have tried to do things differently only to be foiled by countless unexpected events beyond your control, or by you yourself. It is better to succeed with changing one small habit than to fail at an attempt to change everything at once.

Keep a record of your progress, every day if possible

If putting pen to paper seems too much like hard work, do bear in mind that many of us, when we are trying to change old habits, remember only our failures and forget the times when things went well. Writing things down will underline your successes and help you to work out what to do when things went wrong.

Appendix 7 Giving Up Vomiting as a Way to Control Your Weight or Deal with Stress

What is wrong with vomiting to control your weight?

You cannot completely stop food from being absorbed

Vomiting is a very ineffective way of emptying the stomach. It removes only some of the food eaten, together with a great deal of water. Some of the food will still be absorbed, and although your stomach may feel emptier, you may soon feel hungry again.

Vomiting strengthens the vicious cycle of an eating disorder

The habit of vomiting locks people into their cycle of eating disorder. There are three reasons for this:

1 Knowing that you can vomit after meals gives you the false reassurance that you can undo the effects of eating. If you binge, you will be less inclined to stop. If you are underweight and need to gain weight, vomiting when you eat can remove the anxiety about gaining weight but prevents you from learning to eat without fear.
2 If you vomit, you empty your stomach and will soon feel hungry again. You may crave food and if you already have a binge habit, this will lead you into further bingeing.
3 Once vomiting after food has become a habit, people who use it begin to believe that if they do not vomit they will gain weight. They learn to link the feeling of emptiness after vomiting with reassurance and relief, and they grow to feel more and more uncomfortable about the opposite feeling, that of having a full stomach. They become increasingly dependent on being able to vomit. They may even plan their routine around making sure that they will have the opportunity to vomit.

Knowing that they intend to vomit, many binge eaters decide that in order to make vomiting worthwhile they may as well eat a large amount of food. Some feel that they can vomit only after they have eaten a large amount of food and have a full stomach.

So, the decision to vomit sometimes creates a feeling of inevitability and some sufferers will go ahead and fill up on a range of foods that they would normally not allow themselves to eat. This serves only to keep the binge–vomit cycle going and can lead ultimately to increased weight gain.

The dangers of vomiting

Besides its ineffectiveness as a means of weight control, vomiting is physically dangerous. Repeated vomiting upsets the body's fluid balance and depletes the body of important minerals such as potassium and sodium. Low potassium can cause muscular cramps and weakness, kidney damage, heart arrhythmias and even, in severe cases, sudden cardiac arrest. In addition, vomit contains hydrochloric acid, which is produced by the stomach to digest food. The presence of this acid in the mouth gradually damages the teeth by eroding away tooth enamel. This enamel cannot be replaced, although if you stop vomiting, the teeth are no longer damaged.

Vomiting also causes some of the saliva-producing glands around the face to swell. One of these glands is the parotid gland. When this gland is swollen, it gives the face a rounder appearance, and many people see themselves as having a fat face, which only further convinces them that they are fat and need to lose weight. The belief that they are fat only serves to keep them stuck in their pattern of eating disorder.

Some ways to control vomiting

The habit of vomiting to control weight can be extremely powerful and the first task of the person with an eating disorder is to decide that they really want to stop. For some people who binge eat, the vomiting stops or becomes less frequent automatically during treatment as the number of binges becomes less. In fact, in some treatment programmes aimed at treating bulimia nervosa, no specific advice is given with regard to vomiting as in many cases once people have cut down their bingeing the vomiting disappears of its own accord.

However, other people need to take more definite steps to cut down the vomiting. What follows are some ideas that people have found useful.

1   *Keeping a record.* First, you should keep a record, together with any bingeing, of instances of vomiting: the date and time; the place; the situation (who with, what were you doing at the time or what had you been doing just before?); how you were feeling; what you were thinking about just beforehand; what you had eaten/drunk just before vomiting.
2   *Delaying tactics.* The urge to vomit is usually strongest soon after a meal. One very important strategy is to concentrate on lengthening the time between eating and vomiting. So, if you tend to vomit immediately after eating, try giving yourself increasing periods of time between eating and vomiting. Ideally, you should try to create a time delay of at least an hour after eating. You can tell yourself: 'I can vomit, but I have to wait for an hour.' If this is impossible, you can start with five minutes, moving quickly to ten minutes, then fifteen, and so on. In the meantime, your task is to relax as far as possible and give yourself time to become used to the feeling of the food inside you.
3   *Distraction.* The aim is to break the association of vomiting with eating or with a feeling of fullness, and in order to do this you need to become used to the physical feeling of being full and give yourself time to experience the emotions that go with it. If at first, this makes you feel very anxious, one strategy is to distract yourself from the feelings. You can take yourself out of the situation altogether. Go to a place where

it is impossible to be sick, find a job or activity to do, such as talking to a friend, going for a walk, sending an email, even clearing out a cupboard or drawer. If you cannot remove yourself physically, an alternative strategy is to use the time to work on some complicated idea in your head – working on a mathematical puzzle, visualising a place you have been to, concentrating on imagining every detail.

4   *Relaxation*. Another way of coping with this time is to find a way to relax and allow the difficult feelings to wash over you. You might try using a physical relaxation technique, either lying down or sitting somewhere comfortably. Ask your therapist for specific advice about this.

5   *Going with the feelings*. Another, perhaps more effective strategy in the long run, is to allow yourself to experience the often difficult feelings you have immediately before vomiting. Some people say that they do not feel anything: there is simply an urge to vomit. But if they stop and listen to what is going though their heads, many people are able to focus more clearly on the powerful, sometimes painful, ideas and feelings that can trigger their behaviour again and again.

Some people are able to recognise thoughts about being fat and the fear of going out of control if they allow themselves to eat. Try writing these down. Other people notice that the vomiting has become a way to get relief from painful feelings. These can be, for example: intense anger, with someone else or with oneself; anxiety or excitement (not necessarily always negative); feelings of self-hatred or shame, which are very common in people who have an eating disorder. You may recognise other feelings. It is important to recognise that however scary and intense the feelings are, they are only feelings. They are not facts. Vomiting may seem to distract you or get them out of your system temporarily, but talking about them and looking for ways to deal with them together with your therapist can help to change them permanently.

Appendix 8   Learning to be Assertive about What You Eat: A Bill of Rights

Sometimes the biggest problem for a person with an eating disorder can be learning to follow their own food desires. This is where it helps to be assertive. Being assertive means to ask for what you want in a straightforward way, without being either aggressive or manipulative.

Some of us (and not only dieters) have a great deal of difficulty in telling other people what we want from them or simply in saying 'No'.

We all have basic rights with regard to ourselves and other people. Below are some examples of these rights. You may be able to add others to the list.

1   I have the right to state my own food needs.
    So often, other people tell us when we are supposed to be hungry, or when we are supposed to be full up: 'You haven't eaten all day, have another helping'; 'You've been eating all afternoon, haven't you had enough?'
2   I have the right to decide how much I want to eat and when, regardless of any social or work situation I may find myself in.
    Come on, don't be a spoil sport. We are all here to enjoy ourselves. Have a cream cake/another drink. You do not have to eat to make other people feel comfortable.
3   I have the right to express how I feel.
    If you feel hungry, it is OK to say so. If you are not hungry, it is your right to say so. 'I'm not hungry, I won't have any thank you.'
4   I have the right to say 'yes' or 'no' for myself.
    Once people know that you have a problem around food, they can develop an annoying habit of telling you what you should be eating. For example: 'It's not good for you to cut out sweet things altogether. You'd better have some of these to give you some energy'; or, 'You won't want any cake, will you?' It is up to you to choose what is appropriate for you to eat, and if you want to eat something that is not allowed on your diet, you have the right to choose to eat it.
5   I have the right to make mistakes.
    It is only human to make a mistake. You do not have to feel guilty every time you forget your plan and eat more or less than you intended to.
6   I have the right to ask for what I want.
    Sometimes this may conflict with what other people want or expect. If you are with others, it is often easiest to go along with what they want; but at home, you have the right to say what you want on the menu; in a restaurant you do not have to eat the same as everyone else; and in someone else's house you have the right to state a preference: 'No pudding for me thank you, but I'd love a peach from the fruit bowl.'
7   I have the right to decline responsibility for satisfying other people's needs.
    It is often considered a slight to another person not to eat the food he or she has provided. However, it is not necessary to put the feelings of another person before one's own good health. You can show your appreciation for another person in words, without necessarily eating every scrap of the food he or she has provided: 'It looks lovely, but I won't/can't eat another thing thank you.'

8 I have the right to deal with others without being dependent on them for approval. *We are often afraid to ask for what we want or to stand up for our rights for fear of an other person's disapproval. This extends sometimes even beyond our close family and friends to our dealings with people we do not know. We hesitate to leave food on our plate in the restaurant or to send back the chips that we did not order for fear of upsetting the waiter. The more often you practise assertion skills, the easier it gets to ask for what you want without fear of the disapproval of other people, and the more you gain in confidence in your self.*

Adapted from Anne Dickson, *A Woman in Your Own Right: Assertiveness and You*, London: Quartet Books, 1982, pp. 29–36, with the kind permission of the publisher.

References

Agras, W.S. (1993) Short-term psychological treatments for binge eating. In C.G. Fairburn and T. Wilson (eds), *Binge Eating: Nature, Assessment and Treatment*. New York and London: Guilford Press. pp. 270–286.

American Psychiatric Association (1980) *Diagnostic and Statistical Manual of Mental Disorders* (3rd edn) (*DSM-III*). Washington, DC: American Psychiatric Association.

American Psychiatric Association (1987) *Diagnostic and Statistical Manual of Mental Disorders* (3rd edn, revised) (*DSM-III-R*). Washington, DC: American Psychiatric Association.

American Psychiatric Association (1994) *Diagnostic and Statistical Manual of Mental Disorders* (4th edn) (*DSM-IV*). Washington, DC: American Psychiatric Association.

Andres, R., Muller, D.C. and Sorkin, J.D. (1993) Long-term effects of change in body weight on all-cause mortality: a review. *Annals of Internal Medicine*, 119(7 pt 2): 737–743.

Antelman, S.M., Roland, N.E. and Fisher, A.E. (1976) Stimulation-bound ingestive behavior: a view from the tail. *Physiology and Behavior*, 17: 743–748.

Beck, A.T. (1967) *Depression: Clinical, Experimental and Theoretical Aspects*. New York: Harper and Row.

Beck, A.T. (1972) *Depression: Causes and Treatment*. Philadelphia: University of Pennsylvania Press.

Beck, A.T., Freeman, A. and Associates (1990) *Cognitive Therapy of Personality Disorders*. New York: Guilford Press.

Beck, A.T., Rush, A.J., Shaw, B.F. and Emery, G. (1976) *Cognitive Therapy of Depression*. Chichester and New York: John Wiley and Sons.

Beck, A.T., Weissman, A., Lester, D. and Trexler, L. (1974) The measurement of pessimism: the Hopelessness Scale. *Journal of Consulting and Clinical Psychology*, 42: 861–865.

Beck, J.S. (1995) *Cognitive Therapy: Basics and Beyond*. New York: Guilford Press.

Bennett-Levy, J., Butler, G., Fennell, M., Hackman, A., Mueller, M. and Westbrook, D. (2004) *Oxford Guide to Behavioural Experiments in Cognitive Therapy*. Oxford: Oxford University Press.

Bernstein, E.M. and Putnam, F.W. (1986) Development, reliability, and validity of a dissociation scale. *Journal of Nervous and Mental Diseases*, 174(12): 727–735.

Black, R.M., Davis, C. and Kennedy, S.H. (1993) Alterations in metabolism and energy expenditure in eating disorders. In A.S. Kaplan and P.E. Garfinkel (eds), *Medical Issues and the Eating Disorders: The Interface*. New York: Brunner/Mazel. pp. 144–164.

Blackburn, G.L., Wilson, G.T., Kanders, B.S., Stein, L.J., Lavin, P.T., Adler, J. and Brownell, K.D. (1989) Weight cycling: the experience of human dieters. *American Journal of Clinical Nutrition*, 49: 1105–1109.

Blouin, J.H., Carter, J., Blouin, A.G., Tener, L., Schnare-Hayes, K., Zuro, C., Barlow, J. and Perez, E. (1994) Prognostic indicators in bulimia nervosa treated with cognitive-behavioral group therapy. *International Journal of Eating Disorders*, 15(2): 113–123.

Bo-Linn, G.W., Santa Ana, C.A., Morawski, S.G. and Fordtran, J.H. (1983) Purging and calorie absorption in bulimic patients and normal women. *Annals of Internal Medicine*, 99(1): 14–17.

Brewerton, T.D., Dansky, B.S., Kilpatrick, D.G. and O'Neill, P. (2000) Which comes first in the pathogenesis of bulimia nervosa: dieting or bingeing? *International Journal of Eating Disorders*, 28(3): 259–264.

Brownell, K.D., Nelson Steen, S. and Wilmore, J.H. (1987) Weight regulation practices in athletes: analysis of metabolic and health effects. *Medicine and Science in Sports and Exercise*, 19(6): 546–556.

Bruch, H. (1974) *Eating Disorders: Obesity, Anorexia Nervosa and the Person Within*. London: Routledge and Kegan Paul.

Bulik, C.M., Sullivan, P.F. and Kendler, K.S. (2002) Medical and psychiatric morbidity in obese women with and without binge eating. *International Journal of Eating Disorders*, 32(1): 72–78.

Bulik, C.M., Beidel, D.C., Duchmann, E., Weltzin, T.E. and Kaye, W.H. (1992) Comparative psychopathology of women with bulimia nervosa and obsessive compulsive disorder. *Comprehensive Psychiatry*, 33(4): 262–268.

Burns, D. (1980) *Feeling Good: The New Mood Therapy*. New York: Signet Books.

Carlat, D.J. and Camargo, C.A. (1991) Review of bulimia nervosa in males. *American Journal of Psychiatry*, 148: 831–843.

Cash, T.F. (1997) *The Body Image Workbook: An 8-Step Program for Learning To Like Your Looks*. Oakland, CA: New Harbinger Publications.

Cash, T.F. (2002) The situational inventory of body-image dysphoria: psychometric evidence and development of a short form. *International Journal of Eating Disorders*, 32(3): 362–366.

Cash, T.F. and Fleming, E.C. (2002) The impact of body image experience: development of the Body Image Quality of Life Inventory. *International Journal of Eating Disorders*, 31(4): 455–460.

Channon, S., De Silva, P., Hemsley, D. and Perkins, R. (1989) A controlled trial of cognitive-behavioural and behavioural treatment of anorexia nervosa. *Behaviour Research and Therapy*, 27(5): 529–535.

Chen, E., Touyz, S.W., Beumont, P.J.V., Fairburn, C.G., Griffiths, R., Butow, P., Russell, J., Schotte, D., Gertler, R. and Basten, C. (2003) Comparison of group and individual cognitive behavioural therapy for patients with bulimia nervosa. *International Journal of Eating Disorders*, 33(3): 241–254.

Christenson, L. (1993) Effects of eating behavior on mood: a review of the literature. *International Journal of Eating Disorders*, 14(2): 171–183.

Ciliska, D. (1998) Evaluation of two nondieting interventions for obese women. *Western Journal of Nursing Research*, 20(1): 119–135.

Colton, P., Woodside, D.B. and Kaplan, A.S. (1999) Laxative withdrawal in eating disorders: treatment protocol and 3 to 20 month follow-up. *International Journal of Eating Disorders*, 25: 311–317.

Connors, M.E. and Morse, W. (1993) Sexual abuse and eating disorders: a review. *International Journal of Eating Disorders*, 13(1): 1–11.

Cooper, M.J. and Fairburn, C.G. (1992) Thoughts about eating, weight and shape in anorexia nervosa and bulimia nervosa. *Behaviour Research and Therapy*, 30(5): 501–511.

Cooper, M.J. and Hunt, J. (1998) Core beliefs and underlying assumptions in bulimia nervosa and depression. *Behaviour Research and Therapy*, 36(9): 895–898.

Cooper, M.J., Todd, G. and Wells, A. (2000) *Bulimia Nervosa: A Cognitive Therapy Programme for Clients*. London: Jessica Kinglsey.

Cooper, M.J., Todd, G. and Wells, A. (2002) Content, origins, and consequences of dysfunctional beliefs in anorexia nervosa and bulimia nervosa. In R. Leahy and E.T. Dowd (eds), *Clinical Advances in Cognitive Psychotherapy: Theory and Application*. New York: Springer. pp. 399–417.

Cooper, M.J., Wells, A. and Todd, G. (2004) A cognitive model of bulimia nervosa. *British Journal of Clinical Psychology*, 43: 1–16.

Cooper, M.J., Cohen-Tovee, E., Todd, G., Wells, A. and Tovee, M. (1997) The Eating Disorder Belief Questionnaire: preliminary development. *Behaviour Research and Therapy*, 35(4): 381–388.

Cooper, P.J. and Fairburn, C.G. (1993) Confusion over the core psychopathology of bulimia nervosa. *International Journal of Eating Disorders*, 13(4): 385–389.

Cooper, P.J., Coker, S. and Fleming, C. (1996) An evaluation of the efficacy of supervised cognitive behavioural self-help for bulimia nervosa. *Journal of Psychosomatic Research*, 40(3): 281–287.

Cooper, P.J., Taylor, M.J., Cooper, Z. and Fairburn, C.G. (1987) The development and validation of the Body Shape Questionnaire. *International Journal of Eating Disorders*, 6: 485–494.

Cooper, Z., Cooper, P.J. and Fairburn, C.G. (1989) The validity of the eating disorder examination and its subscales. *British Journal of Psychiatry*, 154: 807–812.

Craighead, L.W. and Agras, W.S. (1991) Mechanisms of action in cognitive-behavioural and pharmacological interventions for obesity and bulimia nervosa. *Journal of Consulting and Clinical Psychology*, 59(1): 115–125.

Crisp, A.H. (1980) *Let Me Be*. New York: Academic Press.

Crisp, A.H. and McLelland, L. (1996) *Anorexia Nervosa: Guidelines for Assessment and Treatment in Primary and Secondary Care* (2nd edn). Hove: Psychology Press.

Crowther, J.H. and Sherwood, N. (1997) Assessment. In D.M. Garner and P.E. Garfinkel (eds), *Handbook of Psychotherapy for Eating Disorders* (2nd edn). New York and London: Guilford Press. pp. 34–49.

Da Costa, M. and Halmi, K.A. (1992) Classifications of anorexia nervosa: question of subtypes. *International Journal of Eating Disorders*, 11(4): 305–313.

Dare, C. and Crowther, C. (1995) Psychodynamic models of eating disorder. In G. Szmukler, C. Dare and J. Treasure (eds), *Handbook of Eating Disorders: Theory, Treatment and Research*. Chichester and New York: John Wiley and Sons.

Dare, C. and Eisler, I. (1997) Family therapy for anorexia nervosa. In D.M. Garner and P.E. Garfinkel (eds), *Handbook of Treatment for Eating Disorders* (2nd edn). New York and London: Guilford Press. pp. 307–324.

Davis, M., McKay, M. and Robbins Eshelman, E. (1995) *The Relaxation and Stress Reduction Workbook* (4th edn). Oakland, CA: New Harbinger Publications.

Davis, R., Olmsted, M., Rockert, W., Marqes, T. and Dolhanty, J. (1997) Group psycho-education for bulimia nervosa with and without additional psychotherapy process sessions. *International Journal of Eating Disorders*, 22: 25–34.

De Zwaan, M., Aslam, Z. and Mitchell, J. (2002) Research on energy expenditure in individuals with eating disorders: a review. *International Journal of Eating Disorders*, 31(4): 361–369.

Devlin, M.J., Goldfein, J.A. and Dobrow, I. (2003) What is this thing called BED? Current status of binge eating disorder nosology. *International Journal of Eating Disorders*, 34: S2–S18.

Dickson, A. (1982) *A Woman in Your Own Right: Assertiveness and You*. London: Quartet Books.

Eisler, I., Dare, C., Hodes, M., Russell, G.F.M., Dodge, E. and Le Grange, D. (2000) Family therapy for adolescent anorexia nervosa: the results of a controlled comparison of two family interventions. *Journal of Child Psychology and Psychiatry*, 41: 727–736.

Eisler, I., Dare, C., Russell, G.F.M., Szmukler, G.I., Le Grange, D. and Dodge, E. (1997) Family and individual therapy in anorexia nervosa: a five year follow-up. *Archives of General Psychiatry*, 54: 1025–1030.

Fairburn, C.G. (1981) A cognitive behavioral approach to the management of bulimia. *Psychological Medicine*, 11: 707–711.

Fairburn, C.G. and Beglin, S. (1990) Studies of the epidemiology of bulimia nervosa. *American Journal of Psychiatry*, 147: 401–408.

Fairburn, C.G. and Walsh, B.T. (2002) Atypical eating disorders (eating disorder not otherwise specified). In C.G. Fairburn and K.D. Brownell (eds), *Eating Disorders and Obesity: A Comprehensive Handbook* (3rd edn). New York and London: Guilford Press. pp. 171–177.

Fairburn, C.G., Hay, P. and Welch, S. (1993) Binge eating and bulimia nervosa: distribution and determinants. In C.G. Fairburn and G.T. Wilson (eds), *Binge Eating: Nature, Assessment and Treatment*. New York and London: Guilford Press. pp. 123–143.

Fairburn, C.G., Marcus, M.D. and Wilson, G.T. (1993) Cognitive-behavioral therapy for binge eating and bulimia nervosa: a comprehensive treatment manual. In C.G. Fairburn and G.T. Wilson (eds), *Binge Eating: Nature, Assessment and Treatment*. New York and London: Guilford Press. pp. 361–404.

Fairburn, C.G., Cooper, Z., Doll, H. and Welch, S. (1999) Risk factors for anorexia nervosa: three integrated case-control comparisons. *Archives of General Psychiatry*, 56(5): 468–476.

Fairburn, C.G., Peveler, R.C., Jones, R., Hope, R.A. and Doll, H.A. (1993) Predictors of 12-month outcome in bulimia nervosa and the influence of attitudes to shape and weight. *Journal of Consulting and Clinical Psychology*, 61(4): 696–698.

Fairburn, C.G., Norman, P.A., Welch, S., O'Connor, M.E., Doll, H. and Peveler, R.C. (1995) A prospective study of outcome in bulimia nervosa and the long-term effects of three psychological treatments. *Archives of General Psychiatry*, 52: 304–312.

Fallon, P. and Wonderlich, S.A. (1997) Sexual abuse and other forms of trauma. In D.M. Garner and P.E. Garfinkel (eds), *Handbook of Psychotherapy for Eating Disorders* (2nd edn). New York and London: Guilford Press. pp. 394–414.

Favaro, A. and Santonastaso, P. (1996) Purging behaviors, suicide attempts, and psychiatric symptoms in 398 eating disordered subjects. *International Journal of Eating Disorders*, 20(1): 99–103.

Fennell, M. (1989) Depression. In K. Hawton, P.M. Salkovskis, J. Kirk and D.M. Clark (eds), *Cognitive Behaviour Therapy for Psychiatric Problems: A Practical Guide*. Oxford: Oxford Medical Publications. pp. 169–234.

Fichter, M.M. and Quadflieg, N. (1999) Six-year course and outcome of anorexia nervosa. *International Journal of Eating Disorders*, 26(4): 359–385.

Fitzgibbon, M.L. and Blackman, L.R. (2004) Binge eating disorder and bulimia nervosa: differences in the quality and quantity of binge eating episodes. *International Journal of Eating Disorders*, 27: 238–243.

Folsom, V., Krahn, D., Nairn, K., Gold, L., Demitrack, M.A. and Silk, K.R. (1993) The impact of sexual and physical abuse on eating disordered and psychiatric symptoms: a comparison of eating disordered and psychiatric inpatients. *International Journal of Eating Disorders*, 13(3): 249–257.

Fonesca, H., Ireland, M. and Resnick, M.D. (2002) Familial correlates of extreme weight control behaviours among adolescents. *International Journal of Eating Disorders*, 32(4): 441–448.

Freeman, C.P. (1995) Cognitive therapy. In G. Szmukler, C. Dare and J. Treasure (eds), *Handbook of Eating Disorders: Theory, Treatment and Research*. Chichester and New York: John Wiley and Sons. pp. 309–331.

Freeman, C.P. (1997) Paper given at Conference on Setting up Local Services for People with Eating Disorders, London.

Freeman, C.P. and Gard, M.C.E. (1994) Eating disorders in a young homeless population. Unpublished manuscript cited in Gard and Freeman (1996).

Gard, M.C.E. and Freeman, C.P. (1996) The dismantling of a myth: a review of eating disorders and socioeconomic status. *International Journal of Eating Disorders*, 20(1): 1–12.

Garfinkel, P.E., Lin, E., Goering, P., Spegg, D., Goldbloom, D., Kennedy, S., Kaplan, A.S. and Woodside, D.B. (1996) Should amenorrhoea be necessary for the diagnosis of anorexia nervosa? *British Journal of Psychiatry*, 168: 500–506.

Garner, D.M. (1986) Cognitive therapy for anorexia nervosa. In K.D. Brownell and J.P. Foreyt (eds), *Handbook of Eating Disorders*. New York: Basic Books. pp. 301–327.

Garner, D.M. (1991) *Eating Disorders Inventory-2*. Odessa, FL: Psychological Assessment Resources.

Garner, D.M. (1997) Psychoeducational principles in treatment. In D.M. Garner and P.E. Garfinkel (eds), *Handbook of Psychotherapy for Eating Disorders* (2nd edn). New York and London: Guilford Press. pp. 145–177.

Garner, D.M. and Bemis, K. (1982) A cognitive-behavioral approach to anorexia nervosa. *Cognitive Therapy and Research*, 6: 123–150.

Garner, D.M. and Bemis, K. (1986) Cognitive therapy for anorexia nervosa. In D.M. Garner and P.E. Garfinkel (eds), *Handbook of Psychotherapy for Anorexia Nervosa and Bulimia*. New York: Guilford Press. pp. 107–146.

Garner, D.M. and Garfinkel, P.E. (1979) The Eating Attitudes Test: an index of the symptoms of anorexia nervosa. *Psychological Medicine*, 9: 273–279.

Garner, D.M., Garner, M.V. and Rosen, L.W. (1993) Anorexia nervosa 'Restrictors' who purge: implications for subtyping anorexia nervosa. *International Journal of Eating Disorders*, 13(2): 171–185.

Garner, D.M., Olmstead, M.P. and Polivy, J. (1983) Development and validation of a multi-dimensional eating disorder inventory for anorexia nervosa and bulimia. *International Journal of Eating Disorders*, 2(2): 15–34.

Garner, D.M., Garfinkel, P.E., Schwartz, D. and Thompson, M. (1980) Cultural expectations of thinness in women. *Psychological Reports*, 47: 483–491.

Garrow, J.S.G. (1988) Is obesity an eating disorder? *Journal of Psychosomatic Research*, 12(6): 585–590.

Geary, A. (2001) *The Food and Mood Handbook*. London: Thorsons.

Geller, J. and Drab, D.L. (1999) The readiness and motivation interview: a symptom-specific measure of readiness for change in the eating disorders. *European Eating Disorders Review*, 7: 259–278.

Geller, J., Johnston, C. and Madsen, K. (1997) The role of shape and weight in self-concept: The Shape and Weight Based Self-Esteem Inventory. *Cognitive Therapy & Research*, 21(1): 5–24.

Gilbert, S. (1986) *Pathology of Eating: Psychology and Treatment*. London and New York: Routledge and Kegan Paul.

Goodsitt, A. (1986) Self-psychology and the treatment of anorexia nervosa. In D.M. Garner and P.E. Garfinkel (eds), *Handbook of Psychotherapy for Anorexia Nervosa and Bulimia*. New York and London: Guilford Press. pp. 55–82.

Gormally, J., Black, S., Daston, S. and Rardin, D. (1982) The assessment of binge eating severity among obese persons. *Addictive Behaviors*, 7: 47–55.

Grant, J.E., Won Kim, S. and Eckert, E. (2002) Body dysmorphic disorder in patients with anorexia nervosa: prevalence, clinical features, and delusionality of body image. *International Journal of Eating Disorders*, 32(3): 291–300.

Greeno, C.G. and Wing, R.R. (1994) Stress-induced eating. *Psychological Bulletin*, 115(3): 444–464.

Grilo, C.M., Sanislow, C.A., Shea, T., Skodol, A.E., Stout, R.L., Pagano, M.E., Yen, S. and McGlashan, T.H. (2003) The natural course of bulimia nervosa and eating disorder not otherwise specified is not influenced by personality disorders. *International Journal of Eating Disorders*, 34(3): 319–330.

Groesz, L.M., Levine, M.P. and Murnen, S.K. (2002) The effect of experimental presentation of thin media images on body satisfaction: a meta-analytic review. *International Journal of Eating Disorders*, 31(1): 1–16.

Haley, J. (1976) *Problem-solving Therapy*. San Francisco: Jossey-Bass.

Halmi, K.A., Eckert, E., Marchi, P., Sampugnaro, V., Apple, R. and Cohen, J. (1991) Comorbidity of psychiatric diagnoses in anorexia nervosa. *Archives of General Psychiatry*, 48: 712–718.

Hastings, T. and Kern, J.M. (1994) Relationships between bulimia, childhood sexual abuse, and family environment. *International Journal of Eating Disorders*, 15(2): 103–111.

Hawkins, R.C. and Clement, P.F. (1980) Development and construct validation of a self-report measure of binge eating tendencies. *Addictive Behaviors*, 5: 219–226.

Heard, H.L. and Linehan, M.M. (1994) Dialectical behavior therapy: an integrative approach to the treatment of borderline personality disorder. Society for the Exploration of Psychotherapy Integration, *Newsletter* March 1994: 55–69.

Heatherton, T.F. and Baumeister, R.F. (1991) Binge eating as escape from self-awareness. *Psychological Bulletin*, 110: 86–108.

Henderson, M. and Freeman, C.L.P. (1987) A self-rating scale for bulimia: the BITE. *British Journal of Psychiatry*, 150: 18–24.

Herman, C.P. and Mack, D. (1975) Restrained and unrestrained eating. *Journal of Personality*, 43: 647–660.

Herman, C.P. and Polivy, J. (1980) Restrained eating. In A. Stunkard (ed.), *Obesity*. Philadelphia: Saunders. pp. 208–225.

Herzog, D.B., Greenwood, D.N., Dorer, D., Flores, A.T., Ekeblad, E.R., Richards, A., Blais, M.A. and Keller, M.B. (2000) Mortality in eating disorders: a descriptive study. *International Journal of Eating Disorders*, 28(1): 20–26.

Herzog, D.B., Keller, M.B., Sacks, N.R., Yey, C.H. and Lavori, P.W. (1992) Psychiatric co-morbidity in treatment-seeking anorexics and bulimics. *Journal of American Academic Child and Adolescent Psychiatry*, 31(5): 810–818.

Herzog, T., Hartmann, A., Sandholz, A. and Stammer, H. (1991) Prognostic factors in outpatient psychotherapy of bulimia. *Psychotherapy and Psychosomatics*, 56: 48–55.

Hill, A.J., Oliver, S. and Rogers, P.J. (1992) Eating in the adult world: the rise of dieting in childhood and adolescence. *British Journal of Clinical Psychology*, 31: 95–105.

Hoek, H.W. and Van Hoeken, D. (2003) Review of the prevalence and incidence of eating disorders. *International Journal of Eating Disorders*, 34: 383–396.

Hsu, L.K.G., Holben, B. and West, S. (1992) Nutritional counselling in bulimia nervosa. *International Journal of Eating Disorders*, 11(1): 55–62.

Hulley, A.J. and Hill, A.J. (2001) Eating disorders and health in elite women distance runners. *International Journal of Eating Disorders*, 30(3): 312–317.

Huon, G. (1994) Dieting, binge eating, and some of their correlates among secondary school girls. *International Journal of Eating Disorders*, 15(2): 159–164.

Jacobson, E. (1974) *Progressive Relaxation*. Chicago: University of Chicago Press, Midway Reprint.

James, I.A. and Barton, S. (2004) Changing core beliefs with the continuum technique. *Behavioural and Cognitive Psychotherapy*, 32(4): 431–442.

Jeffery, R.W., Adlis, S.A. and Foster, J.L. (1991) Prevalence of dieting among working men and women: the healthy worker project. *Health Psychology*, 10(4): 274–281.

Jones, R., Peveler, R.C., Hope, R.A. and Fairburn, C.G. (1993) Changes during treatment for bulimia nervosa: a comparison of three psychological treatments. *Behaviour Research and Therapy*, 31: 479–485.

Kaplan, A.S. and Katz, M. (1993) Medical illnesses associated with weight loss and binge eating. In A.S. Kaplan and P.E. Garfinkel (eds), *Medical Issues and the Eating Disorders*. New York: Brunner/Mazel. pp. 17–38.

Kaye, W.H., Gwirtsman, H.E., Obarzanek, E. et al. (1986) Caloric intake necessary for weight maintenance in anorexia nervosa: nonbulimics require greater caloric intake than bulimics. *American Journal of Clinical Nutrition*, 44: 435–443.

Keefe, P.H., Wyshogrod, D., Weinberger, E. and Agras, W.S. (1984) Binge eating and outcome of behavioural treatment of obesity: a preliminary report. *Behaviour Research and Therapy*, 22: 319–322.

Kellum, J.M., De Maria, E.J. and Sugerman, H.J. (1998) The surgical treatment of morbid obesity. *Current Problems in Surgery*, 35(9): 791–858.

Key, A., George, C.L., Beattie, D., Stammers, K., Lacey, H. and Waller, G. (2002) Body image treatment within an inpatient program for anorexia nervosa: the role of mirror exposure in the desensitisation process. *International Journal of Eating Disorders*, 31(2): 185–190.

Keys, A., Brozek, J., Henschel, A., Mickelson, O. and Taylor, H.L. (1950) *The Biology of Human Starvation* (Vols 1 and 2). Minneapolis: University of Minnesota Press.

Klesges, R.C., Klem, M.L., Hanson, C., Eck, L.H., Ernst, J., O'Laughlin, D., Garrott, A. and Rife, R. (1990) The effects of applicants' health status and qualifications on simulated hiring decisions. *International Journal of Obesity*, 14: 527–535.

Kovacs, D., Mahon, J. and Palmer, R.L. (2002) Chewing and spitting out food among eating disordered patients. *International Journal of Eating Disorders*, 32(1): 112–115.

Kral, J.G. (1995) Surgical interventions for obesity. In K.D. Brownell and C.G. Fairburn (eds), *Eating Disorders and Obesity: A Comprehensive Handbook*. New York and London: Guilford Press. pp. 510–515.

Lacey, J.H. and Evans, C.D. (1986) The impulsivist – a multi-impulsive personality disorder. *British Journal of Addictions*, 81(5): 641–649.

Lask, B. and Bryant-Waugh, R. (1986) Childhood onset anorexia nervosa. In R. Meadow (ed.), *Recent Advances in Paediatrics* (Vol. 8). Edinburgh: Churchill Livingstone. pp. 21–31.

Latner, J.D. and Wilson, G.T. (2004) Binge eating and satiety in bulimia nervosa and binge eating disorder: effects of macronutrient intake. *International Journal of Eating Disorders*, 36(4): 402–415.

Le Grange, D., Eisler, I., Dare, C. and Russell, G.F.M. (1992) Evaluation of family treatments in adolescent anorexia nervosa: a pilot study. *International Journal of Eating Disorders*, 12(4): 347–357.

Lehman, A.K. and Rodin, J. (1989) Styles of self-nurturance and disordered eating. *Journal of Consulting and Clinical Psychology*, 57(1): 117–122.

Levine, M.D., Marcus, M.D. and Moulton, P. (1996) Exercise in the treatment of binge eating disorder. *International Journal of Eating Disorders*, 19(2): 171–177.

Lindberg, L. and Hjern, A. (2003) Risk factors for anorexia nervosa: a national cohort study. *The International Journal of Eating Disorders*, 34(4): 397–408.

Linehan, M.M. (1993a) *Cognitive Behavioral Treatment of Borderline Personality Disorder*. New York and London: Guilford Press.

Linehan, M.M. (1993b) *Skills Training Manual for Treating Borderline Personality Disorder*. New York and London: Guilford Press.

Lock, J. (2002) Treating adolescents with eating disorders in the family context: empirical and theoretical considerations. *Child and Adolescent Psychiatric Clinics of North America*, 11: 331–342.

Lock, J., Le Grange, D., Agras, W.S. and Dare, C. (2001) *Treatment Manual for Anorexia Nervosa: A Family-based Approach*. New York and London: Guilford Press.

Long, C.G., Hinton, C. and Gillespie, N.K. (1994) Selective processing and body size words: application of the stroop test with obese restrained eaters, anorexics, and normals. *International Journal of Eating Disorders*, 15(3): 279–283.

Loro, A.D. Jr. and Orleans, C.S. (1981) Binge eating in obesity: preliminary findings and guidelines for behavioural analysis and treatment. *Addictive Behavior*, 6: 155–166.

Lucas, A.R., Melton, L.J., Crowson, C.S. and O'Fallon, W.M. (1999) Long-term fracture risk among women with anorexia nervosa: a population-based cohort study. *Mayo Clinic Proceedings*, 74(10): 972–977.

MacBrayer, E.K., Smith, G.T., MacCarthy, D.M., Demos, S. and Simmons, J. (2000) The role of family of origin food-related experiences in bulimic symptomatology. *International Journal of Eating Disorders*, 30(2): 149–160.

McCann, J.B., Stein, A., Fairburn, C.G. and Dunger, D.B. (1994) Eating habits and attitudes of mothers of children with non-organic failure to thrive. *Archives of Diseases in Childhood*, 70: 234–236.

McKisack, C. and Waller, G. (1996) Why is attendance variable at groups for women with bulimia nervosa? The role of eating psychopathology and other characteristics. *International Journal of Eating Disorders*, 20(2): 205–209.

McKisack, C. and Waller, G. (1997) Factors influencing the outcome of group psychotherapy for bulimia nervosa. *International Journal of Eating Disorders*, 22(1): 1–13.

McLelland, L. and Crisp, A. (2001) Anorexia nervosa and social class. *International Journal of Eating Disorders*, 29(2): 150–156.

Maddox, G.L., Back, K.W. and Liederman, V.R. (1968) Overweight as social deviance and disability. *Journal of Health and Social Behaviour*, 9: 287–298.

Maiman, L.A., Wang, V.L., Becker, M.H., Finlay, J. and Simonson, M. (1979) Attitudes towards obesity and the obese among professionals. *Journal of the American Dietetic Association*, 74(3): 331–336.

Marcus, M.D. (1995) Paper given at International Conference on Eating Disorders, London, April 1995.

Marcus, M.D., Wing, R.R. and Fairburn, C.G. (1995) Cognitive treatment of binge eating versus behavioural weight control in the treatment of binge eating disorder. *Annals of Behavioural Medicine*, 17: S090.

Marcus, M.D., Wing, R.R. and Lamparski, D.M. (1985) Binge eating and dietary restraint in obese patients. *Addictive Behaviors*, 10: 163–168.

Marcus, M.D., Smith, D., Santelli, R. and Kaye, W. (1992) Characterisation of eating disordered behavior in obese binge eaters. *International Journal of Eating Disorders*, 12(3): 249–255.

Marzillier, J. (2004) The myth of evidence based psychotherapy. *The Psychologist*, 17(7): 392–395.

Meyer, C. and Waller, G. (2000) Subliminal activation of abandonment and eating-related schemata: relationship with eating disordered attitudes in a nonclinical population. *International Journal of Eating Disorders*, 27(3): 328–334.

Miller, W.C., Niederpruem, M.G., Wallace, J.P. and Lindeman, A.K. (1994) Dietary fat, sugar, and fiber predict body fat content. *Journal of the American Dietetic Association*, 94(6): 612–615.

Miller, W.R. and Rollnick, S. (1991) *Motivational Interviewing: Preparing People to Change Addictive Behavior*. New York and London: Guilford Press.

Milos, G., Spindler, A., Ruggiero, G., Klaghofer, R. and Schnyder, U. (2002) Comorbidity of obsessive compulsive disorders and duration of eating disorders. *International Journal of Eating Disorders*, 31(3): 284–289.

Minuchin, S., Rosman, B.L. and Baker, L. (1978) *Psychosomatic Families: Anorexia Nervosa in Context*. Cambridge, MA and London: Harvard University Press.

Mitchell, J.E. (1991) A review of the controlled trials of psychotherapy for bulimia nervosa. *Journal of Psychosomatic Research*, 35(suppl. 1): 23–32.

Mitchell, J.E. (1992) Subtyping of bulimia nervosa. *International Journal of Eating Disorders*, 11(4): 327–332.

Mitchell, J.E., Raymond, N. and Specker, S. (1993) A review of the controlled trials of pharmacotherapy and psychotherapy in the treatment of bulimia nervosa. *International Journal of Eating Disorders*, 14(3): 229–247.

Mizes, J.S., Christiano, B., Madison, J., Post, G., Seime, R. and Varnado, P. (2000) Development of the Mizes Anorectic Cognitions Questionnaire – Revised: psychometric properties and factor structure in a large sample of eating disorder patients. *International Journal of Eating Disorders*, 28(4): 415–421.

Newton, J.R., Freeman, C.P. and Munro, J. (1993) Impulsivity and dyscontrol in bulimia nervosa: is impulsivity an independent phenomenon or a marker of severity? *Acta Psychiatrica Scandinavica*, 87: 389–394.

NICE (National Institute for Clinical Excellence) (2004) *Eating Disorders: Core Interventions in the Treatment and Management of Anorexia Nervosa, Bulimia Nervosa and Related Eating Disorders*. Clinical Guideline 9. London: National Institute for Clinical Excellence.

Nielson, S. (2001) Epidemiology and mortality of eating disorders. *Eating Disorders*, 24: 201–214.

Nisbett, R.E. (1972) Hunger, obesity and the ventromedial hypothalamus. *Psychological Review*, 79: 433–453.

Oberrieder, H., Walker, R., Monroe, D. and Adeyabju, M. (1995) Attitude of dietetics students and registered dietitians toward obesity. *Journal of the American Dietetic Association*, 95 (8): 914–916.

Ohanian, V. (2002) Imagery rescripting within cognitive behavior therapy for bulimia nervosa: an illustrative case report. *International Journal of Eating Disorders*, 31(3): 352–357.

Orbach, S. (1978) *Fat is a Feminist Issue: The Anti-Diet Guide to Permanent Weight Loss*. New York and London: Paddington Press.

Padesky, C.A. (1994) Schema change processes in cognitive therapy. *Clinical Psychology and Psychotherapy*, 1: 267–278.

Padesky, C.A. (2001) Transforming Personality: In-depth Training in Cognitive Therapy of Personality Disorders (workshop). Institute of Education, London.

Padesky, C.A. (2002) Cognitive Therapy Unplugged: Fine-tuning Essential Therapist Skills (workshop). Institute of Education, London.

Palmer, R.L., Birchall, H., McGrain, L. and Sullivan, V. (2002) Self-help for bulimic disorders: a randomised controlled trial comparing minimal guidance with face-to-face or telephone guidance. *British Journal of Psychiatry*, 181: 230–235.

Palmer, R.L., Oppenheimer, R., Chaloner, D.A. and Howells, K. (1990) Childhood sexual experiences with adults reported by women with eating disorders: an extended series. *British Journal of Psychiatry*, 156: 699–703.

Palmer, R.L., Birchall, H., Damani, S., Gatward, N., McGrain, L. and Parker, L. (2003) A dialectical behaviour therapy program for people with an eating disorder and borderline personality disorder – description and outcome. *International Journal of Eating Disorders*, 33(3): 281–286.

Pike, K.M. and Rodin, J. (1991) Mothers, daughters and disordered eating. *Journal of Abnormal Psychology*, 100: 198–204.

Pike, K.M., Walsh, B.T., Vitousek, K., Wilson, G.T. and Bauer, J. (2003) Cognitive behavior therapy in the posthospitalization treatment of anorexia nervosa. *The American Journal of Psychiatry*, 160(11): 2046–2049.

Polivy, J. and Herman, C.P. (1992) Undieting: a program to help people stop dieting. *International Journal of Eating Disorders*, 11(3): 261–268.

Polivy, J. and Herman, C.P. (1999) Distress and eating: why do dieters overeat? *International Journal of Eating Disorders*, 26: 153–164.

Polivy, J., Zeitlin, S.B., Herman, C.P. and Beal, A.L. (1994) Food restriction and binge eating: a study of former prisoners of war. *Journal of Abnormal Psychology*, 103(2): 409–411.

Prochaska, J.O. and Di Clemente, C.C. (1982) Transtheoretical therapy: toward a more integrative model of change. *Psychotherapy, Theory, Research, and Practice*, 19: 276–288.

Ramacciotti, C.E., Dell'Osso, L., Paoli, R.A., Ciaparelli, A., Coli, E., Kaplan, A.S. and Garfinkel, P. (2002) Characteristics of eating disorder patients without a drive for thinness. *International Journal of Eating Disorders*, 32(2): 206–212.

Rastam, M. (1992) Anorexia nervosa in 51 Swedish adolescents: premorbid problems and comorbidity. *Journal of the American Academy of Child and Adolescent Psychiatry*, 31(5): 819–829.

Ratnasuriya, R.H., Eisler, I., Szmukler, G.I. and Russell, G.F. (1991) Anorexia nervosa: outcome and prognostic factors after 20 years. *British Journal of Psychiatry*, 158: 495–502.

Reas, D.L., Williamson, D.A., Martin, C.K. and Zucker, N.L. (2000) Duration of illness predicts outcome for bulimia nervosa: a long-term follow-up study. *International Journal of Eating Disorders*, 27(4): 428–434.

Richardson, S.A., Hastorf, A.H., Goodman, N. and Dornbusch, S.M. (1961) Cultural uniformity in reaction to physical disabilities. *American Sociological Review*, 26: 241–247.

Rieger, E., Touyz, S.W. and Beumont, P.J.V. (2002) The Anorexia Nervosa Stages of Change Questionnaire (ANSOCQ): information regarding its psychometric properties. *International Journal of Eating Disorders*, 32(1): 24–38.

Rieger, E., Touyz, S.W., Swain, T. and Beumont, P.J.V. (2001) Cross-cultural research on anorexia nervosa: assumptions regarding the role of body weight. *International Journal of Eating Disorders*, 29(2): 205–215.

Robin, A.L., Siegel, P.T., Koepke, T., Moye, A.W. and Tice, S. (1994) Family therapy versus individual therapy for adolescent females with anorexia nervosa. *Developmental and Behavioral Pediatrics*, 15 (2): 111–116.

Robins, C.J. and Chapman, A. (2004) Dialectical behaviour therapy: current status, recent developments, and future directions. *Journal of Personality Disorders*, 18 (1): 73–89.

Rodin, G.M., Johnson, L.E., Garfinkel, P., Daneman, D. and Kenshole, A.B. (1986) Eating disorders in female adolescents with insulin-dependent diabetes mellitus. *International Journal of Psychiatry in Medicine*, 16: 49–57.

Rolls, B.J., Kim-Harris, S., Fischman, M.W., Foltin, R.W., Moran, T.H. and Stoner, S. (1994) Satiety after preloads with different amounts of fat and carbohydrate: implications for obesity. *American Journal of Nutrition*, 60: 476–487.

Rorty, M., Yager, J. and Rossotto, E. (1993) Why and how do women recover from bulimia nervosa? The subjective appraisals of 40 women recovered for a year or more. *International Journal of Eating Disorders*, 14(3): 249–260.

Rosen, J.C. and Leitenberg, H. (1982) Bulimia nervosa: treatment with exposure and response prevention. *Behavior Therapy*, 13: 117–124.

Rosen, J.C., Orosan, P. and Reiter, J. (1995) Cognitive behavior therapy for negative body image in obese women. *Behavior Therapy*, 26: 25–42.

Rosenberg, M. (1965) *Society and the Adolescent Self-Image*. Princeton, NJ: Princeton University Press.

Russell, G.F.M. (1979) Bulimia nervosa: an ominous variant of anorexia nervosa. *Psychological Medicine*, 9: 429–488.

Russell, G.F.M., Szmukler, G.I., Dare, C. and Eisler, I. (1987) An evaluation of family therapy in anorexia nervosa and bulimia nervosa. *Archives of General Psychiatry*, 44: 1047–1056.

Safer, D.L., Telch, C.F. and Agras, W.S. (2001) Dialectical behaviour therapy for bulimia nervosa. *American Journal of Psychiatry*, 158: 632–634.

Saloff-Coste, C.J., Hamburg, P. and Herzog, D.B. (1993) Nutrition and psychotherapy: collaborative treatment of patients with eating disorders. *Bulletin of the Menninger Clinic*, 57(4): 504–516.

Sanders, B. and Becker-Lausen, E. (1995) The measurement of psychological maltreatment: early data on the child abuse and trauma scale. *Child Abuse and Neglect*, 19(3): 315–323.

Schachter, S., Goldman, R. and Gordon, A. (1968) Effects of fear, food deprivation and obesity on eating. *Journal of Personality and Social Psychology*, 10: 91–97.

Schlundt, D.G. and Zimmerig, R.T. (1988) The dieter's inventory of eating temptations: a measure of weight control competence. *Addictive Behaviors*, 13: 151–164.

Schlundt, D.G., Hill, J.O., Sbrocco, T., Pope-Cordle, J. and Sharp, T. (1992) The role of breakfast in the treatment of obesity: a randomised clinical trial. *American Journal of Clinical Nutrition*, 55: 645–651.

Schmidt, U., Troop, N. and Treasure, J. (1999) Events and onset of eating disorders: correcting an 'age-old' myth. *International Journal of Eating Disorders*, 25(1): 83–88.

Segal, Z.V., Williams, M.G. and Teasdale, J.D. (2002) Mindfulness-based cognitive therapy for depression. New York and London: Guilford Press.

Selvini Palazzoli, M. (1974) *Self-starvation: From the Intrapsychic to the Transpersonal Approach to Anorexia Nervosa*. Haywards Heath: Human Context Books.

Selvini Palazzoli, M. (1978) *Self-Starvation: From Individual to Family Therapy in the Treatment of Anorexia Nervosa*. New York: Jason Aronson.

Serdula, M.K., Collins, M.E., Williamson, D.F., Anda, R.F., Pamuk, E. and Byers, T.E. (1993) Weight control practices of US adolescents and adults. *Annals of Internal Medicine*, 119(7 pt 2): 667–671.

Serpell, L. and Treasure, J. (2002) Bulimia nervosa: friend or foe? The pros and cons of bulimia nervosa. *International Journal of Eating Disorders*, 32(2): 164–170.

Serpell, L., Treasure, J., Teasdale, J.D. and Sullivan, V. (1999) Anorexia nervosa: friend or foe? A qualitative analysis of the themes expressed in letters written by anorexia nervosa patients. *International Journal of Eating Disorders*, 25(2): 177–186.

Simopoulos, A.P. (1985) The health implications of overweight and obesity. *Nutrition Reviews*, 43(2): 33–40.

Slade, P.D. (1973) A short anorexic behaviour scale. *British Journal of Psychiatry*, 122: 85.

Slade, P.D. (1982) Towards a functional analysis of anorexia nervosa and bulimia nervosa. *British Journal of Clinical Psychology*, 21(3): 167–179.

Sloan, G. and Leichner, P. (1986) Is there a relationship between sexual abuse or incest and eating disorders? *Canadian Journal of Psychiatry*, 31: 656–660.

Smith, D.E., Marcus, M. and Eldridge, K.L. (1994) Cognitive behavioural treatment of obese binge eaters. *Behavior Therapy*, 25: 635–658.

Smith, M.C. and Thelen, M. (1984) Development and validation of a test for bulimia. *Journal of Consulting and Clinical Psychology*, 52(5): 863–872.

Spitzer, R.L., Devlin, M., Walsh, B.T., Hasin, D., Wing, R., Marcus, M., Stunkard, A., Wadden, T., Yanovski, S., Agras, W.S., Mitchell, J. and Nonas, C. (1992) Binge eating disorder: a multisite field trial of the diagnostic criteria. *International Journal of Eating Disorders*, 11(3): 191–203.

Spitzer, R.L., Yanovski, S., Wadden, T., Wing, R., Marcus, M., Stunkard, A., Devlin, M., Mitchell, J., Hasin, D. and Horne, R.L. (1993) Binge eating disorder: its further validation in a multisite study. *International Journal of Eating Disorders*, 13(2): 137–153.

Spurrell, E.B., Wilfley, D., Tanofsky, M.B. and Brownell, K.D. (1997) Age of onset for binge eating: are there different pathways to binge eating? *International Journal of Eating Disorders*, 21(1): 55–65.

Staffieri, J.R. (1967) A study of social stereotype of body image in children. *Journal of Personality and Social Psychology*, 7: 101–104.

Steen, N.S., Oppliger, R.A. and Brownell, K.D. (1988) Metabolic effects of repeated weight loss and regain in adolescent wrestlers. *Journal of the American Medical Association*, 260(1): 47–50.

Stein, A., Woolley, H., Cooper, S.D. and Fairburn, C.G. (1994) An observational study of mothers with eating disorders and their infants. *Journal of Child Psychology and Psychiatry*, 35(4): 733–748.

Steinhausen, H.C. (1999) Eating disorders. In H.C. Steinhausen and F.C. Verhulst (eds), *Risk and Outcomes in Developmental Psychopathology*. Oxford: Oxford University Press. pp. 210–230.

Striegel-Moore, R.H. (1993) Etiology of binge eating: a developmental perspective. In C.G. Fairburn and G.T. Wilson (eds), *Binge Eating: Nature, Assessment and Treatment*. New York and London: Guilford Press. pp. 144–172.

Strober, M. (2004) Managing the chronic, treatment-resistant patient with anorexia nervosa. *International Journal of Eating Disorders*, 36(3): 245–255.

Stunkard, A.J. (1959) Eating patterns and obesity. *Psychiatric Quarterly*, 33: 284–295.

Stunkard, A.J. and Messick, S. (1985) The three-factor eating questionnaire to measure dietary restraint, disinhibition and hunger. *Journal of Psychosomatic Research*, 1: 71–83.

Sypeck, M.F., Gray, J. and Ahrens, A. (2004) No longer just a pretty face: fashion magazines' depictions of ideal female beauty from 1959 to 1999. *International Journal of Eating Disorders*, 36(3): 342–347.

Telch, C.F., Agras, W.S. and Linehan, M.M. (2001) Dialectical behaviour therapy for binge eating disorder. *Journal of Consulting and Clinical Psychology*, 69: 1061–1065.

Telch, C.F., Agras, W.S. and Rossiter, E.M. (1988) Binge eating increases with increasing adiposity. *International Journal of Eating Disorders*, 7: 115–119.

Telch, C.F., Agras, W.S., Rossiter, E.M., Wilfley, D. and Kenardy, J. (1990) Group cognitive-behavioral treatment for the nonpurging bulimic: an initial evaluation. *Journal of Consulting and Clinical Psychology*, 58(5): 629–635.

Thackwray, D.E., Smith, M.C., Bodfish, J.W. and Meyers, A.W. (1993) A comparison of behavioral and cognitive-behavioral interventions for bulimia nervosa. *Journal of Consulting and Clinical Psychology*, 61(4): 639–645.

Thelen, M.H., Farmer, J., Wonderlich, S. and Smith, M. (1991) A revision of the Bulimia Test: The BULIT-R. *Psychological Assessment: A Journal of Consulting and Clinical Psychology*, 3: 119–124.

Tobin, D.L., Johnson, C.L. and Dennis, A.B. (1992) Divergent forms of purging behaviour in bulimia nervosa patients. *International Journal of Eating Disorders*, 11(1): 17–24.

Tozzi, F., Sullivan, P.F., Fear, J.L., McKenzie, J. and Bulik, C. (2003) Causes and recovery in anorexia nervosa: the patient's perspective. *International Journal of Eating Disorders*, 33(2): 143–154.

Treasure, J. (1997) *Anorexia Nervosa: A Survival Guide for Families, Friends, and Sufferers*. Hove: Psychology Press.

Vanderlinden, J. and Vandereycken, W. (1990) The use of hypnosis in the treatment of bulimia nervosa. *International Journal of Clinical and Experimental Hypnosis*, 38: 101–111.

Vanderlinden, J. and Vandereycken, W. (1997) *Trauma, Dissociation, and Impulse Dyscontrol in Eating Disorders*. Brunner/Mazel Eating Disorders Monographs, No. 9. New York: Brunner/Mazel.

Vanderlinden, J., Van Dyck, R., Vertommen, H. and Vandereycken, W. (1992) The Dissociation Questionnaire (DIS-Q): development and characteristics of a dissociation questionnaire. *Nederlands Tijdschrift voor de Psychologie en Haar Grensgebieden*, 47(3): 134–142.

Vitousek, K., De Viva, I., Slay, L. and Manke, F. (1995) Concerns about change in the eating and anxiety disorders. Paper presented at the Annual Meeting of the American Psychological Association, New York. Also cited in Rieger, Touyz and Beumont (2002).

Waller, G. (1992) Sexual abuse and the severity of bulimic symptoms. *British Journal of Psychiatry*, 161: 90–93.

Waller, G. (1997) Drop-out and failure to engage in individual outpatient cognitive behavior therapy for bulimic disorders. *International Journal of Eating Disorders*, 22: 35–41.

Waller, G. (2003) Schema-level cognitions in patients with binge eating disorder: a case control study. *International Journal of Eating Disorders*, 33(4): 458–64.

Waller, G., Ohanian, V., Meyer, C. and Osman, S. (2000) Cognitive content among bulimic women: the role of core beliefs. *International Journal of Eating Disorders*, 28(2): 235–241.

Walsh, B.T. (1991) Fluoxetine treatment of bulimia nervosa. *Journal of Psychosomatic Research*, 35(Suppl. 1): 33–40.

Walsh, B.T. (2002) Pharmacological treatment of anorexia nervosa and bulimia nervosa. In C.G. Fairburn and K.G. Brownell (eds), *Eating Disorders and Obesity: A Comprehensive Handbook* (2nd edn). New York and London: Guilford Press. pp. 325–329.

Wardle, J. and Marsland, J. (1990) Adolescent concerns about weight and eating: a social-developmental perspective. *Journal of Psychosomatic Research*, 34: 377–391.

Wardle, J. and Watters, R. (2004) Sociocultural influences on attitudes to weight and eating: results of a natural experiment. *International Journal of Eating Disorders*, 35(4): 589–596.

Waugh, E. and Bulik, C.M. (1999) Offspring of women with eating disorders. *International Journal of Eating Disorders*, 25: 123–133.

Weissman, A.N. and Beck, A.T. (1978) Development and validation of the Dysfunctional Attitude Scale: a preliminary investigation. Paper presented at the Annual Meeting of the American Educational Research Association, Toronto, Canada.

Weltzin, T.E., Hsu, L.K.G., Pollice, C. and Kaye, W.H. (1991) Feeding patterns in bulimia nervosa. *Biological Psychiatry*, 30: 1093–1110.

Wilfley, D.E., Wilson, G.T. and Agras, W.S. (2003) The clinical significance of binge eating disorder. *International Journal of Eating Disorders*, 34: S96–S106.

Williams, G.J. and Power, K. (1996) *The Stirling Eating Disorder Scales*. London: The Psychological Corporation.

Williamson, D.F. and Pamuk, E.R. (1993) The association between weight loss and increased longevity: a review of the evidence. *Annals of Internal Medicine*, 119(7 pt 2): 731–736.

Wilson, G.T. (1993a) Binge eating and addictive disorders. In C.G. Fairburn and G.T. Wilson (eds), *Binge Eating: Nature, Assessment and Treatment*. New York and London: Guilford Press. pp. 97–120.

Wilson, G.T. (1993b) Assessment of binge eating. In C.G. Fairburn and G.T. Wilson (eds), *Binge Eating: Nature, Assessment and Treatment*. New York and London: Guilford Press. pp. 227–249.

Wilson, G.T. (1996) Treatment of bulimia nervosa: when CBT fails. *Behavior Research and Therapy*, 34(3): 197–212.

Wilson, G.T., Fairburn, C.G. and Agras, W.S. (1997) Cognitive-behavioral therapy for bulimia nervosa. In D.M. Garner and P.E. Garfinkel (eds), *Handbook of Psychotherapy for Eating Disorders* (2nd edn). New York and London: Guilford Press. pp. 67–93.

Wiseman, C.V., Gray, J.J., Mosimann, J.E. and Ahrens, A.H. (1992) Cultural expectations of thinness in women: an update. *International Journal of Eating Disorders*, 11(1): 85–89.

Wiseman, M.J. (1996) Behaviour change in practice: population strategies. *International Journal of Obesity*, 20(suppl. 1): 531–533.

Wisniewski, L. (2003) The application of dialectical behaviour therapy to the treatment of eating disorders. *Cognitive and Behavioral Practice*, 10: 131–138.

WHO (1992) *The International Classification of Diseases* (10th edn). Geneva: World Health Organisation.

Wolf, E.W. and Crowther, J.H. (1992) An evaluation of behavioral and cognitive behavioral group interventions for the treatment of bulimia nervosa in women. *International Journal of Eating Disorders*, 11(1): 3–15.

Wonderlich, S., Crosby, R., Mitchell, J., Thompson, K., Redlin, J., Demuth, G. and Smyth, J. (2001) Pathways mediating sexual abuse and eating disturbance in children. *International Journal of Eating Disorders*, 29(3): 270–279.

Young, J.E. (1999) *Cognitive Therapy for Personality Disorders*. Sarasota, FL: Professional Resource Press.

Young, J. and Rygh, J. (2003) Young–Rygh Avoidance Inventory (online). New York: Cognitive Therapy Center (available from www.schematherapy.com).

Index

Compiled by INDEXING SPECIALISTS (UK) Ltd., Regent House, Hove Street, Hove, East Sussex
    BN3 2DW. Tel: 01273 738299.
E-mail: richardr@indexing.co.uk Website: www.indexing.co.uk